French Beaded
Christmas Wreath

A One-a-Day Project

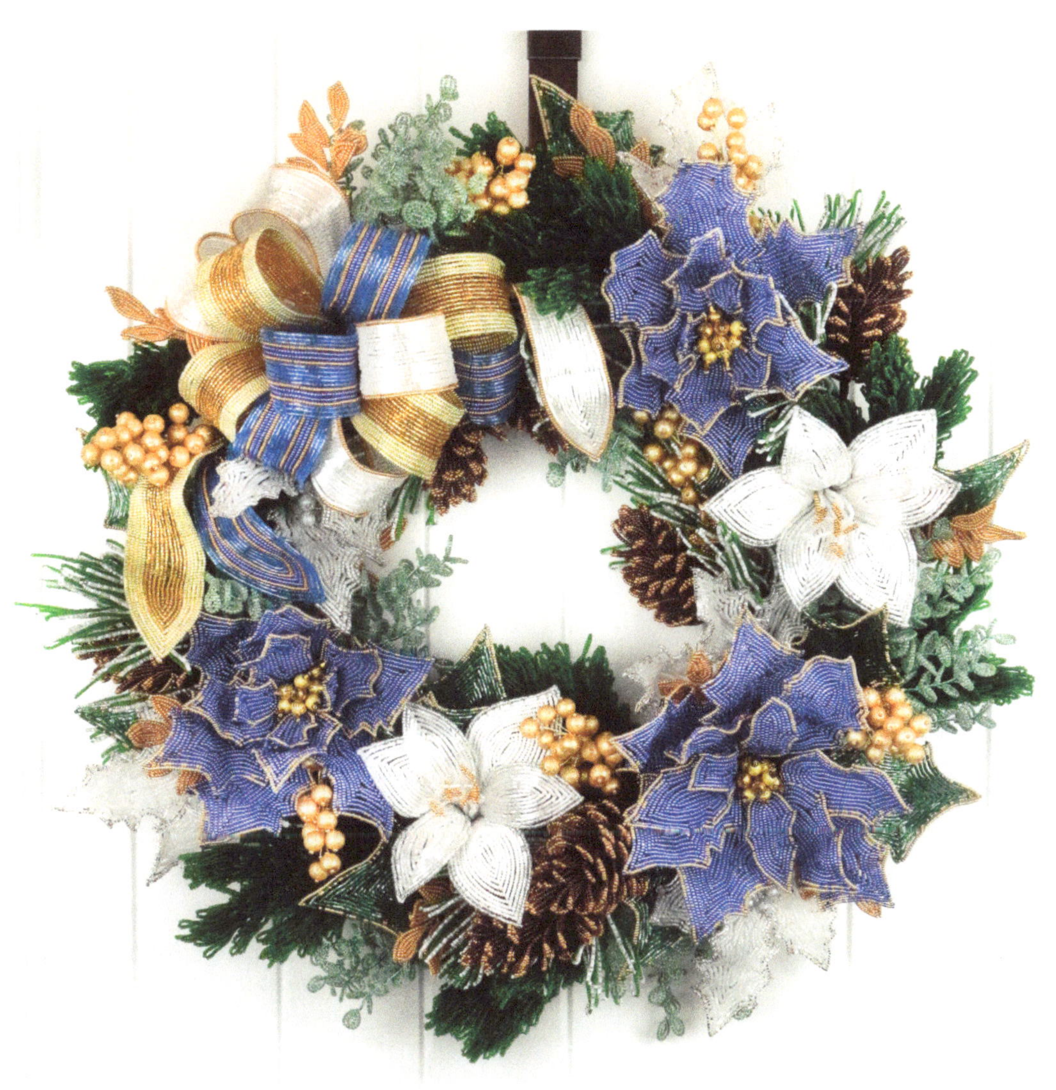

Lauren Harpster

Bead & Blossom

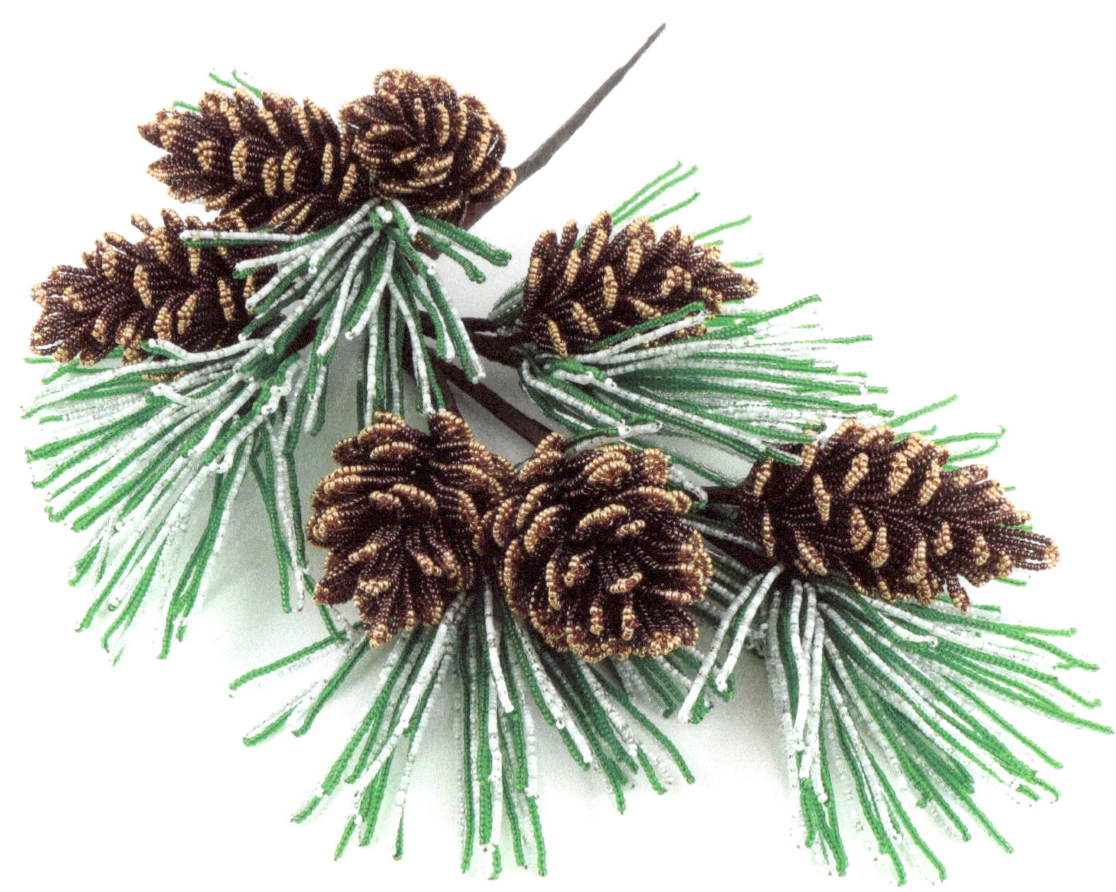

To my sweet husband, Scott, thank you for supporting my efforts to publish again, for celebrating each little success with me, and for being my biggest fan.

To my friend Suzanne Steffenson, thank you for helping to improve my writing, and for tutoring me in making an index.

To my friend Tracy Yu, thank you for helping me test this book before releasing it into the wild.

To each of you, thank you for your support! And for encouraging me and cheering me on through this project and publication.

Designer, Photographer: Lauren Harpster

Editor: Suzanne Steffenson

BeadandBlossom.com

First paperback edition, July 2020.

ISBN: 978-1-7347209-1-4

Bead & Blossom

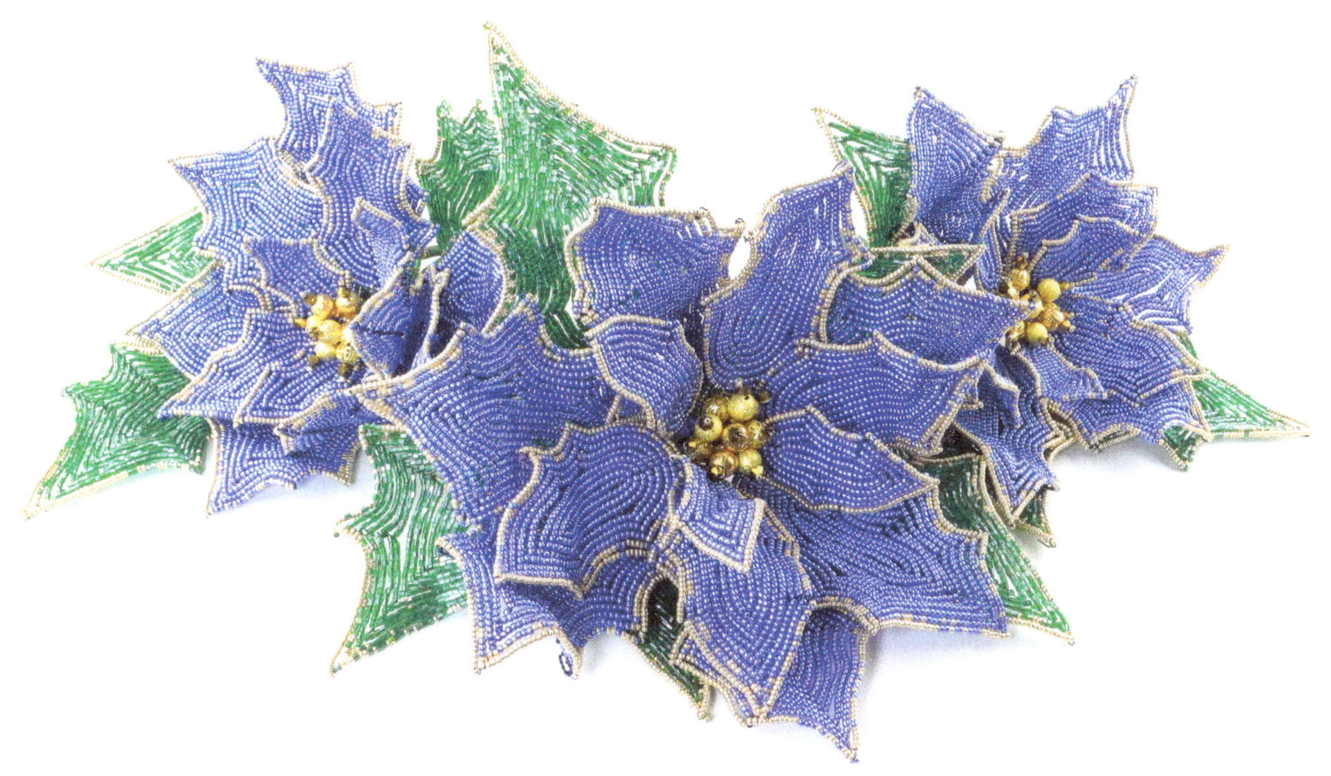

Table of Contents

About the Project

Those familiar with me and my work probably know that I love Christmas! One project that I had on my to-make list for a long time was a Christmas Wreath. However, I never had enough time to make one without neglecting my other work and publications. In 2018 I made my first one-a-day project - a Color Wreath - where I made one piece each day for a whole year and ended up with 365 pieces that I combined into a huge rainbow-colored wreath. That project taught me that by breaking down a huge project into one piece per day it becomes less overwhelming, and I would still have time for other projects.

The wreath taught in this book was my 2019 one-a-day project. My goal was to spend 45 minutes or less every day on this wreath, so some pieces that would have been more tedious have been simplified to use easier techniques that can be done more quickly. Some patterns are easy, while others are more advanced. It may take you more or less time, depending on how comfortable you are with the techniques. You may find that the first few days making a certain part take longer, but by the end, you have gotten faster.

Happy Beading!

How to Use this Book

Naturally, you don't have to make this project one piece each day if you don't want to, but the book is set up for those who do. Each pattern has a green information bar like the one below. You can find this bar located at the top of the page above the materials list. This bar will tell you the difficulty level of each pattern, as well as the techniques you need to know, and the approximate finished size of the piece. There is also a column in this bar called "One-a-day Counts". This list breaks down how many of each branch or stem to make, how many pieces - and therefore also how many days - are in each stem. I've provided these counts to make it easier to customize the wreath. If you don't want holly stems, or if you want extra eucalyptus, for example, you can quickly see how many pieces you need to add to or subtract from other projects to still have 365 pieces in the whole wreath.

DIFFICULTY LEVEL: Advanced	FINISHED SIZES:	ONE-A-DAY COUNTS:
TECHNIQUES USED: • Wire-Back Fringe (WBF) • Basic Frame (BF) • Lacing • Top Wire Extensions • Spokes	Large Poinsettia: 8 inches (20.3 cm) Small Poinsettia: 7 inches (17.8 cm)	2x Small Flowers: 16 pieces each 1x Large Flower: 16 pieces Leaves: 15 pieces Total Days: 63

For the one-a-day project, I count everything that can be made on one length of wire (not counting lacing or support wires) as one piece and therefore, one day. The patterns in this book are written to be used for the wreath, but they also contain component counts and material lists for those who are using the patterns for other arrangements. In the instructions you will see a count like the examples below. In the first example, the counts tell you to make six of that particular component for the wreath project, which equals six days. In the parenthesis you will find a count for how many to make for a single stem. Some patterns have two sizes - large and small - so the parenthesis will give the counts for a single stem in both sizes.

- Example 1 -
Make 6 (3 for each Small Poinsettia)

- Example 2 -
Make 29 (7 per large spray, 4 per small spray)

I have included a Progress Log on the next page to help you keep track of the pieces you have made. Each box represents one piece, and one day. Check off each box as you make components. Some boxes have letter labels that correspond with the component names in the pattern (ex: Unit A is written in the log boxes as "A". "Small Leaf" is labeled as S and "Large Leaf" as L). If you are working through a leap year and need an extra day, add in an extra unit in one of the projects where an extra piece won't be an issue - like the baby eucalyptus or berry stems. If you don't want to write in your book, scan it, print it out, and keep it tucked inside the book.

Progress Log

Poinsettia

Center Pieces

Bracts for Small Flowers: A A A A A A B B B B B B B B C C C C C C
C C C C C C

Bracts for Large Flower: D D D E E E F F F F F F

Leaves: S S S S S S S S L L L L L L L

Gold Leaves

Pinecone Sprays

Needle Units

Needle Tip Units

Scales: A A A A A A A B B B B B B B C C C C C C
C D D D D D D D E E E E E E E E E E E
E E E E E E E E F F F F F F F

Fir Branches

Small Branch Units: A A A A A A A A A A A A A A A A A A A A
A A A A A A B B B B B B B B B B B B B
B B B B B

Holly Stems

Berry Bunches

Leaves: S S S S S L L L L L L L L L L L

Berry Stems

Berry Bunches

Baby Eucalyptus

Eucalyptus Sprigs

Amaryllis Flowers

Pistil/Stamen Pieces

Petals: A A B B B B C C C C C C

Gigantic Bow

Loops: A A A A B B B B C C C C

Tails: A B C

..... SPOKE POINSETTIA .....

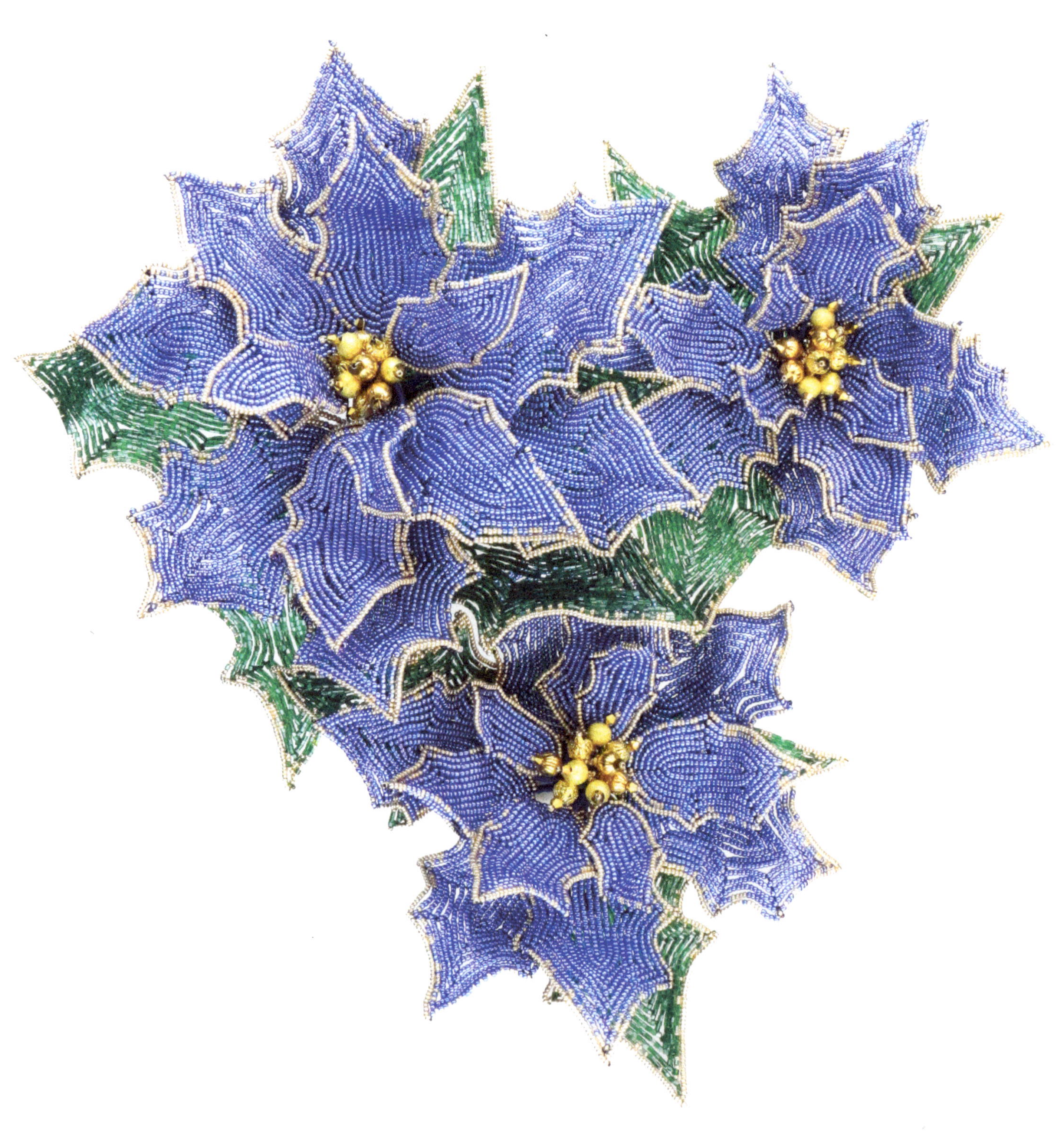

DIFFICULTY LEVEL: Advanced

TECHNIQUES USED:
- Wire-Back Fringe (WBF)
- Basic Frame (BF)
- Lacing
- Top Wire Extensions
- Spokes

FINISHED SIZES:
Large Poinsettia: 8 inches (20.3 cm)
Small Poinsettia: 7 inches (17.8 cm)

ONE-A-DAY COUNTS:
2x Small Poinsettia: 16 pieces each
1x Large Poinsettia: 16 pieces
Leaves: 15 pieces
Total Days: 63

Materials

For the wreath make one Large Poinsettia and two Small Poinsettias.

BEADS:	FULL WREATH	1 LARGE	1 SMALL
Size 11/0 Toho PF586 seed beads for bracts	240 grams (7 hanks)	100 grams (3 hanks)	70 grams (2 hanks)
Size 11/0 metallic light gold seed beads for edging	2 ½ hanks (~90 grams	1 hank (~35 grams)	¾ hank (~27 grams)
Size 11/0 2-cut transparent green luster seed beads	7 hanks (245 grams)	~ 3 hanks (105 grams)	~ 2 hanks (70 grams
8mm round beads for flower center*	27 pieces	9 pieces	9 pieces
4 mm gold bicone beads for flower center	54 pieces	18 pieces	18 pieces
WIRE:			
24 gauge (.5 mm) bract/petal colored copper core wire	360 ft (107 m)	140 ft (43 m)	110 ft (34 m)
22 gauge (.6 mm) bract/petal colored copper core wire	30 ft (9.2 m)	15 ft (4.6 m)	7.5 ft (2.3 m)
30 gauge (.25 mm) bract/petal colored copper core wire	16 ft (4.9 m)	6 ft (1.8 m)	5 ft (1.5 m)
24 gauge (.5 mm) leaf colored copper core wire	150 ft (46 m)	50 ft (15 m)	50 ft (15 m)
30 gauge (.25 mm) leaf colored copper core wire	18 ft (5.5 m)	8 ft (2.4 m)	5 ft (1.5 m)
28 gauge (.3 mm) gold colored copper core wire	9 ft (2.7 m)	3 ft (~1 m)	3 ft (~1 m)
16 gauge (1.3 mm) florist stem wire	15 pieces	2-5 pieces	2-5 pieces
14 gauge galvanized steel wire	3x 8 inch pieces	1 piece	1 piece
OTHER:			
Green floral tape	< 1 roll	< 1 roll	< 1 roll
Bract/petal colored embroidery floss (or floral tape)	< 1 skein	< 1 skein	< 1 skein

NOTES:

If you don't want to use a contrasting color for the edging, I recommend using a bead that is a similar color, but in a different finish than the main bract/petal color. This way there will still be some sort of edging to visually separate one petal from another. Otherwise, the flowers will look like a mass of beads with no definition to the shapes of the petals.

When working with patterns that tell you to cut a specific length of working wire, or string a certain amount of beads, always add a little extra to the length the first couple times you make the piece. The exact length will vary from one person to the next based on individual technique, and having that extra length will help you learn how much wire *you* need to complete the piece.

*For my flower center 8mm beads, I used a mix of three different gold metal beads with fun textures for the flower center - filigree, stardust, and corrugated.

FLOWER CENTER: *Each unit with 3 fringes equals one day.*

I chose not to make my flower centers botanically correct, opting instead for a more decorative look that would add more bling to the wreath.

Wire: *28 gauge gold colored copper core wire*
Beads: *8 and 4 mm gold colored beads, size 11/0 gold seed beads.*

Make 9 (3 for each flower)

Pattern: 3x WBF. For each fringe string 2x 11/0, 1x 4mm bicone, 1x 8 mm round bead, 1x 4mm, 1 x 11/0.

Instructions:

1. Cut approximately 10 inches (25.4 cm) of wire.

2. Leave a 2 inch (5 cm) tail wire, then string 2x 11/0 gold seed beads, followed by 1x 4mm bicone, 1x 8 mm round bead, 1x 4mm bicone, and 1x 11/0 gold seed bead. Skip the last 11/0 gold bead, then pass the working wire back through all of the beads below. (**Photo 1**)

3. Repeat until you have three fringes. (**Photo 2**)

4. Twist the beginning and ending tail wires together. (**Photo 3**)

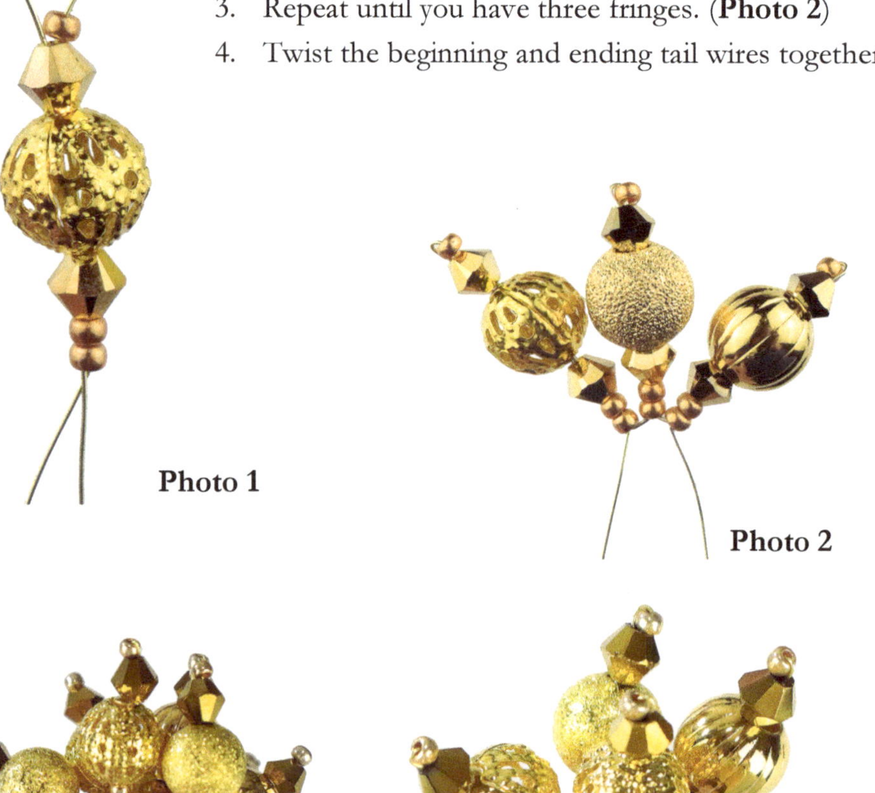

Photo 1

Photo 2

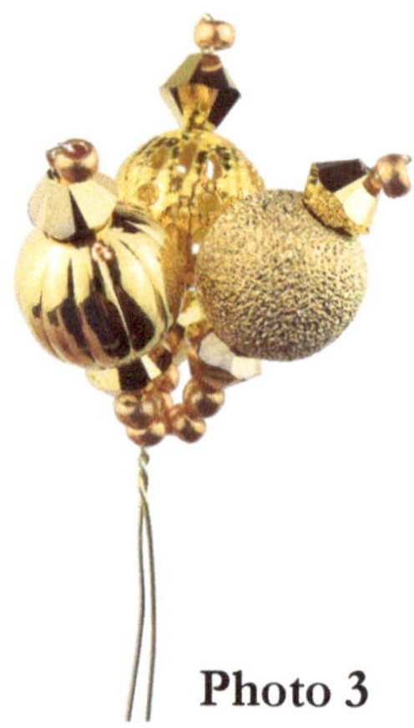

Photo 3

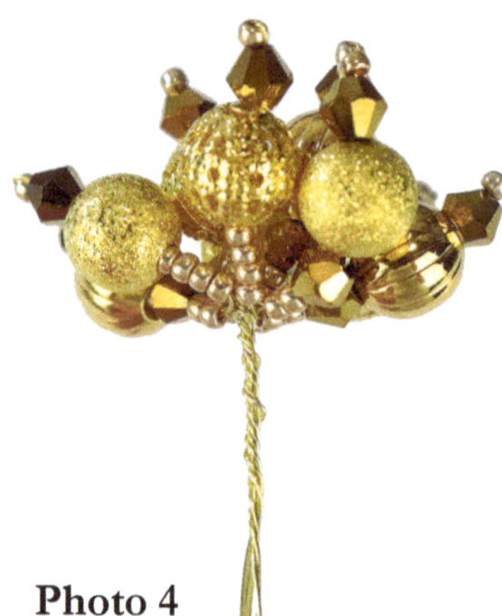

Photo 4

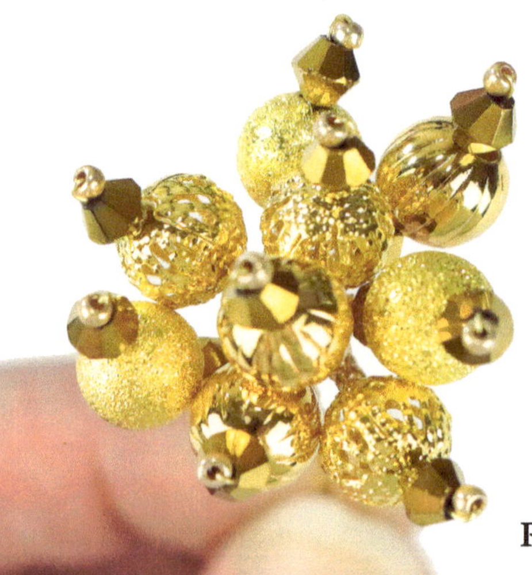

Photo 5

5. Twist the stem wires of three units together to make a completed flower center (**Photos 4 & 5**). You should have enough units to make three flower centers.

BRACTS: *Each bract equals one day.*

Wire: *22, 24, and 30 gauge (.6, .5, and .25 mm) bract/petal colored copper core wire.*
Beads: *Size 11/0 bract/petal colored seed beads, size 11/0 gold seed beads.*

Prep: Make a mix of the bract and edging beads with a 1:1 ratio. Start with approximately 15 grams of the mix, and make more as needed.

As you work through the bract patterns, I recommend stringing about 10 feet (3 m) of the bract colored beads beads onto the spool at a time. This will be enough for a few bracts. Before making another bract, check to make sure you still have several feet of beads strung on the spool. If not, string more beads before you begin. Leave the remaining bract color beads either on the hank or in the spinner bowl to use while making the edging.

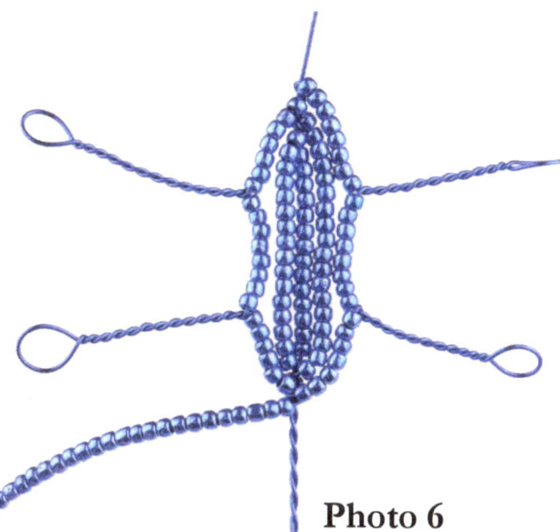

Photo 6

Bract A:

Make 6 (3 for each Small Poinsettia)

Pattern: 9 row BF, ⅞ inch (2.2 cm) BR - RB PT.

- **SPOKES - Rows 4 & 5: 2 spokes in each row, 1 inch (2.5 cm) long, spaced evenly.**
- **EXTENSIONS: Add 1 bead to the top wire after rows 5 and 7 (2 beads total).**
- **Three bottom wires**

Instructions:

1. Working from the spool, construct a Basic Frame using ⅞ inch (2.2 cm) + 2 beads for the Basic Row. Make the top wire at least 1 inch (2.5 cm) long. Move the top 2 beads to the end of the top wire and bend the wire back to keep them out of the way. These beads will be used later for top wire extensions.

2. Wrap rows 2 & 3 with a round bottom and pointed top.

3. Make 2 spokes each in rows 4 & 5. Each spoke should be one inch (2.5 cm) long Space them so they divide the rows evenly. (**Photo 6**)

4. Wrap row 6 around both of the spokes in row 4 at a 45 degree angle to make a nice point. Before wrapping row 6 at the top wire, slide one of the beads on the top wire down so it sits above row 5. Wrap row 7 around all spokes and the bottom wire. (**Photo 7**)

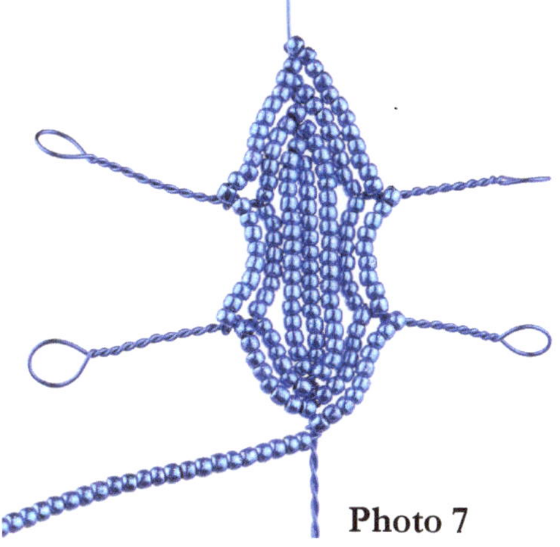

Photo 7

5. Move the beads on the working wire further down onto the spool. Measure and cut approximately 10 inches (25.4 cm) of bare working wire.

6. String approximately 6 inches (15.2 cm) of the mixed beads onto the working wire. Move the last top wire extension bead down, then and wrap rows 8 & 9 around.

7. Twist the working wire into the two bottom wires. Try to twist smoothly to prevent a lumpy stem wire. Clip the top and spoke wires short and fold them back.

A finished Bract A for the Small Poinsettia is shown in **Photo 8**. *See the note on Alterations in the Bract C instructions.*

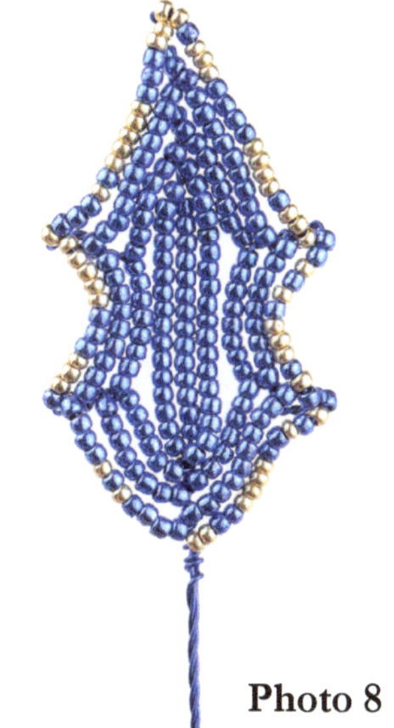

Photo 8

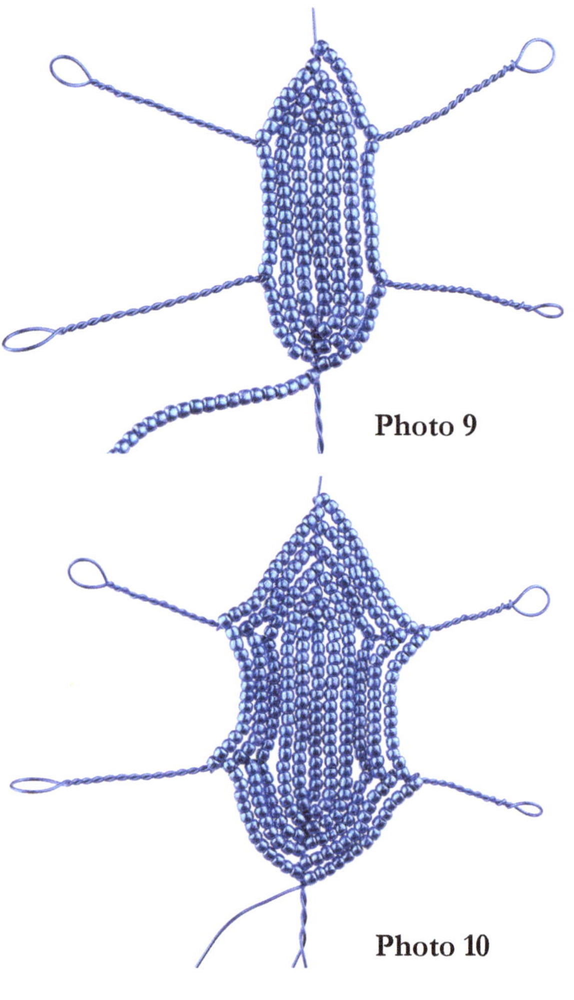

Photo 9

Photo 10

Bract B:

Make 8 (4 for each Small Poinsettia)

Pattern: 15 row BF, 1 inch (2.5 cm) BR, RB PT.

- **SPOKES - Rows 6 & 7: 2 spokes in each row, 2 inches (5 cm) long, spaced evenly.**
- **EXTENSIONS: Add 1 bead to the top wire after rows 11 and 13 (2 beads total).**
- **Three bottom wires**
- **Lace once across the center.**

Instructions:

1. Working from the spool, construct a Basic Frame using 1 inch (2.5 cm) + 2 beads for the Basic Row. Make the top wire at least 1 ½ inches (3.8 cm) long. Move the top 2 beads to the end of the top wire and bend the wire back to keep them out of the way. These beads will be used later for top wire extensions.

2. Wrap rows 2-5 with a round bottom and pointed top.

3. Make two 2 inch (5 cm) spokes each in rows 6 & 7. Position the spokes so they divide the rows somewhat evenly. (**Photo 9**)

4. Wrap rows 8-11 around, wrapping at a point at each spoke and the top wire, and round at the bottom wire. (**Photo 10**)

5. Measure and cut approximately 20 inches (50.8 cm) of bare working wire.

6. For rows 12 & 13, string 1-1 ½ inches (2.5 - 3.8 cm) of the bract color, then a similar length of the mixed beads. Alternate until you have strung approximately 8 inches (20.3 cm) of beads total. (**Photo 11**)

7. Bring one bead down from the top wire, then wrap rows 12 & 13.

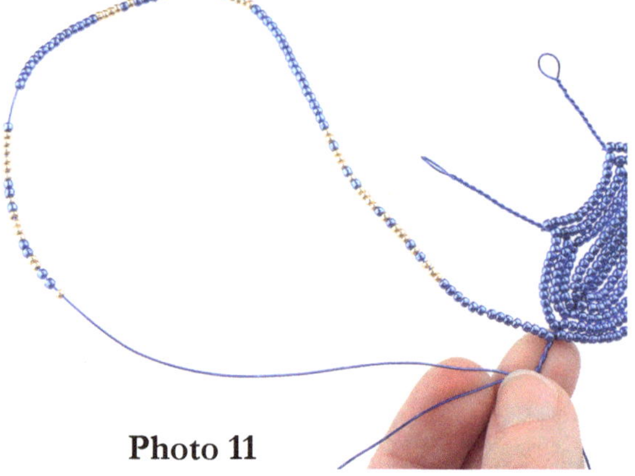

Photo 11

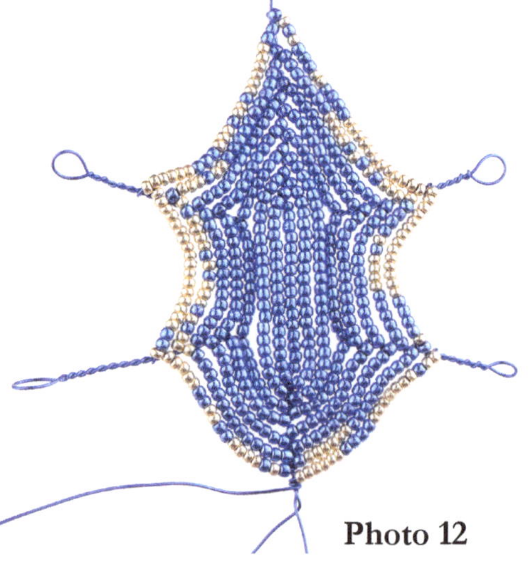

Photo 12

8. Remove any excess beads from the working wire. Move the last bead on the top wire down. For the last two rows you need to line up beads in rows 14 & 15 with beads in rows 12 & 13. It's easiest to string a couple inches at a time as you wrap around. Line up a string of mixed beads with sections in the previous rows that are bract-colored. Line up a string of gold beads with sections in the previous rows that are mixed. (**Photo 12**)

9. Twist the working wire into the bottom wire. Cut the top and spoke wires and fold them back.

10. Cut approximately 5 inches (12.7 cm) of 30 gauge bract-colored wire and lace across the center.

A finished Bract B for the Small Poinsettia is shown in **Photo 13.** *See the note on Alterations in the Bract C instructions.*

Bract C:

Make 12 (6 for each Small Poinsettia)

Pattern: 19 row BF, 1 inch (2.5 cm) BR, RB PT.
- Use 22 gauge wire for the basic wire, 24 gauge wire for the working wire.
- Add a 22 gauge support wire after row 3.
- **SPOKES:**
  - **Rows 6 & 7: 2x spokes in each row, 2 inches (5 cm) long, spaced evenly.**
  - **Row 12: 1x 1 inch (2.5 cm) spoke halfway between the 2nd spoke and top wire.**
  - **Row 13: 1x 1 inch (2.5 cm) spoke halfway between the 3rd and 4th spokes.**
- **EXTENSIONS: Add 1 bead to the top wire after rows 13, 15, and 17 (3 beads total).**
- **Five bottom wires**
- **Lace once across the center.**

Instructions:

1. Cut two 10 inch (25.4 cm) lengths of 22 gauge wire. Bend one in half and set it aside to use later as a support wire. The second one will be the Basic Wire for the bract. String 1 inch (2.5 cm) + 3 beads for the Basic Row onto the second 22 gauge wire.

2. Attach the 24 gauge spool wire strung with bract colored beads to the bottom half of the 22 gauge basic wire by twisting them together. (**Photo 14**)

3. Move the top 3 beads up to the end of the top wire and bend it back to keep them out of the way for now.

4. Wrap rows 2 & 3 with a pointed top and round bottom.

5. After row 3, insert the bent 22 gauge wire from step 1 into the front of the petal so the wire ends are on either side of the basic row (**Photo 15**). *In Photos 15 and 16 the 22 gauge support wire is shown in gold.* Push the wire all the way through so the bend in the center catches around the wire below the lowest bead on the Basic Row.

6. Fold the 22 gauge wire ends down to join with the bottom wire, but do not twist them together (**Photo 16**). From now on, all rows wrapped around the bottom wire should be wrapped around all four wires.

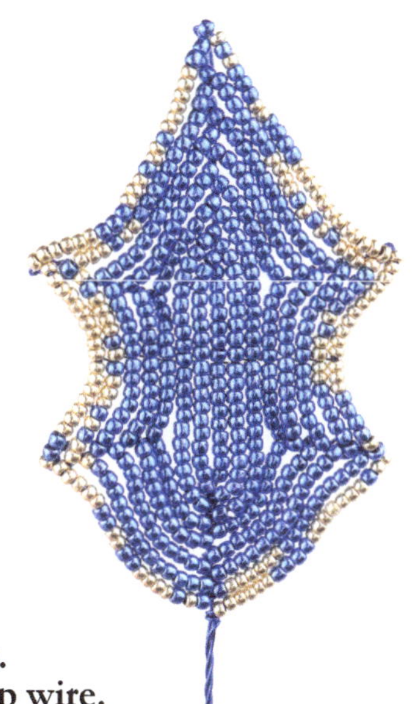

Photo 13

Photo 14

Photo 15

Photo 16

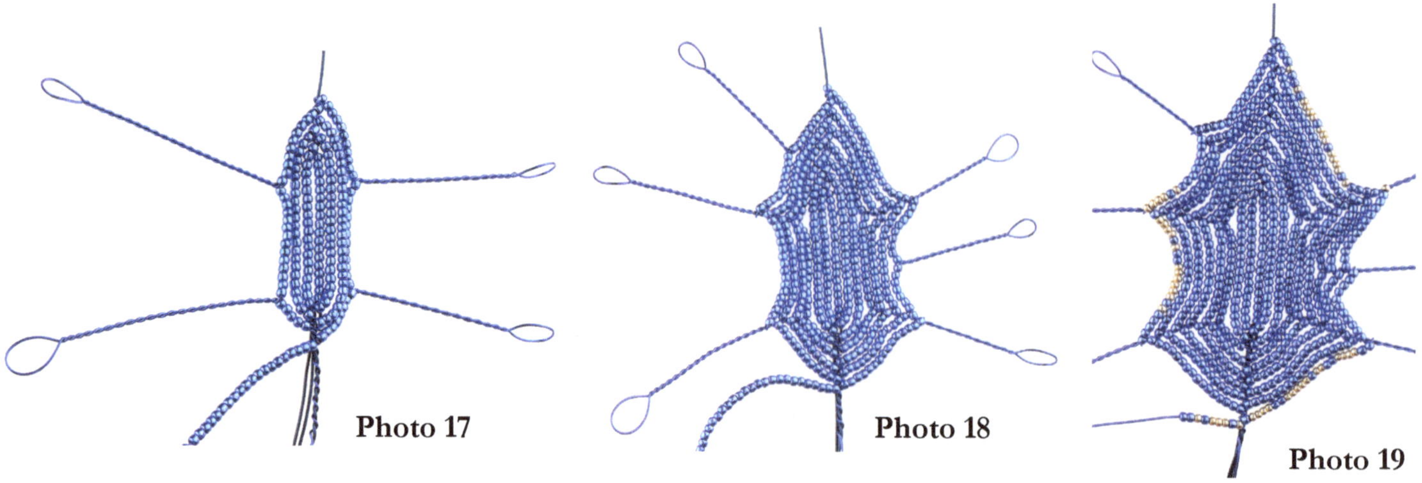

Photo 17 **Photo 18** **Photo 19**

7. Make two spokes each in rows 6 & 7, distributing them evenly through the rows. Each spoke should be approximately 2 inches (5 cm) long. (**Photo 17**)

8. Wrap rows 8-11 around all spokes and the top wire, wrapping at a 45 degree angle at each spoke to make them pointed.

9. Wrap row 12 adding one spoke halfway between the second spoke and the top wire. For row 13, add one spoke halfway between the third and fourth spokes. Each spoke should be approximately 1 inch (2.5 cm) long. (**Photo 18**)

10. Move one of the beads on the top wire down, then wrap rows 14 & 15.

11. Cut approximately 26 inches (66 cm) of bare working wire from the spool. String approximately 11 inches (28 cm) of beads following the same alternating pattern of the bract-colored beads and the mixed beads that was used in Bract B. Bring one bead down from the top wire, then wrap rows 16 & 17. (**Photo 19**)

12. Remove any excess beads from the working wire. String beads as needed for rows 18 & 19, lining up mixed beads with a section of bract-colored beads, and gold beads with a section of mixed beads in the previous rows. Bring the last bead on the top wire down before wrapping row 18.

13. Clip and fold the top and spoke wires. Twist the working wire together with the four bottom wires to make five total bottom wires. Cut approximately 6 inches (15.2 cm) of 30 gauge wire and lace across the center. You may need to lace on a slant to avoid running into the spoke wire on the right side.

A finished Bract C for the Small Poinsettia is shown in **Photo 20.**

Photo 20

Photo 21

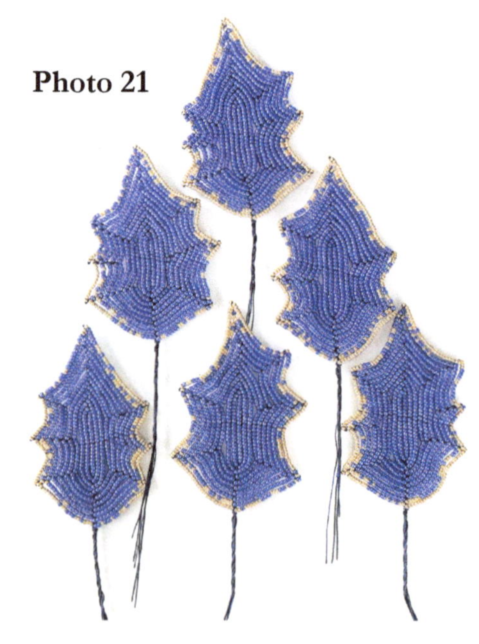

Bract D:

Make 3 (3 per large poinsettia)

Pattern: 11 row BF, 1 ⅛ inch (2.9 cm) BR, RB PT.

- **SPOKES:**
  - Row 4: 1x 1 inch (2.5 cm) spoke, placed half-way.
  - Row 5: 2x 1 inch spokes, evenly spaced.
- **EXTENSIONS: Add 1 bead to the top wire after rows 7 and 9 (2 beads total).**
- **Three bottom wires**

Instructions:

1. Construct a Basic Frame using 1 ⅛ inch (2.9 cm) +2 beads for the Basic Row. Make the top wire at least 1 ¼ inches (3.2 cm) long. Move the top two beads to the end of the top wire and bend it back to hold them out of the way.

2. Wrap rows 2 & 3 with a round bottom and pointed top.

3. For row 4 make one 1 inch (2.5 cm) long spoke somewhere near the center of the row. In row 5 make two 1 inch long spokes spacing them evenly through the row. (**Photo 22**)

4. Wrap rows 6 & 7, making sharp points at each spoke.

5. Cut 1 foot (30.5 cm) of bare working wire. String approximately 8 inches (20.3 cm) of beads, alternating between 1-1 ½ inches of plain bract colored beads and a similar length of the mixed beads. Slide down one of the beads on the top wire, then wrap rows 8 & 9.

6. Remove any excess beads from the working wire. Slide down the last bead on the top wire, then wrap rows 10 & 11. String beads as needed so gold beads line up with a section of mixed beads, and mixed beads line up with bract colored beads in the previous rows.

7. Twist the working wire into the bottom wire. Cut the top and spoke wires and fold them back.

Photo 23 shows a finished Bract D for the Large Poinsettia. *See the note on Alterations in the Bract C instructions.*

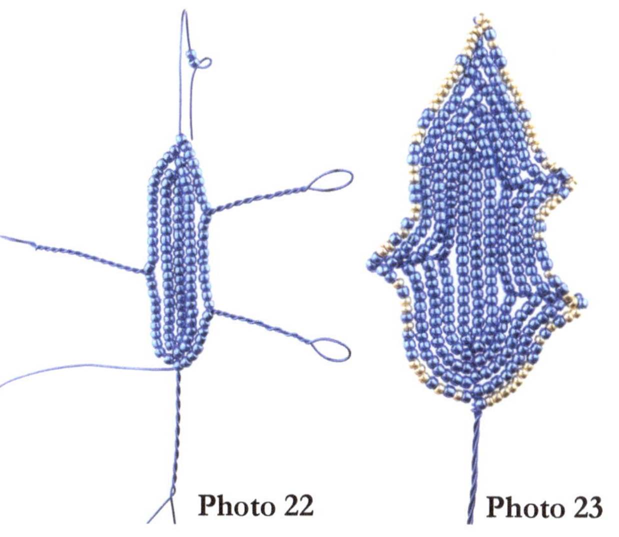

Photo 22   **Photo 23**

Bract E

Make 4 (4 per large poinsettia)

Pattern: 17 row BF, 1 ¼ inch (3.2 cm) BR, RB PT.
- **SUPPORT WIRE: 10 inch (25.4 cm) 22g support wire after row 3.**
- **SPOKES - Rows 6 & 7: 2 spokes each, 2 inches (5 cm) long, evenly spaced.**
- **EXTENSIONS: Add 1 bead to the Top Wire after rows 11, 13 and 15 (3 beads total).**
- **Lace once across the center.**
- **Five bottom wires**

Instructions:

1. Cut a 10 inch (25.4 cm) length of 22 gauge wire and fold it in half to use later as a support wire.

2. Construct a Basic Frame using 1 ¼ inch (3.2 cm) +3 beads for the Basic Row. Make the top wire at least 1 ¾ inches (4.5 cm) long. Move the top 3 beads to the end of the top wire and bend the wire back to hold them out of the way. Wrap rows 2-3.

3. After row 3, add the 22 gauge support wire from step 1. Follow the same steps as the Bract C instructions.

4. For row 6, make two 2 inch (5 cm) long spokes, spacing them evenly through the rows. Make row 7 a mirror image. (**Photo 24**)

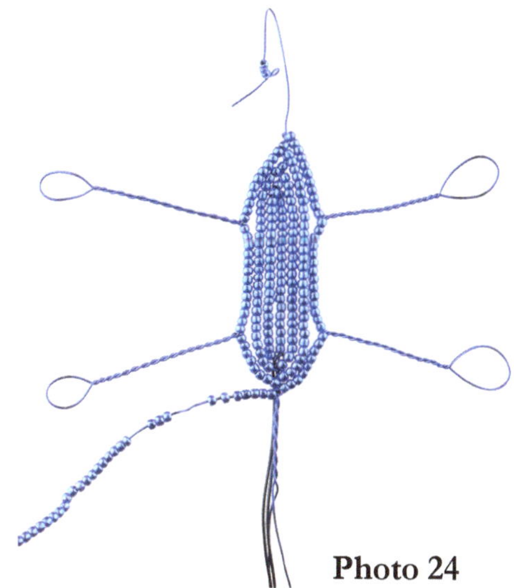

Photo 24

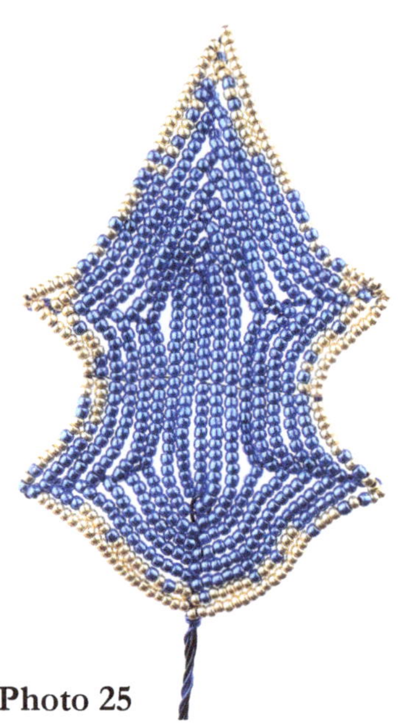

Photo 25

5. Wrap rows 8 -11, making a sharp point at each of the spokes.

6. Slide down one of the beads on the top wire, then wrap rows 12 & 13.

7. Cut approximately 22 inches (55.9 cm) of bare working wire. String 9 inches (23 cm) of beads, alternating between an inch or two of plain bract colored beads and an inch or two of the mixed beads. Slide down one of the beads on the top wire, then wrap rows 14 & 15.

8. Remove any excess beads from the working wire. Bring down the last bead on the top wire. String beads as needed for rows 16 & 17 so plain gold beads line up with sections of mixed beads, and mixed beads line up with the sections of plain bract colored beads in the previous rows.

9. Twist the working wire into the four bottom wires. Cut the top wire and spoke wires short and fold them back.

10. Cut a 6 inch (15.2 cm) length of 30 gauge (.25 mm) bract colored wire and lace across the center of the bract.

Photo 25 shows the finished Bract E for the Large Poinsettia. *See the note on Alterations in the Bract C instructions.*

Bract F

Make 6 (6 per large poinsettia)

Pattern: 21 row BF, 1 ½ inch (3.8 cm) BR, RB PT.
- **22 gauge basic wire, 24 gauge working wire.**
- **SUPPORT WIRE: 10 inch (25.4 cm) 22g support wire after row 3.**
- **SPOKES:**
  - **Rows 6 & 7: 2 spokes in each row, 2 inches (5 cm) long, evenly spaced.**
  - **Rows 10 & 11: 1 spoke in each row, 1 ½ inches (3.8 cm) long, placed between previous spokes.**
- **EXTENSIONS: Add 1 bead to the Top Wire after rows 15, 17 and 19 (3 beads total).**
- **Lace once across the center.**
- **Five bottom wires**

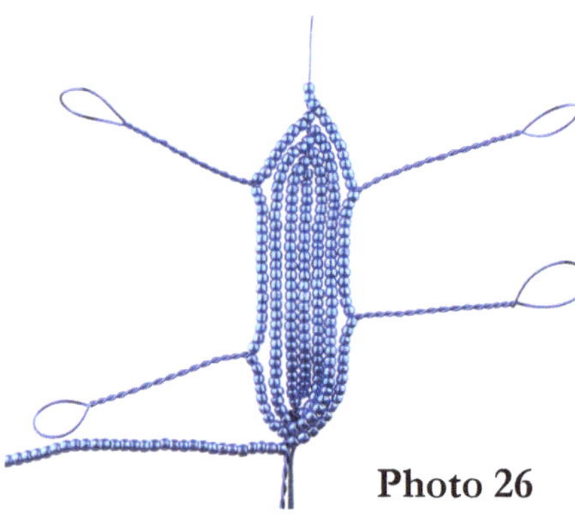

Photo 26

Instructions:

1. Cut two 10 inch (25.4 cm) lengths of 22 gauge wire. Bend one in half to use later as a support wire. Use the other as the Basic Wire.

2. String 1 ½ inches (3.8 cm) + 3 beads onto the 22 gauge basic wire, then attach the 24 gauge working wire below by twisting them together. Move the top 3 beads to the end of the top wire and fold the wire back to keep them out of the way for now. Wrap rows 2-3 with a round bottom and pointed top.

3. Insert the 22 gauge support wire into the front of the bract between the last two rows of beads along the bottom wire. (*See Small Poinsettia Bract C instructions.*)

4. In row 6 make two 2 inch (5 cm) long spokes, spacing them somewhat evenly through the row. Make row 7 similar to row 6. (**Photo 26**)

5. Wrap rows 8 & 9, making a sharp point at each of the spokes.

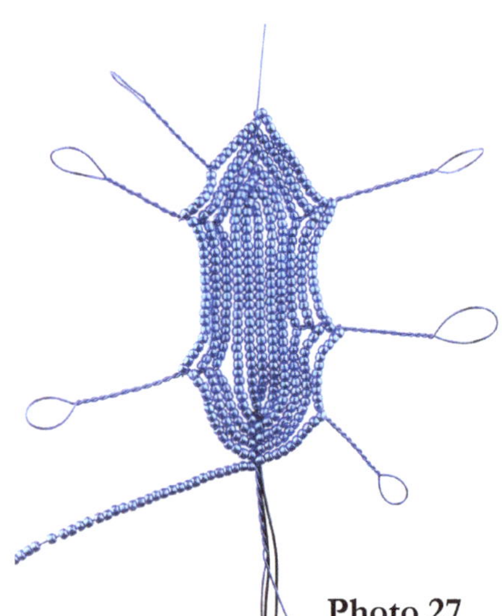

Photo 27

6. In row 10, make one 1 ½ inch (3.8 cm) long spoke, positioning it between the second spoke and the top wire. In row 11 make another spoke of the same length, positioning it between the fourth spoke and the bottom wire. (**Photo 27**)

7. Wrap rows 12-15 around all spokes and frame wires. Bring down 1 bead on the top wire, then wrap rows 16 & 17.

8. Cut approximately 28 inches (71 cm) of bare working wire. String 11 inches (28 cm) of beads, alternating between an inch or two of plain bract colored beads and an inch or two of the mixed beads. Slide down one bead on the top wire, then wrap rows 18 & 19.

9. Remove any excess beads from the working wire. Bring the last bead down from the top wire, then wrap rows 20 & 21. Line up the bead colors with rows 18 & 19 so plain gold beads line up with the sections of mixed beads, and mixed beads line up with plain bract colored beads.

10. Twist the working wire into the bottom wire and support wires to make five bottom wires. Cut the top and spoke wires short and fold them back.

11. Cut a 7 inch (17.8 cm) length of 30 gauge (.25 mm) bract colored wire and lace across the center of the bract. You may need to lace at a slant to avoid the center spoke wires.

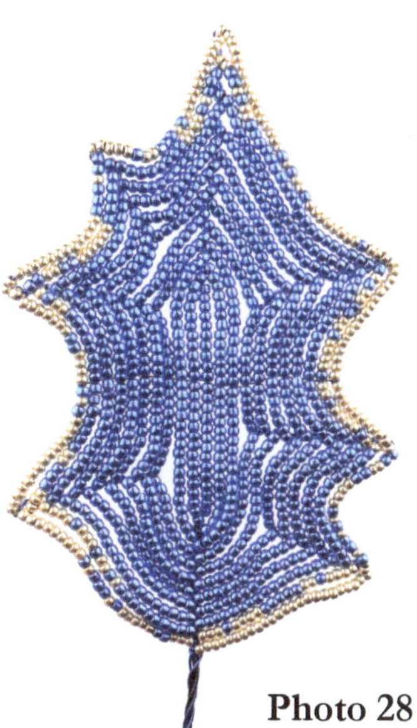

Photo 28

Photo 28 shows the finished Bract F for the Large Poinsettia. *See the note on Alterations in the Bract C instructions.*

POINSETTIA LEAVES: *Each leaf equals one day.*

The leaves for the Poinsettia are made using the same basic procedure as the bracts, but a little larger.

Wire: *24, and 30 gauge (.5, and .25 mm) green copper core wire.*
Beads: *Size 11/0 2-cut green seed beads, size 11/0 gold seed beads.*

Small Leaf
Make 8 (or 2-3 per flower).

Pattern: 23 row BF, 1 inch (2.5 cm) BR, RB PT.
- **SPOKES:**
  - **Rows 8 & 9: 2 spokes in each row, 1 ½ inch (3.8 cm) long, evenly spaced**
  - **Row 14: 1 spoke, 1 ½ inches long, halfway between the second spoke and the top wire.**
  - **Row 15: 1 spoke, 1 ½ inches long, halfway between the fourth spoke and the bottom wire.**
- **EXTENSIONS: Add 1 bead to the top wire after rows 15, 17, 19, and 21 (4 beads total).**
- **Reduce to two bottom wires.**
- **Lace once across the center.**

Prep: Make another mix for the leaf edging. Make approximately 20 grams of the gold/green bead mix with a 1:1 ratio.

Just like the bracts, string 10 or so feet of the main leaf colored beads at a time and make as many leaves as you can with that length.

Instructions

1. Construct a Basic Frame using 1 inch (2.5 cm) + 4 beads for the Basic Row. Make the top wire at least 2 ¼ inches (5.7 cm) long. Move the top 4 beads to the end of the top wire, and bend it back to keep the beads out of the way. These will be used later as top wire extension beads.

2. Wrap rows 2-7 with a round bottom and pointed top.

3. In rows 8 & 9, make two spokes each. Each spoke needs to be approximately 1 ½ inches (3.8 cm) long. Space the spokes so they divide the rows somewhat evenly. (**Photo 29**)

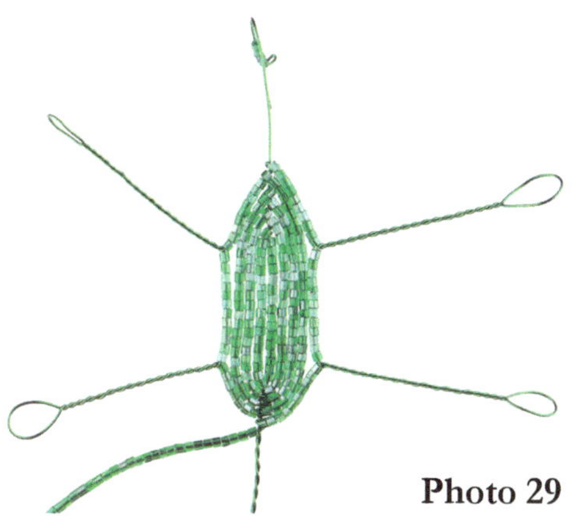

Photo 29

4. Wrap rows 10-13, making a sharp point at each spoke.

5. In row 14, make one 1 ½ inch (3.8 cm) spoke, positioning it between second spoke in row 8 and the top wire. In row 15, make spoke of the same length, positioning it between the second spoke in row 9 and the bottom wire. (**Photo 30**)

6. Wrap rows 16-19, moving one bead down on the top wire before wrapping rows 16 and 18. Wrap at a sharp point at each spoke.

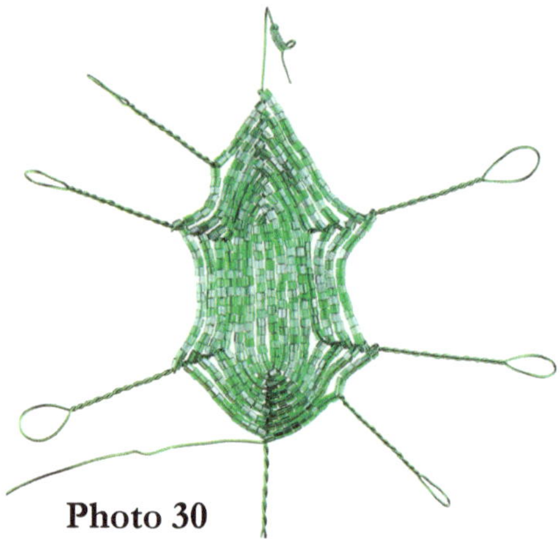

Photo 30

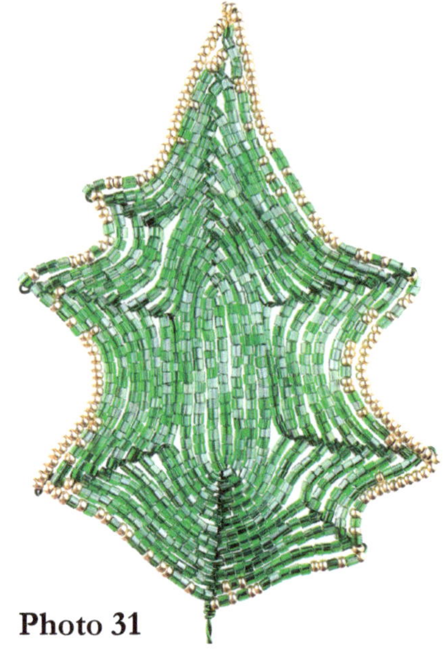

7. Cut approximately 30 inches (76.2 cm) of bare working wire. String 1-1 ½ inches of the mixed beads, then a similar length of the green beads. Continue stringing beads alternating between the mix and the green beads until you have approximately 12 inches (30.5 cm) total. Move one bead down from the top wire and wrap rows 20 & 21.

8. Remove any excess beads from the working wire. Move the last bead on the top wire down. String beads as needed to complete rows 22 & 23. Line up a length of gold beads with a length of mixed beads in the previous rows, and string mixed beads to line up with the green sections in the previous rows.

9. Reduce to two bottom wires. Cut and fold the top and spoke wires. Cut approximately 7 inches (17.8 cm) of 30 gauge green wire and lace across the center of the leaf.

A finished Leaf A is shown in **Photo 31**.

Photo 31

Large Leaf
Make 7 (or 2-3 per poinsettia)

Pattern: 27 row BF, 1 ¾ inch (4.5 cm) BR, RB PT.
- **SPOKES:**
  - **Rows 10 & 11: 2 spokes in each row, 2 inches (5 cm) long, evenly spaced**
  - **Row 16: 1 spoke, 1 ¼ inches (3.2 cm) long, placed halfway between the two spokes in row 10.**
  - **Row 17: 1 spoke, 1 ¼ inches (3.2 cm) long, placed halfway between the top wire and the first spoke in row 11.**
- **EXTENSIONS: Add 1 bead to the Top Wire after rows 17, 19, 21, 23, and 25 (5 beads total).**
- **Reduce to two bottom wires.**
- **Lace once across the center, and once in a V-shape at the top of the leaf.**

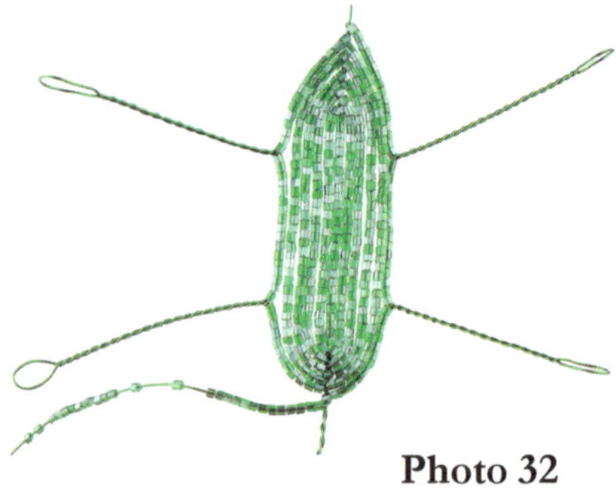

Photo 32

1. Construct a Basic Frame using 1 ¾ inches (4.5 cm) + 5 beads for the Basic Row. Make the top wire at least 2 ¾ inches (7 cm) long. Move the top 5 beads to the end of the top wire, and bend the wire back to keep the beads out of the way. These will be used later as top wire extension beads.

2. Wrap rows 2-9 with a round bottom and pointed top.

3. In rows 10 & 11, make two spokes each. Each spoke needs to be approximately 1 ¾ inches (4.5 cm) long. Space the spokes so they divide the rows somewhat evenly. (**Photo 32**)

4. Wrap rows 12-15, wrapping at a sharp point at each spoke.

5. In row 16, make one 1 ¼ inch (3.2 cm) spoke somewhere between the two previously made spokes. In row 17, make one spoke the same length halfway between the top wire and the first spoke. (**Photo 33**)

6. Wrap rows 18-23, moving one bead down from the top wire after rows 17, 19, and 21. Make a sharp point at each spoke.

7. Cut approximately 35 inches (89 cm) of bare working wire. String approximately 16 inches (40.6 cm) of beads, alternating between 1-1 ½ inches of the mix and a similar length of the green beads. Move one bead down from the top wire, then wrap rows 24 & 25.

8. Remove any excess beads. Bring down the last bead on the top wire. For rows 26 & 27, string beads as needed. Line up a length of gold beads with mixed beads in the previous rows, and mixed beads with a length of green beads in the previous rows.

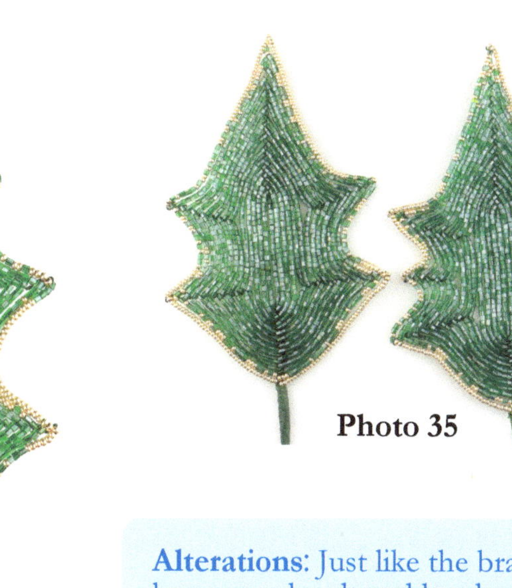

Photo 33

9. Reduce to two bottom wires. Cut the top and spoke wires and fold them back. Cut approximately 8 inches (20.3 cm) of 30 gauge green wire and lace across the center of the leaf. You may need to slant the lacing just a little to avoid running into the spoke wires. Cut another length of 30 gauge green wire and lace in a V-shape at the top of the leaf. Position the middle of the V about 2 beads down from the top of the Basic Row.

A finished Leaf B is shown in **Photo 34**.

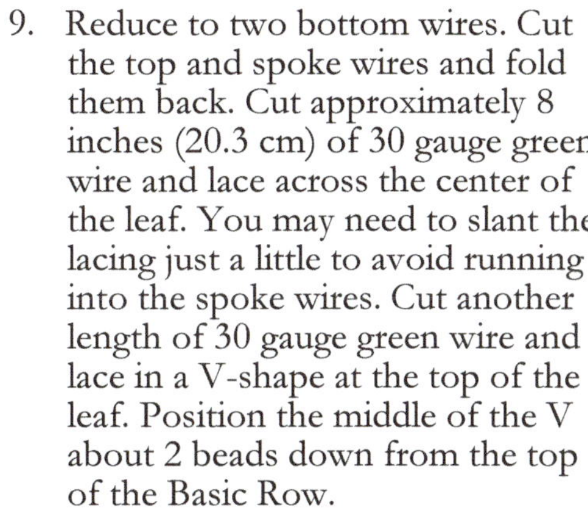

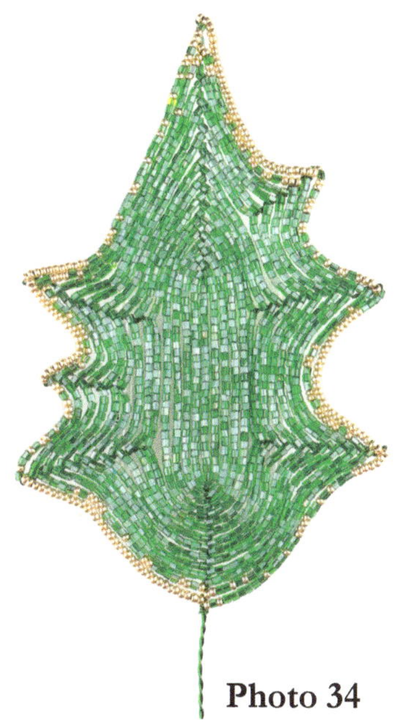

Photo 34

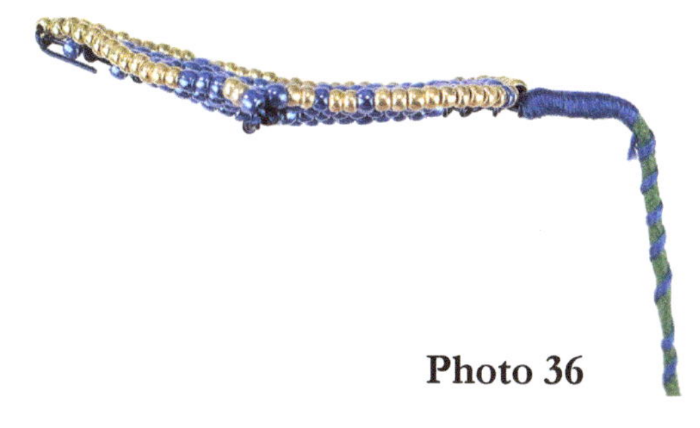

Photo 35

Alterations: Just like the bracts, the leaves can be altered by changing the position and number of spokes (**Photo 35**).

ASSEMBLY:

The instructions use Small Poinsettia bracts A, B, C. For the Large Poinsettia substitute bracts D, E, F.

1. Cut a long length of floral tape in half length-wise to make thinner tape. Use this tape to wrap the stem wires on each Flower Center, Bract, and Leaf.

2. Cut a few feet of bract-colored embroidery floss and divide it in half to make two three-strand lengths. Wrap the stems on each bract with the floss to approximately ¼ inch (6.4 mm) below the bract. Bend each bract stem at a 90 degree angle just below the floss. (**Photo 36**)

3. Prepare the 14 gauge galvanized steel stem wires by wrapping them with a layer of floral tape. This creates extra grip on the stem's surface so components will be less likely to slip around.

4. Use half-width tape to attach the Flower Center to one of the 14 gauge stem wires, wrapping all the way down to the end of the flower center's stem wire. (**Photo 37**)

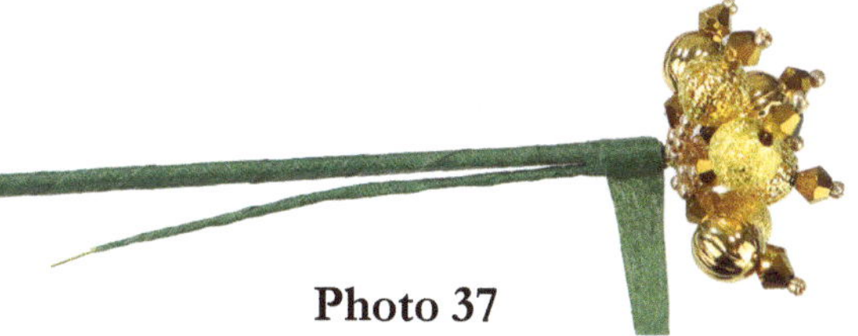

Photo 36

Photo 37

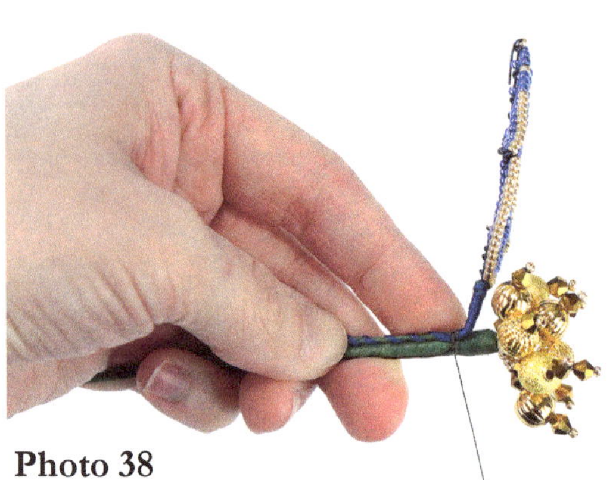

Photo 38

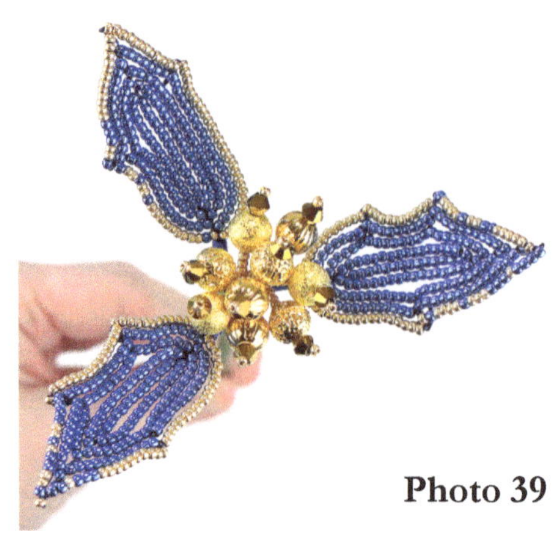

Photo 39

5. Cut a few feet of 30 gauge green wire to use as an assembly wire, and use it to attach one Bract A approximately ¼- ½ inch (6.4 - 12.7 mm) below the poinsettia's Flower Center. (**Photo 38**)

6. Wrap the wire tightly 3-4 time just below the point where the stems join. Then, add in the other two Bract A one at a time, spacing them evenly around the Flower Center. (**Photo 39**)

7. Wrap the assembly wire down the stem at least 1 inch (2.5 cm). Tie off the assembly wire, trim the end off, and cover the stem with a layer of floral tape.

8. Cut several more feet of 30 gauge green wire. Lay a tail of the 30 gauge wire against the bract stem wire and wind it tightly a few times just below the floss (**Photo 40**).

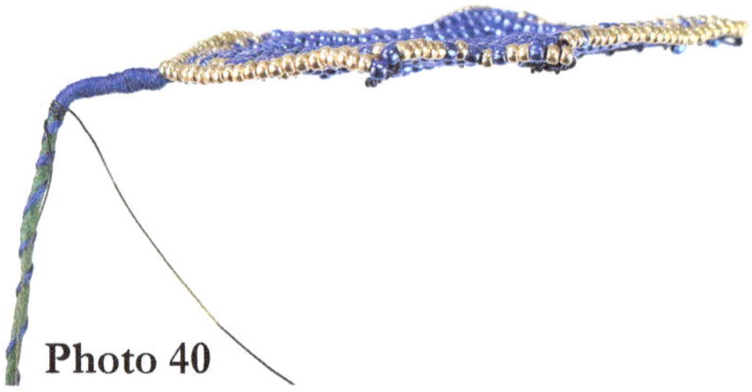

Photo 40

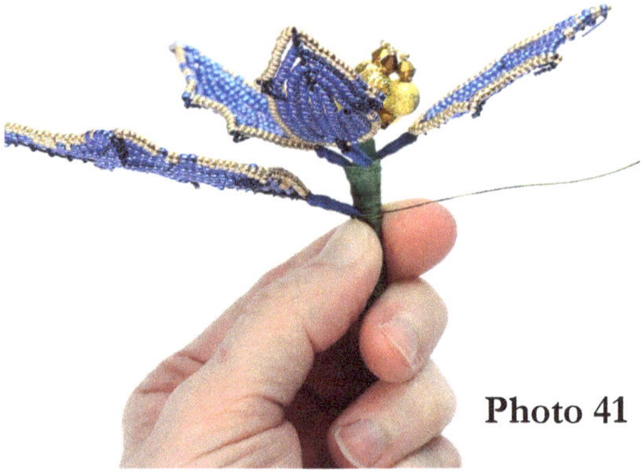

Photo 41

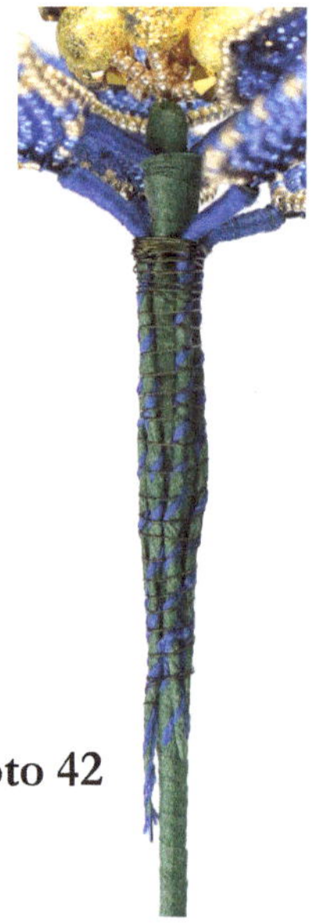

9. Attach the bract approximately ½ inch (12.7 mm) below the layer of Bract As. (**Photo 41**)

10. Wind the wire tightly around the petal 3-5 times, then add in the other bracts, one at a time, winding the wire around each one 3-5 times before adding in the next. Continue winding the wire down the stem 1-2 inches (2.5-5 cm). Space the bracts evenly around the Flower Center. (**Photo 42**)

11. Cover the exposed wires with a layer of floral tape.

12. Cut several feet of 30 gauge wire and attach it to one of the Bract C as shown on the previous page.

13. Attach three Bract Cs approximately ½ inch (12.7 mm) below the layer of Bract Bs, following the same procedure as before. Space them evenly around the Flower Center (**Photo 43**). After attaching the third bract, continue wrapping the assembly wire down the stem 1-2 inches (2.5 -5 cm), then clip it off. Cover the exposed wires with floral tape.

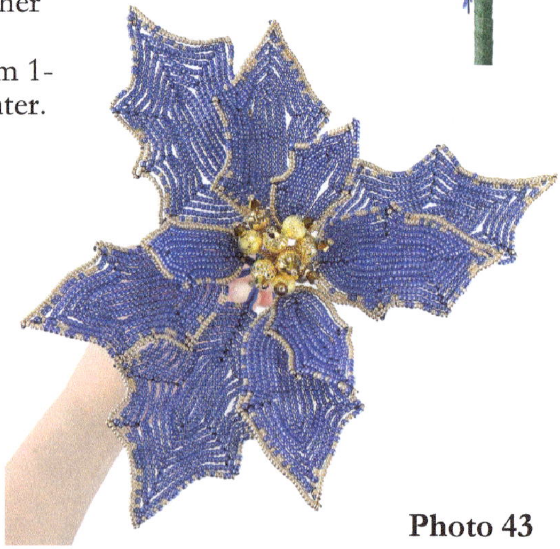

Photo 42

Photo 43

14. Cut several feet of 30 gauge wire and attach the last three Bract Cs between the three previous Bract C. Follow the same procedure as before. The new bracts should be positioned on the same level as the previous layer, not below them. Cover the stem again with floral tape. (**Photo 44**)

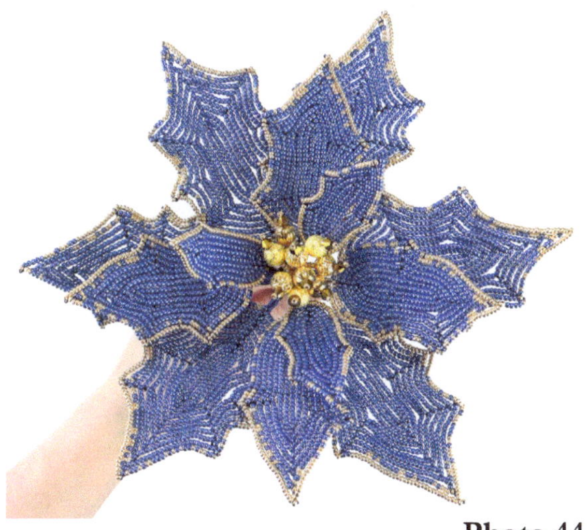

Photo 44

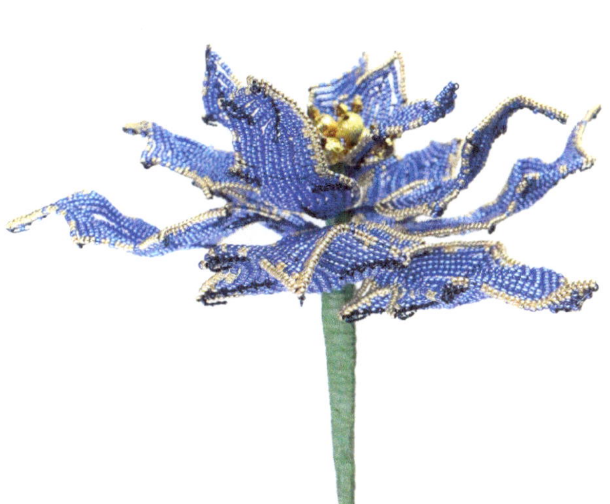

Photo 45

15. Shape each bract by twisting, bending and curling them so they are no longer flat. This is essential to making more natural-looking flowers. (**Photo 45**)

16. Repeat the entire process to assemble the remaining two poinsettias.

Leaf Assembly:

The poinsettia leaves are attached to the wreath frame separately from the flowers. In other arrangements, you may want to attach the leaves directly to the flower stem. In either case, follow the instructions below to attach the leaves to stem wires. If you are attaching the leaves directly to the flower stem for use in another arrangement, use 30 gauge wire to attach them to the flower stem beginning a few inches below the flower head.

1. Prepare all the 16 gauge stem wires by wrapping them with floral tape.

2. Cut about 1 foot (30.5 cm) of 30 gauge green wire. Lay a short tail of the 30 gauge wire against one of the 16g stem wires, then wind it a couple times around the end of the stem wire to secure it. (**Photo 46**)

3. Lay a leaf against the stem wire, positioning the tip of the stem wire directly below the basic row on the leaf.

4. Use the 30g wire to sew the leaf to the stem by looping the wire around between rows on the bottom wire. Check the front often to make sure the wire has gone all the way down between two rows of beads. (**Photo 47**)

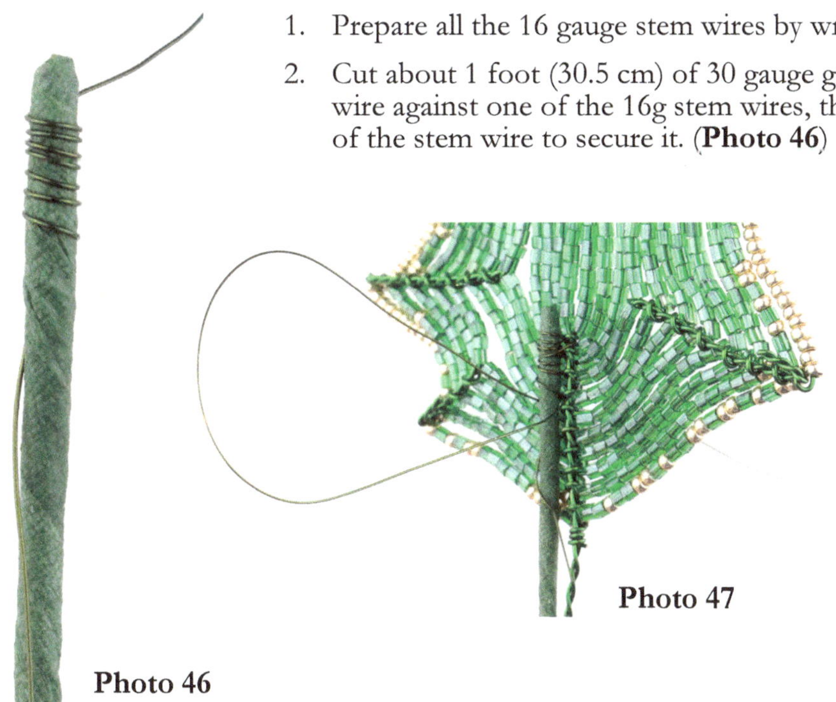

Photo 47

Photo 46

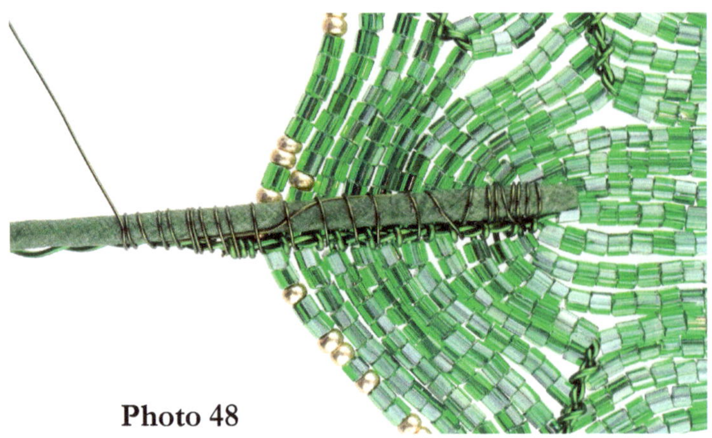

Photo 48

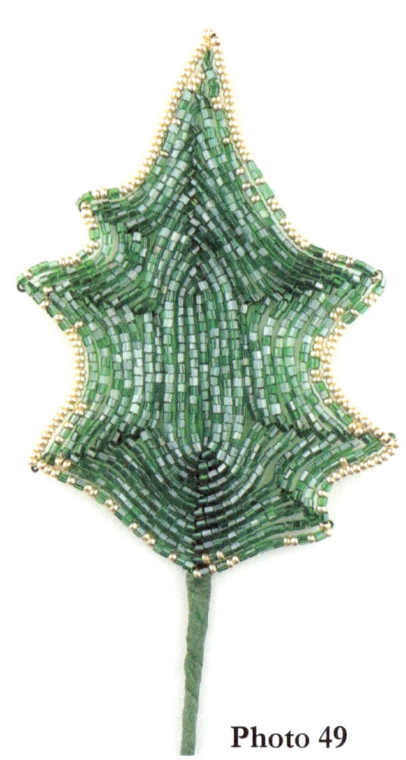

Photo 49

5. Continue all the way down the leaf. Once you reach the bottom, wrap the 30 gauge wire around the leaf wire and 16g stem (**Photo 48**).

6. Wrap the stem with floral tape to cover the wires (**Photo 49**).

7. Repeat for each of the remaining poinsettia leaves.

Bonus Project: Poinsettia Tree Topper

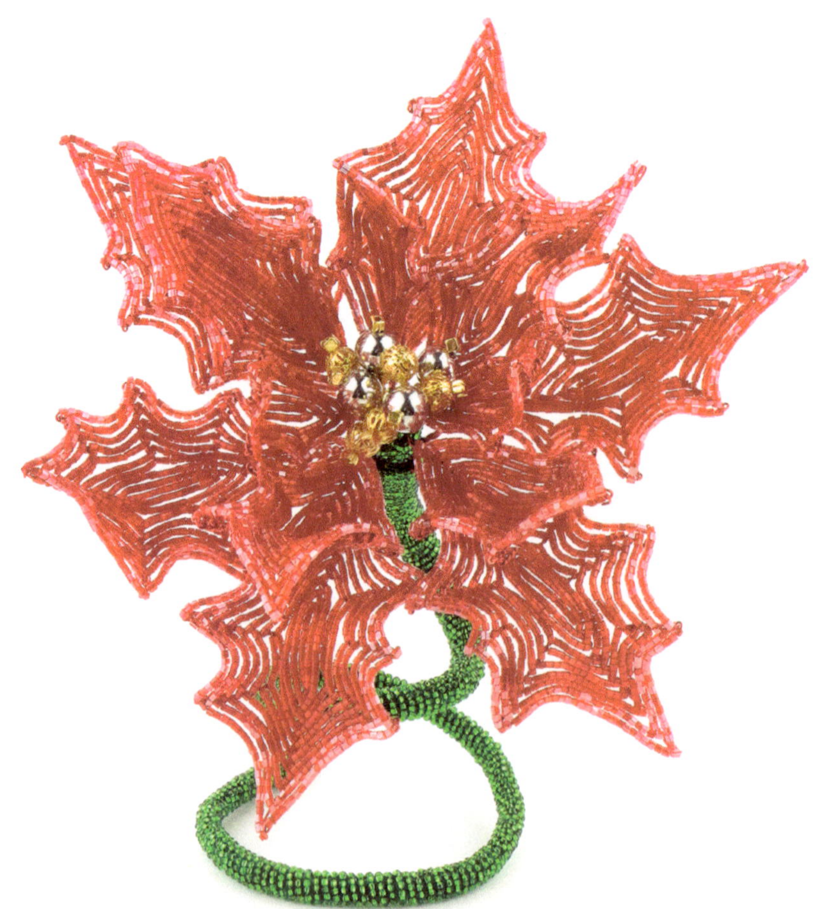

Additional Techniques Required
*   Beehive

Additional Materials
In addition to the materials for one Small Poinsettia listed at the beginning of the Spoke Poinsettia pattern, you will need:

*   28 grams 11/0 silver-lined green
*   20 ft (6 m) 26 gauge (.4 mm) green colored copper core wire
*   A length of 14 gauge galvanized steel stem wire to 18 inches (45.7 cm) long.

For the bracts on my tree topper poinsettia, I used Czech 11/0 2-cut red satin seed beads for the main color, with Czech 11/0 2-cut transparent red luster beads for the edging color. Though the color of the beads is the same, using a different finish on the edging beads will help distinguish between individual petals and add a little bit of a highlight around the edges.

I've also used a mix of silver and gold metal beads for the flower center. Using small jingle bells could be fun!

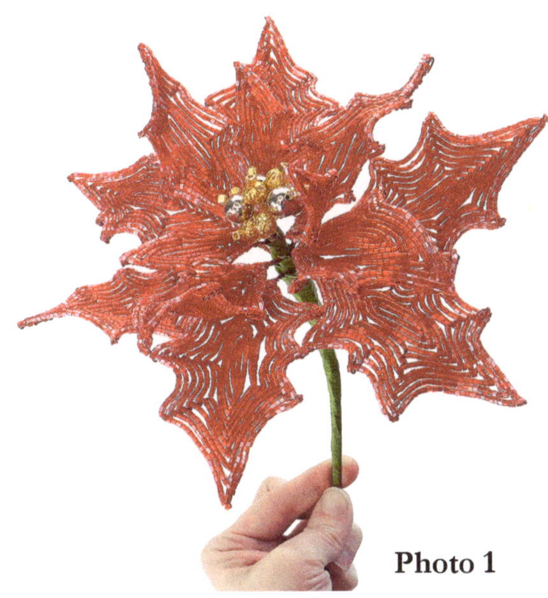

Photo 1

Use the Spoke Poinsettia pattern to make one Small Poinsettia assembled on a stem that is 18 inches (45.7 cm) long. (**Photo 1**)

You should have 3x Bract A, 4x Bract B, and 6x Bract C, along with 3 center pieces. You do not need any leaves.

NOTE: I have not tested this tree topper design with a Large Poinsettia, which is heavier. It is possible that it will work just fine, but may require a little more attention to adjusting the stem for balance.

BEADING THE STEM:

Stem End Cap Pattern: 9 row BBF, 1 bead BR, RB RT

1. String all the green seed beads onto 26 gauge copper core wire.

2. Construct a Basic Frame with a 1 bead Basic Row. The Top wire should be at least 3 inches (7.6 cm) long.

3. Wrap rows 2 & 3, then bend the top and bottom wires back 90 degrees. (**Photo 2**)

4. Wrap rows 4-9 down the top and bottom wires to create a little "cap" that will cover the end of the poinsettia stem. Remove one of the Bottom Wires by clipping it just below the wrap of the last row. Do not tie off or remove the working wire or top wire. (**Photo 3**)

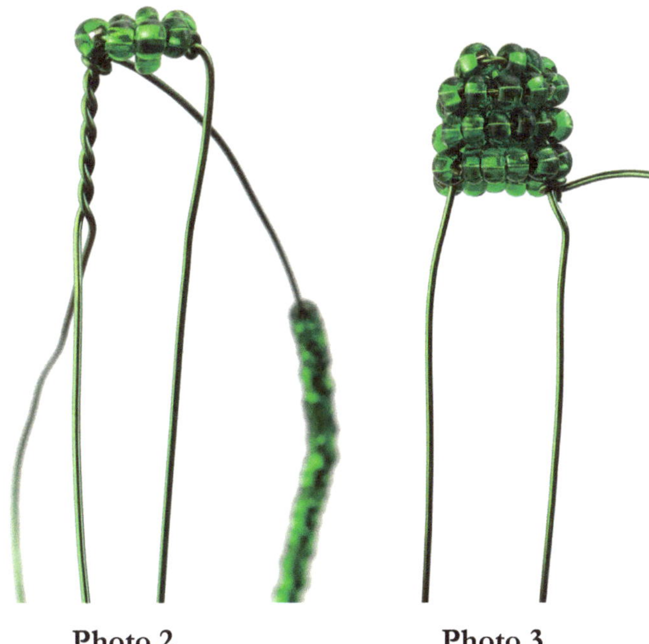

Photo 2   **Photo 3**

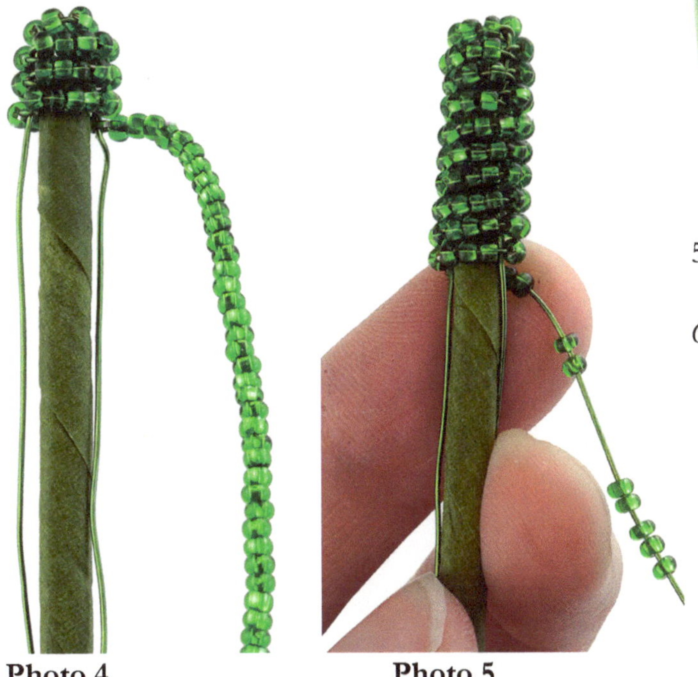

Photo 4   **Photo 5**

5. Insert the bottom end of the poinsettia's stem into the center of the cap. (**Photo 4**)

6. Push more beads onto the working wire from the spool. Hold the cap tightly in place, then wrap beads around the stem. Make sure you are wrapping in the same direction as you were wrapping rows. Also make certain you wrap over the top and bottom wires as this will secure the cap in place. (**Photo 5**)

7. Continue wrapping all the way up the stem, between the layers of bracts, to just beneath the first layer of bracts. Secure the end of the wire by wrapping it a few times around the stem wire on the closest bract, then clip it from the spool. (**Photo 6**)

8. Curl the stem into a spiral shape. Because the flower is front-heavy, make sure the stem curls forward for the best support. You may need to play with it a bit to get the proper shape. The spiral should be tighter at the top and wider at the bottom to fit around the cone-shape of a Chrismas tree. (**Photo 7**) Test the tree topper on a flat surface to make sure it can stand up on it's own. If not, alter the shape and angle of the flower head and the spiral stem until it is well balanced.

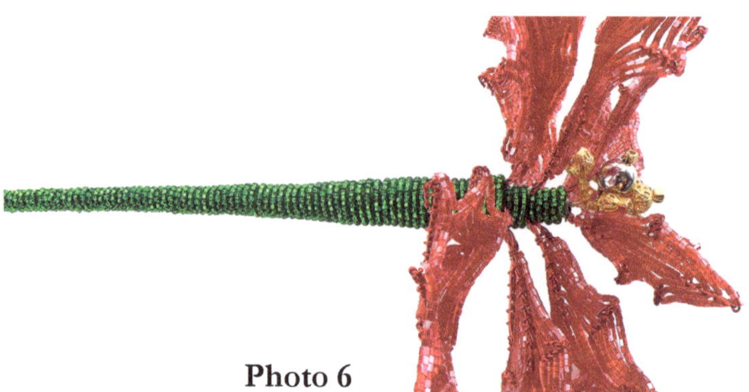

Photo 6

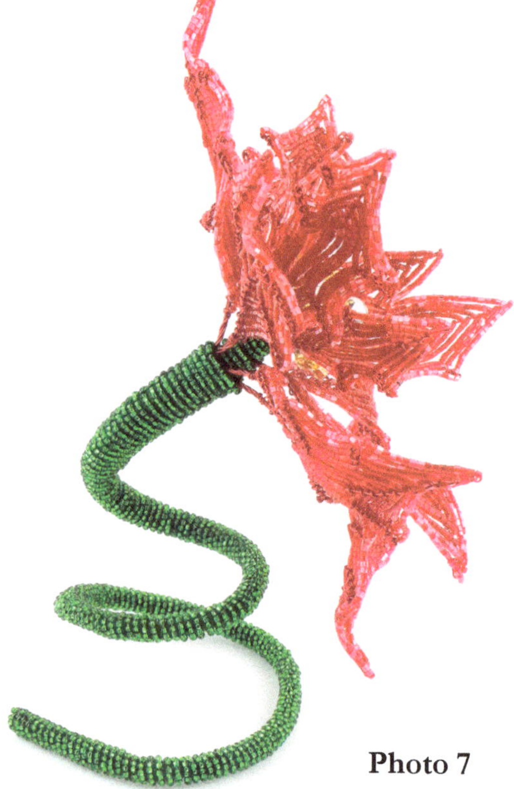

Photo 7

..... GOLD LEAVES .....

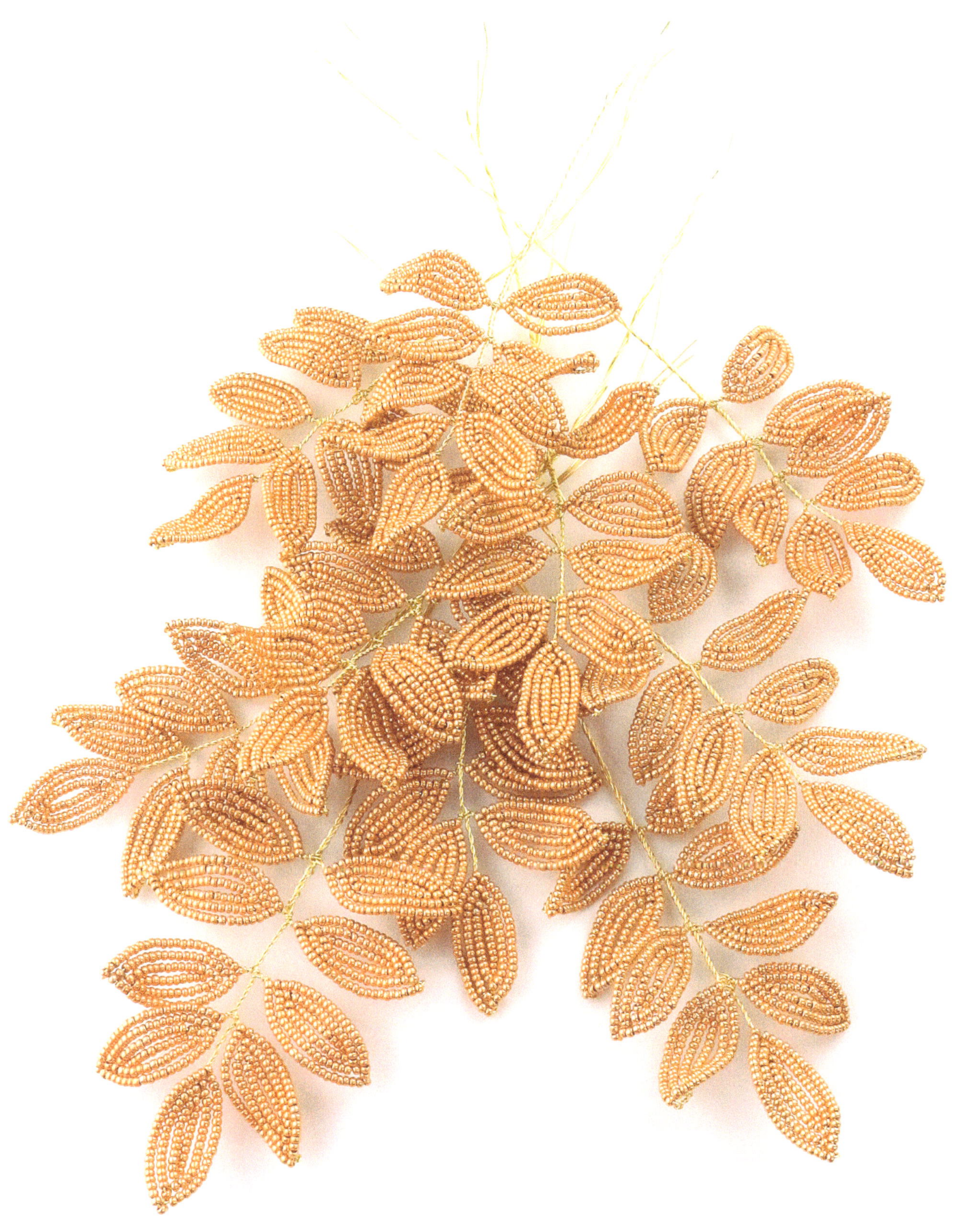

Materials

For the full wreath you will need ten of these simple gold leaf stems.

BEADS:	FULL WREATH	1 STEM
Size 11/0 metallic gold seed beads	100 grams	10 grams
WIRE:		
24 gauge (.5 mm) gold colored copper core wire	80 ft (24.4 m)	8 ft (2.4 m)
22 gauge (.6 mm) gold colored copper core wire	10 ft (3 m)	1 ft (30.5 cm)

Make 10. *One full stem with 9 leaves equals one day.*
Pattern: 9x 8 row CBF, 10 bead BR, PB PT
- **Made vertically, with one leaf at the tip, and the rest in pairs spaced ¾ inch (1.9 cm) apart.**

Instructions:

1. String all of the gold beads onto the 24 gauge wire. Leave a 7 inch (17.8 cm) tail wire, then make the first Continuous Basic Frame using 10 beads for the Basic Row. (**Photo 1**)

2. Wrap rows 2-8 with a pointed bottom and pointed top. Then twist the working wire and tail wire together approximately ¾ inch (1.9 cm) below the leaf. (**Photo 2**)

3. On one side of the twisted wire (right or left, it doesn't matter), leave a ½ inch (1.3 cm) space of bare wire, then construct a second CBF. (**Photo 3**)

4. Wrap rows 2-8. The bottom of the leaf should be very close to the main twisted wire stem. (**Photo 4**) If there is any excess space below the leaf, just twist the working wire with that bottom wire a couple times until you reach the center twisted stem.

TIP: Measure the distance between the bottom of the first leaf's basic row and the last row on the bottom wire. Use this measurement as a gauge for how much bare wire you need to leave below the next leaf's basic row. I used ½ inch, but your measurement might be slightly different.

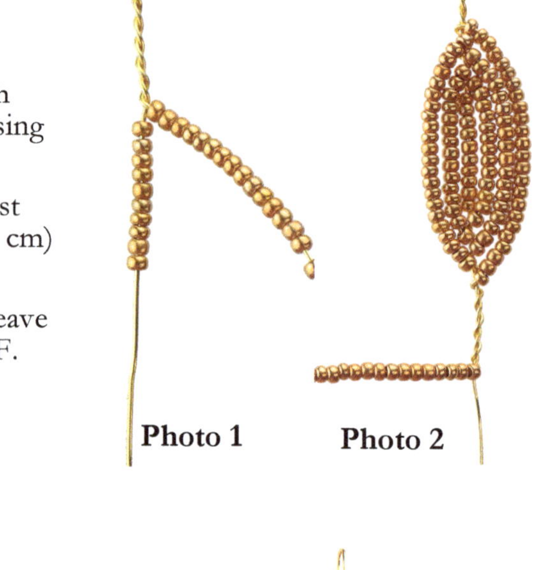

Photo 1   Photo 2

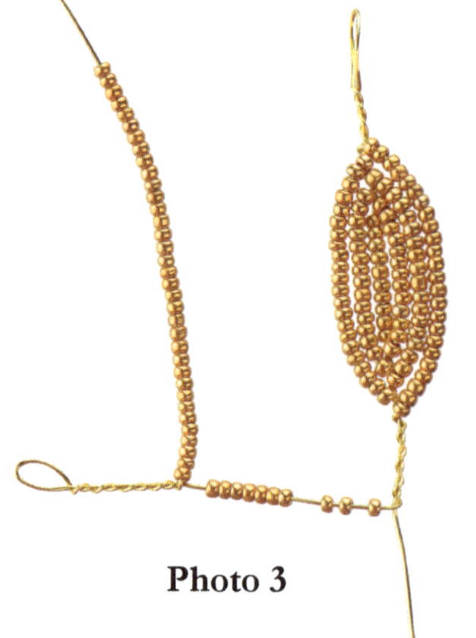

Photo 3

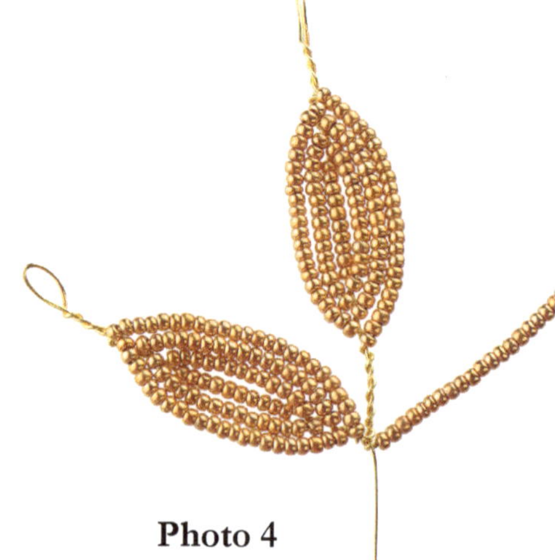

Photo 4

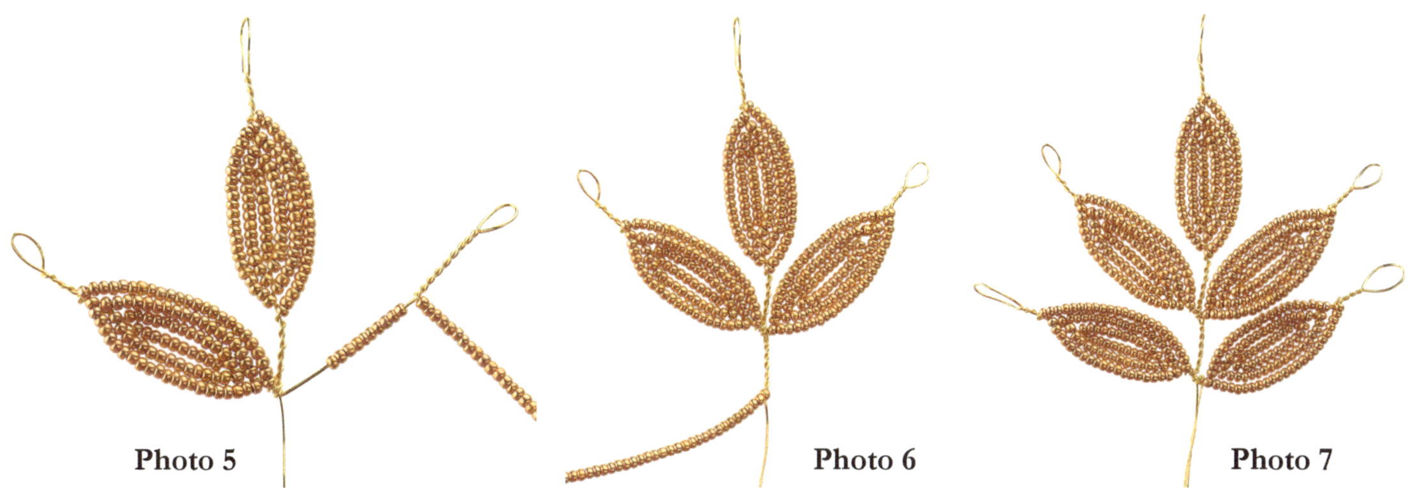

Photo 5   Photo 6   Photo 7

5. Switch the working wire to the opposite side of the stem by wrapping around it once. Leave a ½ inch (1.3 cm) space of bare wire and make the third leaf. (**Photo 5**)

6. Twist the tail and working wires together approximately ¾ inch (1.9 cm) below the pair of leaves. (**Photo 6**)

7. Repeat steps 3-6 to make another pair of leaves, but do not twist the wires below the last set of leaves yet. (**Photo 7**)

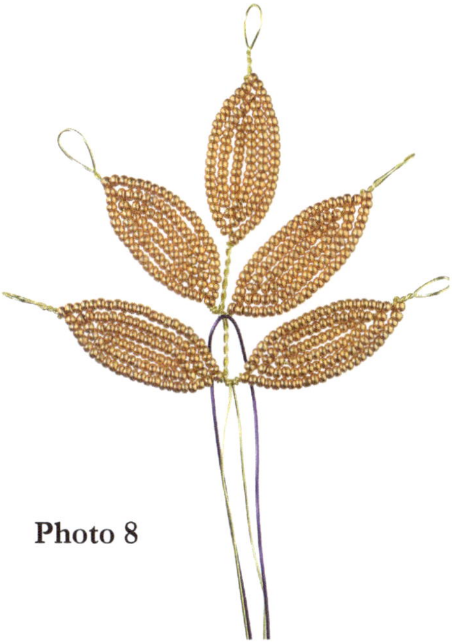

8. Cut a 12 inch (30.5 cm) length of 22 gauge gold wire and fold it in half. Add it into the stem by positioning the center fold in the wire directly above the last set of leaves on the main twisted stem. In **Photo 8** the new 22 gauge support wire is shown in purple.

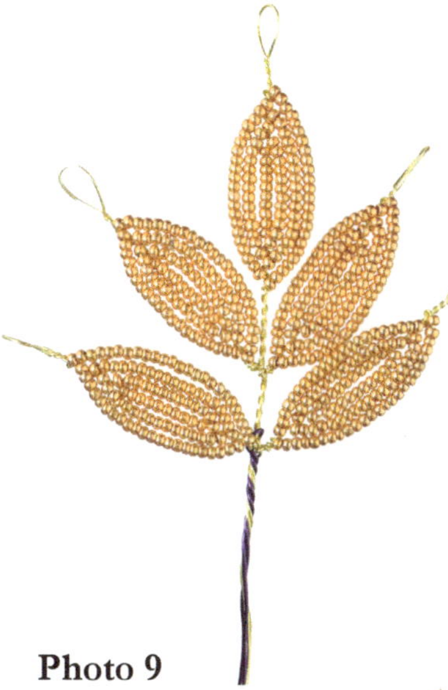

9. Fold both ends of the new wire down with the working wire and tail wire and twist all four wires together approximately ¾ inch (1.9 cm) below the last set of leaves. (**Photo 9**)

Photo 8   **Photo 9**

10. Continue making two more sets of leaves, following the same procedure as before, but with 4 wires making up the stem between sets. (**Photo 10**)

11. Clip all the leaf top wires and fold them back.

The finished leaf stem is shown in **Photo 11.**

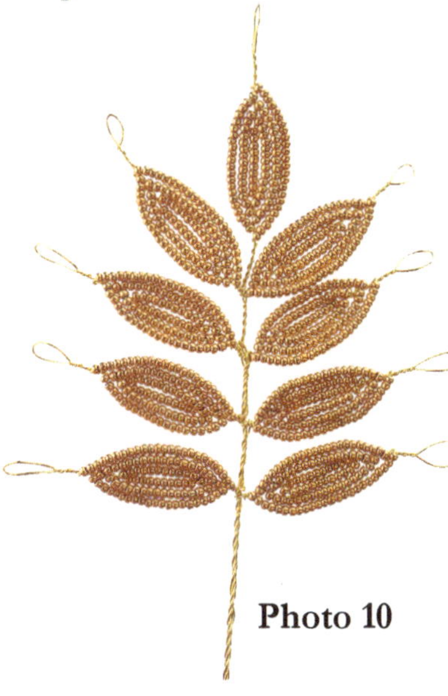

Photo 10 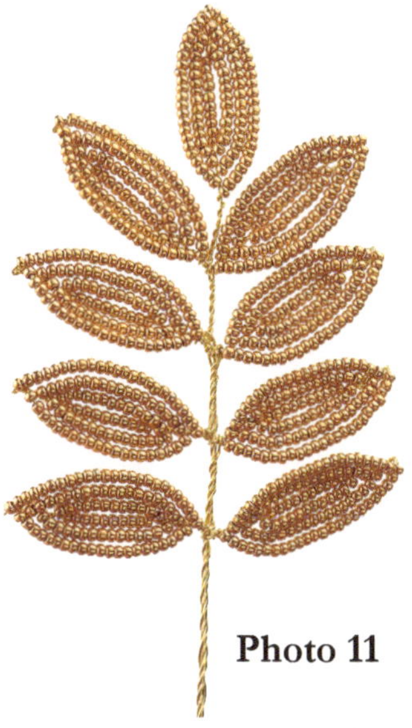   **Photo 11**

..... Pinecone Sprays .....

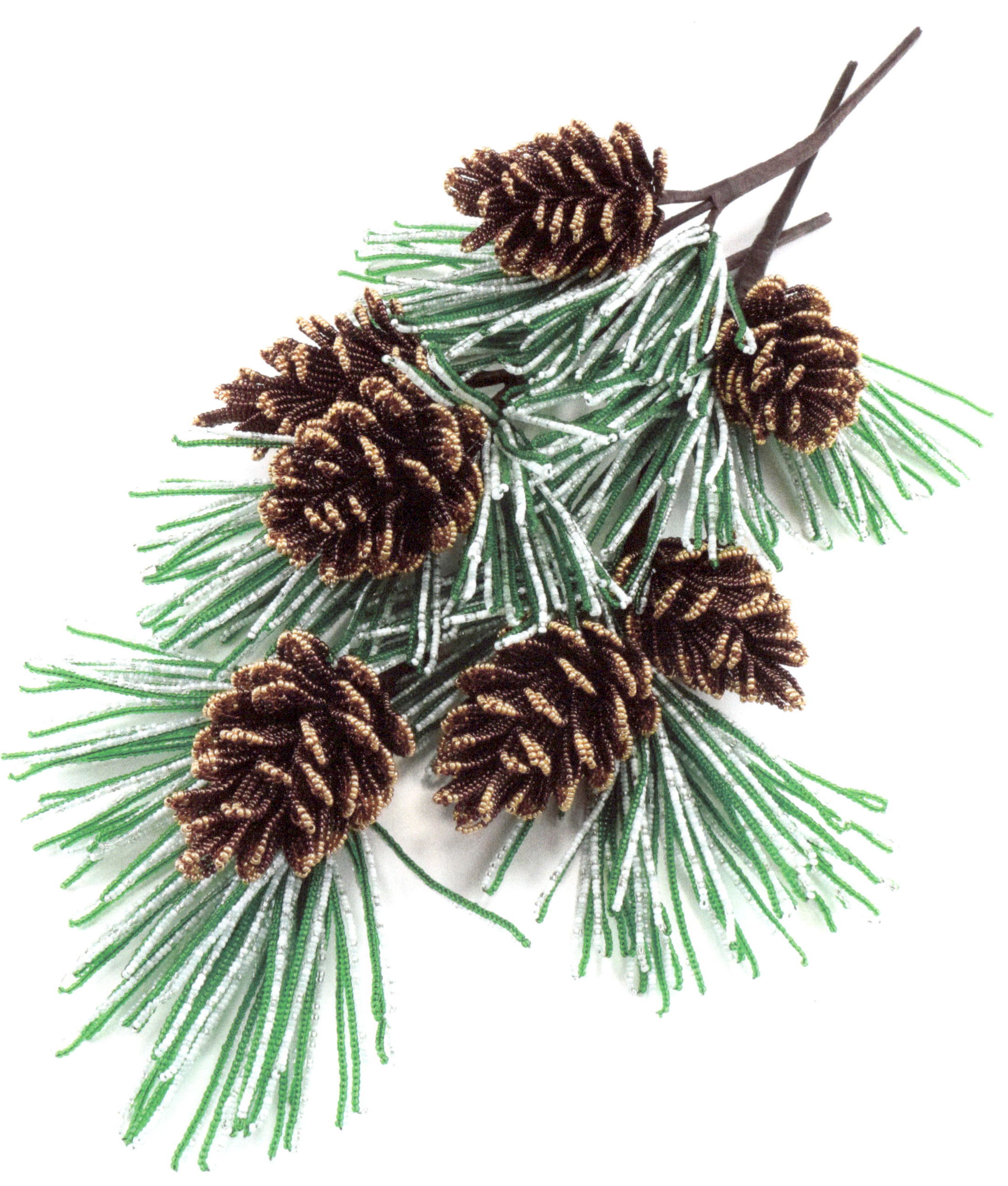

Materials

For the wreath, make two large sprays with two pinecones each, and three small sprays with one pinecone each.

BEADS:	FULL WREATH	SMALL SPRAY	LARGE SPRAY
Size 11/0 Matsuno opaque iris dark bronze (metallic brown) seed beads	245 grams	35 grams	70 grams
Size 11/0 metallic gold seed beads	50 grams	10 grams	20 grams
Size 11/0 transparent green seed beads	150 grams	30 grams	30 grams
Size 11/0 mixed white seed beads*	150 grams	30 grams	30 grams
WIRE:			
24 gauge (.5 mm) brown colored copper core wire	280 ft (83 m)	40 ft (13 m)	80 ft
24 gauge (.5 mm) green colored copper core wire	170 ft (52 m)	35 ft (11 m)	35 ft
30 gauge (.25 mm) brown colored copper core wire	50 ft (16 m)	7 ft (3 m)	7 ft
16 gauge (1.29 mm) florist stem wire	17 pieces	3 pieces	4 pieces
OTHER:			
Brown floral tape	< 1 roll	< 1 roll	< 1 roll

NOTES:

*For my white seed beads, I mixed three different types: opaque white luster, white ceylon, and silver-lined crystal for a little twinkle. Feel free to substitute your own finishes. They don't need to be equal parts.

PINE NEEDLES: *Each unit equals one day.*

Wire: *24g (.5 mm) green*
Beads: *white mix, transparent green*

Prep: The loops will be half green and half white. This shading pattern makes it look like a layer of snow or frost has collected on the needles. String beads onto the spool - 3 inches (7.6 cm) of green, then 3 inches of white. Alternate between green and white until you have enough for the unit. You can string for one unit at a time, or all of them at once.

After stringing the beads this way, you will not need to measure and cut wire. Work from the spool, folding one green segment plus one white segment together to make a loop.

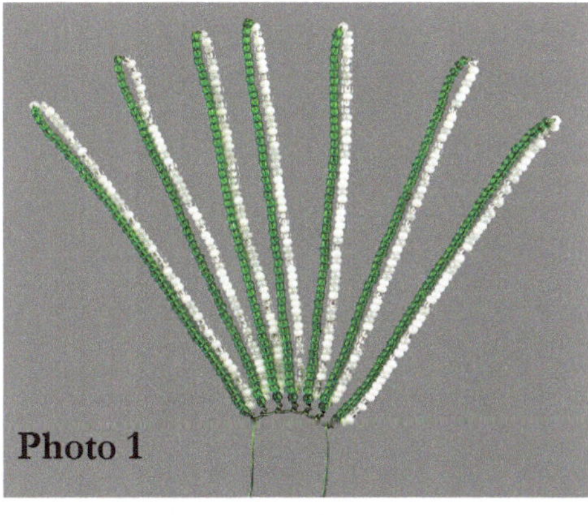

Photo 1

Needle Unit:

Make 30 (6 per large or small spray).

Pattern: 7x CL using 6 inches (15.2 cm) of beads per loop (3 inches of green, 3 inches of white).

Instructions:

1. Leave a 2 inch (5 cm) starting tail wire, then make the continuous loops according to the pattern above. Pinch each of the loops closed to make them flat and skinny. (**Photo 1**)

2. Close the unit into a circle by wrapping the working wire around the first loop. Then twist the two wires together in the center below.

The finished Needle Unit is shown in **Photo 2**.

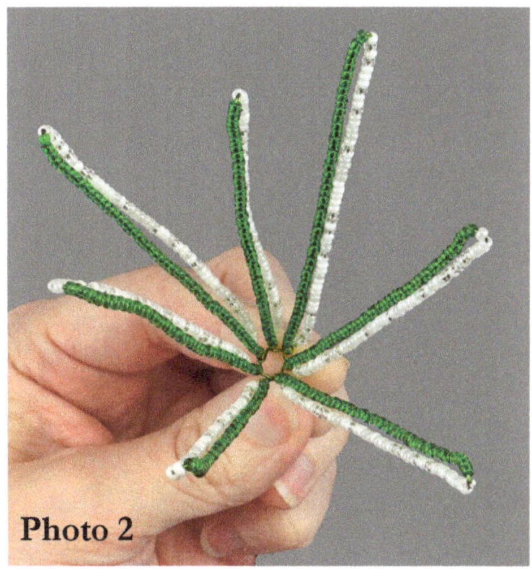

Photo 2

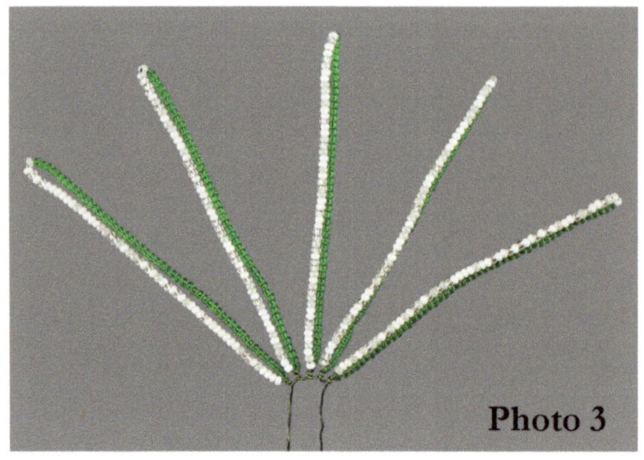

Photo 3

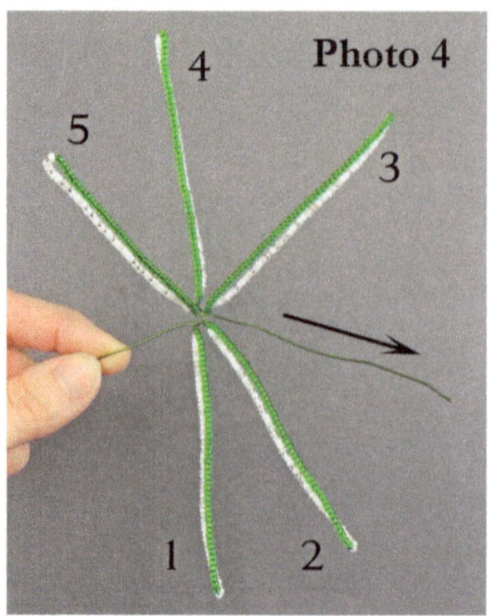

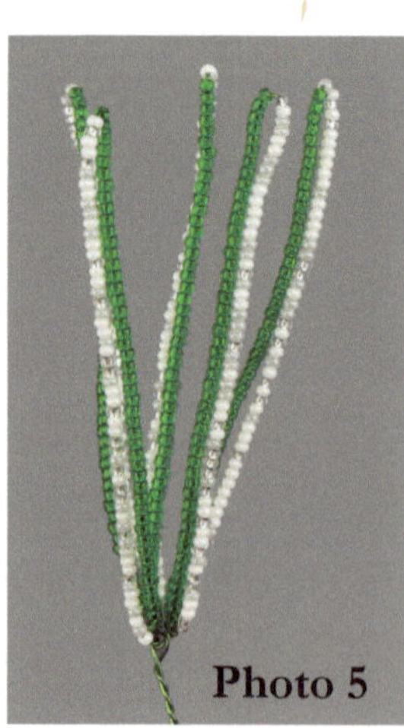

Photo 5

Needle Tip Unit:

Make 10 (2 per small or large spray).

Pattern: 5x CL using 6 inches (15.2 cm) of beads per loop (3 inches of green, 3 inches of white).

1. Make the continuous loop unit according to the pattern above. Pinch each of the loops closed to make them flat and skinny. (**Photo 3**)

2. Close the unit by crossing the working wire over between the second and third loops (**Photo 4**). This pulls the last loop into position in the center of the unit. Loop the starting tail wire around the fourth loop to close the four outer loops into a circle around the center loop. Twist the beginning and ending tail wires together below the unit.

The finished Needle Tip Unit is shown in **Photo 5**.

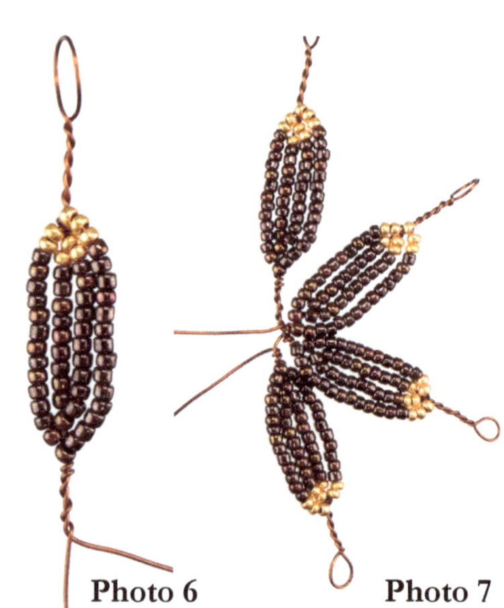

Photo 6   Photo 7

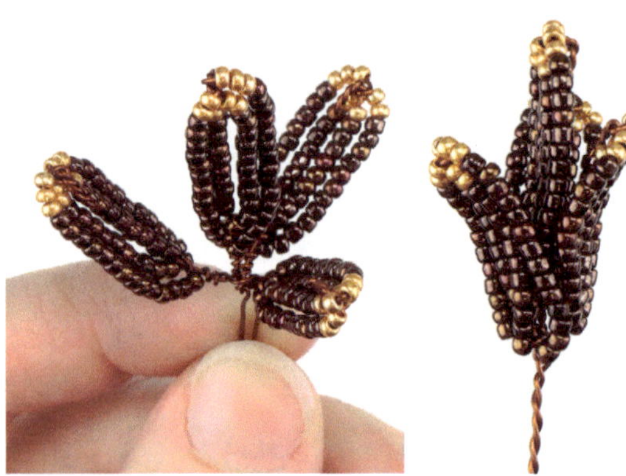

Photo 8   Photo 9

Pinecone Scales: *Each unit equals one day.*

Wire: *24g (.5 mm) brown*
Beads: *opaque iris dark bronze, metallic gold*

Unit A:

Make 7 (1 per pinecone, 1 per small spray, 2 per large spray)

Pattern: 4x 4 row Continuous Basic Frame (CBF), 11 bead BR, PB RT

Shading Counts:
BR = 10x brown, 1x gold
Row 2= begin with 2x gold, fill the rest with brown
Row 3 = fill in with brown, end with 2x gold
Row 4 = begin with 3x gold, fill in with brown

Instructions:

1. Cut a 2.5 foot (76.2 cm) length of wire. Do not pre-load the beads. Instead add beads to the working wire as needed to complete each row.

2. Leave a 2 inch (5 cm) starting tail wire, then make the first scale according to the pattern above. Twist the two wires below the scale approximately 1/4 inch (6.35 mm). (**Photo 6**)

3. Make the last three scales all in line. (**Photo 7**)

4. Close the unit by wrapping the last three scales around the starting tail wire, directly beneath the 1/4" (6.35 mm) twisted wire. Flip the scales so the undersides are facing toward the center scale. Wrap the working wire around the first of the three lower scales (**Photo 8**). Twist the two wires below.

5. Fold the three lower scales up around the center scale.

A finished Unit A is shown in **Photo 9**.

Unit B:

Make 7 (1 per pinecone, 1 per small spray, 2 per large spray)

Pattern: 5x 4 row CBF, 11 bead BR, PB RT

Shading Counts:
BR = 10x brown, 1x gold
Row 2= begin with 2x gold, fill the rest with brown
Row 3 = fill in with brown, end with 2x gold
Row 4 = begin with 3x gold, fill in with brown

Instructions:

1. Cut a 3.5 foot (1 m) length of wire.

2. Leave a 2 inch (5 cm) starting tail wire, then make all five scales according to the pattern above. (**Photo 10**)

3. Close the unit by wrapping the tail wire around the first scale, then twist the wires together so they stick out on top of the unit instead of underneath as you normally would. This will keep the wire wraps concealed in the finished pinecone.

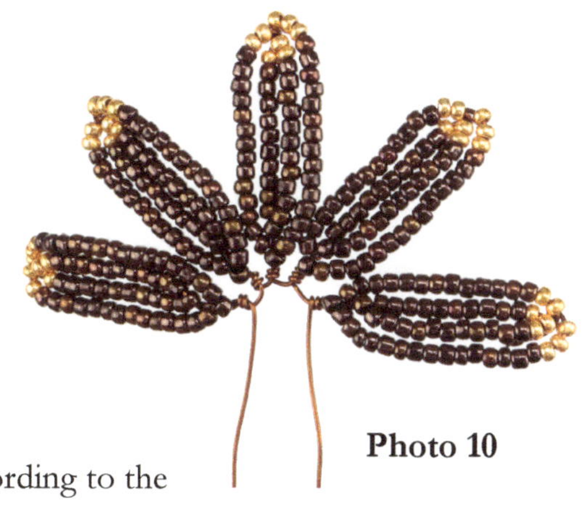

Photo 10

Unit C:

Make 7 (1 per pinecone, 1 per small spray, 2 per large spray)

Pattern: 6x 4 row CBF, 11 bead BR, PB RT

Shading Counts:
BR = 10x brown, 1x gold
Row 2= begin with 2x gold, fill the rest with brown
Row 3 = fill in with brown, end with 2x gold
Row 4 = begin with 3x gold, fill in with brown

Instructions:

1. Cut a 4.5 foot (1.4 m) length of wire.

2. Leave a 2 inch (5 cm) starting tail wire, then make all six scales according to the pattern above. (**Photo 11**)

3. Close the unit by wrapping the tail wire around the first scale, then twist the wires together. Make sure the stem wire is sticking out of the top of the unit, not the underside.

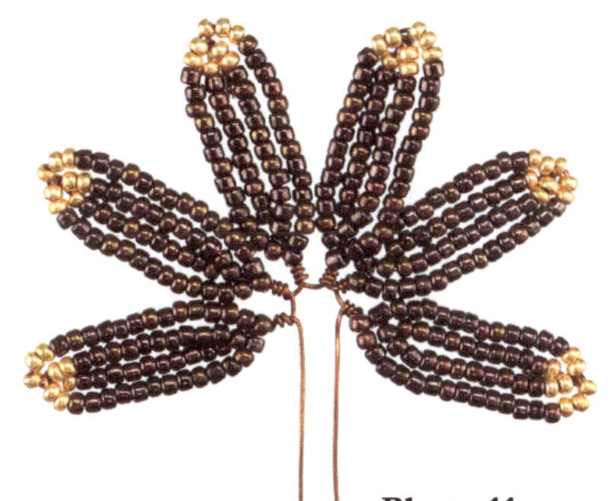

Photo 11

Unit D:

Make 7 (1 per pinecone, 1 per small spray, 2 per large spray)

Pattern: 6x 6 row CBF, 11 bead BR, PB RT

Shading Counts:
BR = 10x brown, 1x gold
Row 2= begin with 2x gold, fill the rest with brown
Row 3 = fill in with brown, end with 2x gold
Row 4 = begin with 3x gold, fill in with brown
Row 5 = fill in with brown, end with 4x gold
Row 6 = begin with 5x gold, fill in with brown

Instructions:

1. Cut a 5 foot (1.5 m) length of wire.

2. Leave a 2 inch (5 cm) starting tail wire, then make all six scales according to the pattern above. A close-up of one scale is shown in **Photo 12**. **Photo 13** shows all six scales. Notice the overlapping pattern of the scales. Pull every other scale forward so it rests in front of both scales on either side.

3. Close the unit by wrapping the tail wire around the first scale, then twist the wires together. Make sure the stem wire is sticking out of the top of the unit, not the underside.

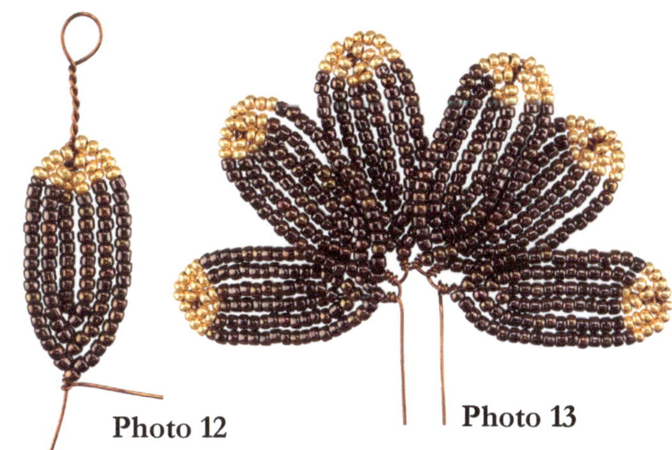

Photo 12   **Photo 13**

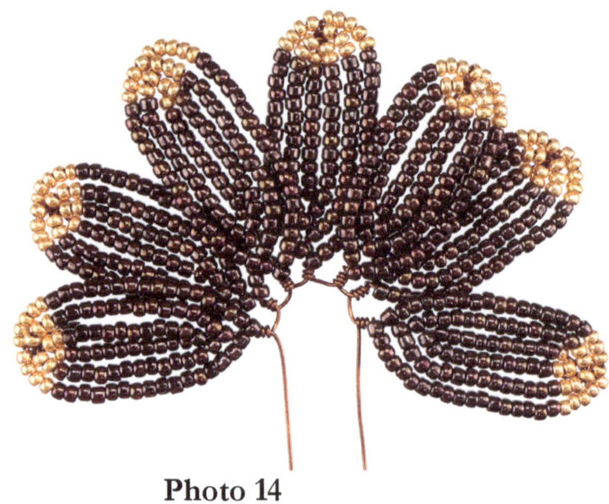

Photo 14

Alterations: Unit E controls the length of the pinecone. If you want a longer pinecone, make more of Unit E. If you want a shorter pinecone, make just one or two per pinecone. This will add or subtract days to a one-a-day project, so be sure to make up the days elsewhere. You will also need more materials.

Unit E:

Make 21 (3 per pinecone, 3 per small spray, 6 per large spray)

Pattern: 7x 6 row CBF, 11 bead BR, PB RT

Shading Counts:
BR = 10x brown, 1x gold
Row 2= begin with 2x gold, fill the rest with brown
Row 3 = fill in with brown, end with 2x gold
Row 4 = begin with 3x gold, fill in with brown
Row 5 = fill in with brown, end with 4x gold
Row 6 = begin with 5x gold, fill in with brown

Instructions:

1. Cut a 6 foot (1.8 m) length of wire.

2. Leave a 2 inch (5 cm) starting tail wire, then make all seven scales according to the pattern above. Pull every other scale forward so it rests in front of both scales on either side. (**Photo 14**)

3. Close the unit into a circle by wrapping the tail wire around the first scale, then twist the wires together. Make sure the stem wire is sticking out of the top of the unit, not the underside.

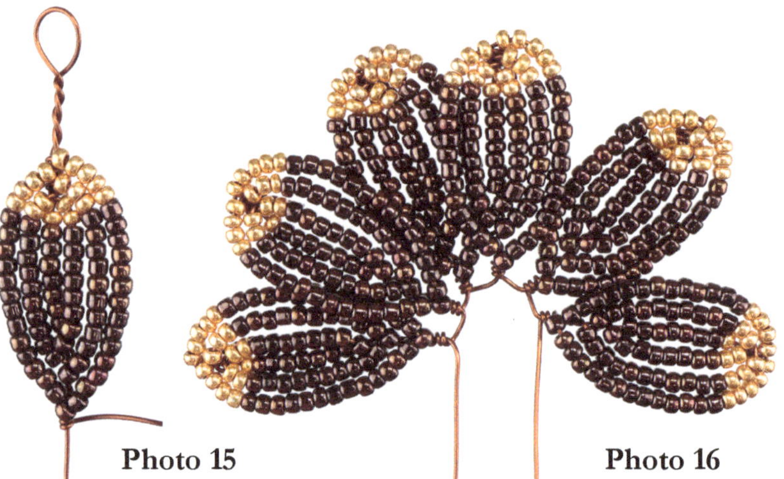

Photo 15   **Photo 16**

Unit F:

Make 7 (1 per pinecone, 1 per small spray, 2 per large spray)

Pattern: 6x 6 row CBF, 8 bead BR, PB RT

Shading Counts:
BR = 7x brown, 1x gold
Row 2= begin with 2x gold, fill the rest with brown
Row 3 = fill in with brown, end with 2x gold
Row 4 = begin with 3x gold, fill in with brown
Row 5 = fill in with brown, end with 4x gold
Row 6 = begin with 5x gold, fill in with brown

Instructions:

1. Cut a 4.5 foot (1.4 m) length of wire.

2. Leave a 2 inch (5 cm) starting tail wire, then make all six scales according to the pattern above. A close-up of one of the scales is shown in **Photo 15**. **Photo 16** shows the completed six scales. Pull every other scale forward so it rests in front of both scales on either side.

3. Close the unit by wrapping the tail wire around the first scale, then twist the wires together. Make sure the stem wire is sticking out of the top of the unit, not the underside.

ASSEMBLY:

Pinecone:

1. Prepare 17x 16 gauge (1.3 mm) stem wires by wrapping them with brown floral tape.

2. Mold all of the pinecone scale units B-F into bell shapes like the one shown in **Photo 17**)

3. Combine scale units A, B, and C, by inserting the stem wire for A into the center of Unit B, then inserting the combined stem wires into the center of Unit C. Pull them all close together, then twist the stems together to secure them. (**Photo 18 & 19**)

4. Cut a long length of brown floral tape in half length-wise to make thinner tape. Use the thin tape to wrap the stem wire on the combined ABC unit.

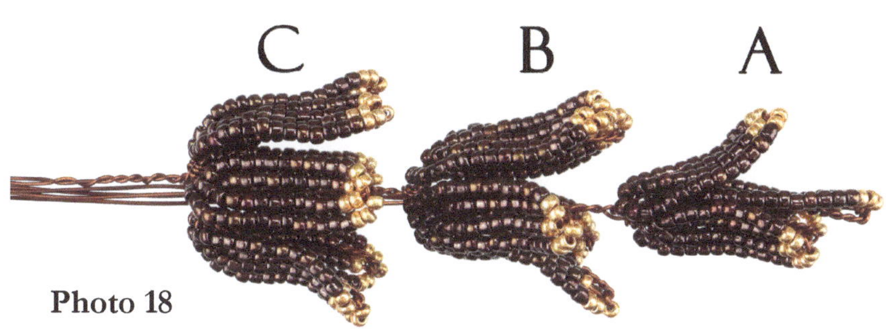

Photo 18

5. Cut a long length of 30g brown wire and use it to attach the ABC unit to the end of one prepared 16g stem wires (**Photo 20**). Then cover the exposed wires with a thin layer of half-width brown floral tape.

6. Insert the end of the stem wire into the center of the D unit, plus 2x E units (**Photo 21**), and push them up below the ABC unit. *Leave approximately ¼ inch (6.35 mm) of space along the main stem between the units so they don't end up too close together*. Carefully rotate the units around the stem as necessary to make sure the scales in one unit are not directly in line with the scales in the next unit. Instead, they should be between the scales in the next unit for proper overlapping. This is a very important step in making the pinecones look natural!

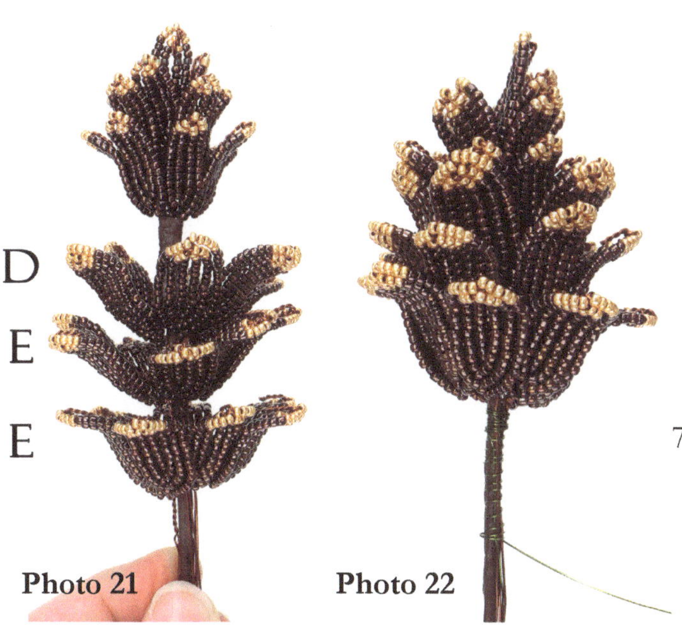

Photo 21   **Photo 22**

7. Cut another long length of 30 gauge brown wire and use it to secure the DEE units in place (**Photo 22**). Cover the exposed wires with a thin layer of half-width floral tape.

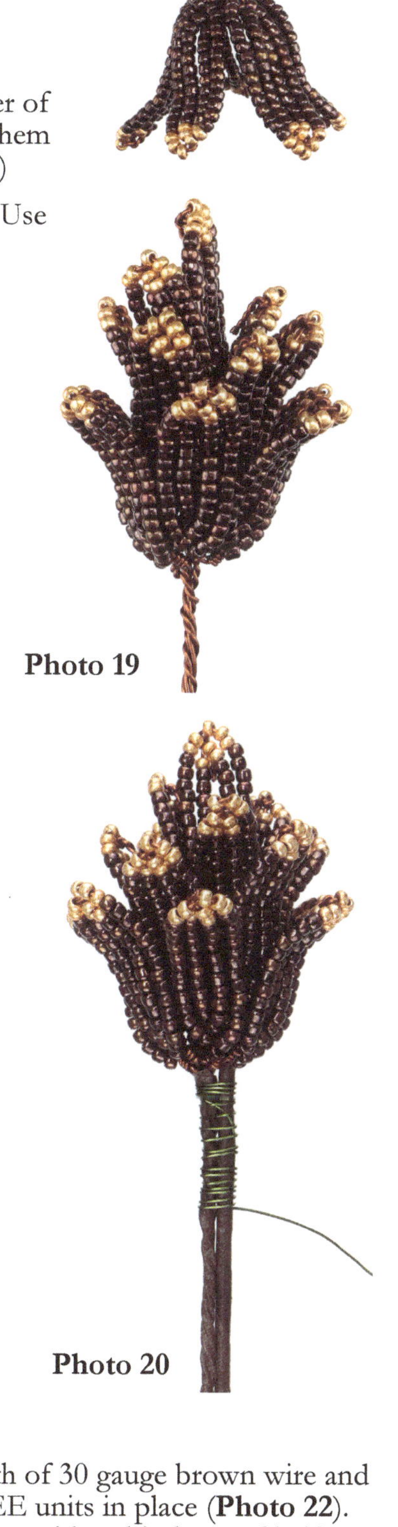
Photo 17

Photo 19

Photo 20

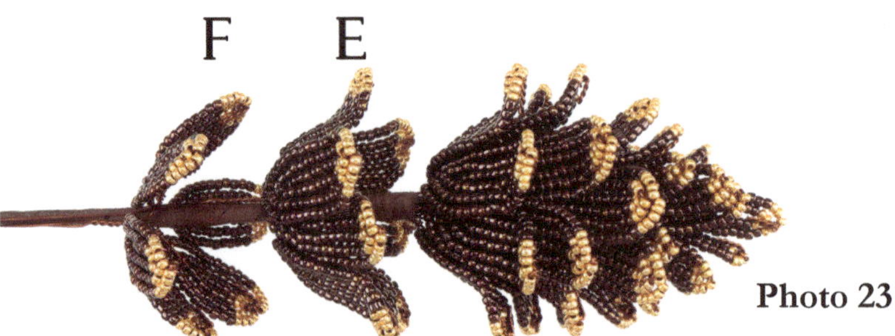

Photo 23

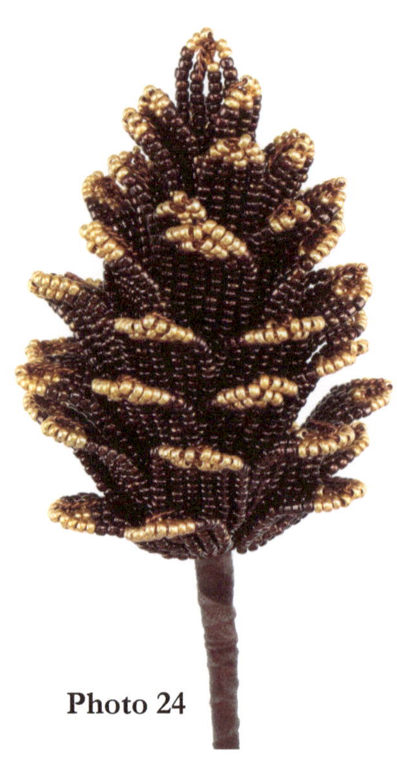

Photo 24

8. Insert the stem wire into the center of the last Unit E, and then Unit F. (**Photo 23**)

9. Move Unit E up under the previous E units, leaving a ¼ inch (6.35 mm) space on the main stem between the units. Then move Unit F directly below the last Unit E. Again make sure the scales are not in line with the scales in previous units.

10. Cut a long length of 30 gauge brown wire, then use it to secure the last two scale units in place. Wrap the wire at least an inch (2.5 cm) below the last scale unit. Then cover the exposed wires with another layer of brown floral tape, and the pinecone is complete. (**Photo 24**)

11. Repeat for the remaining six pinecones.

Needles:

1. Insert the stem wire of one Needle Tip Unit into the center of one Needle Unit. Push them close together, then twist the stem wires together. Use a half-width brown floral tape to wrap the combined stem wires. (**Photo 25**)

2. Repeat step 1 to make a second combined tip/needle unit.

3. Cut a couple feet of 30 gauge brown wire and use it to attach one of the combined tip/needle units from step 1 to the end of one prepared 16 gauge stem wire. (**Photo 26**)

4. Insert the end of the stem wire into the center of 3x needle units and slide them all the way up below the tip/needle combined unit. Use another length of 30g wire to secure them to the stem, then cover the exposed wires with floral tape. (**Photo 27**)

5. Repeat step 3 to attach the second tip/needle unit to a separate 16g stem wire. Then insert the end of the stem into the center of 1x needle unit and slide it all the way up below the tip/needle unit at the end. Use 30g wire to secure it in place, then cover with floral tape. (**Photo 28**)

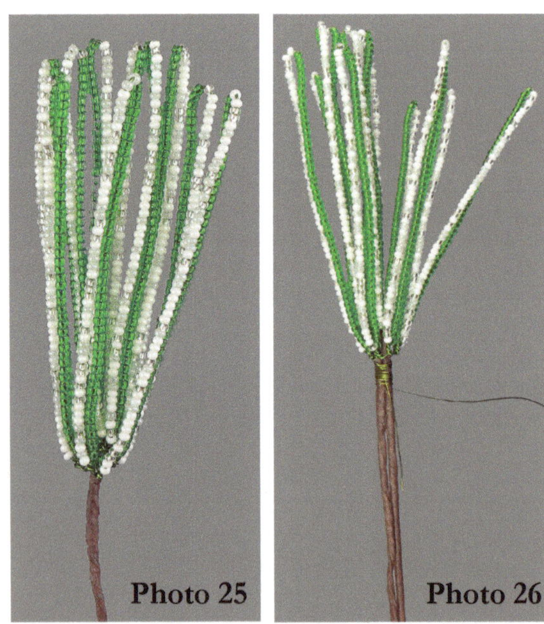

Photo 25   **Photo 26**

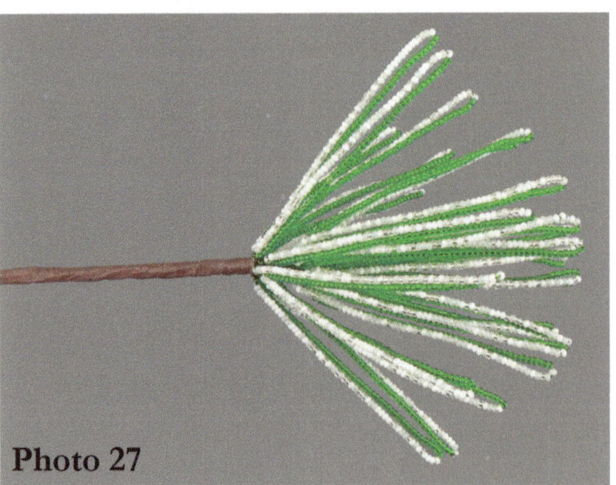

Photo 27

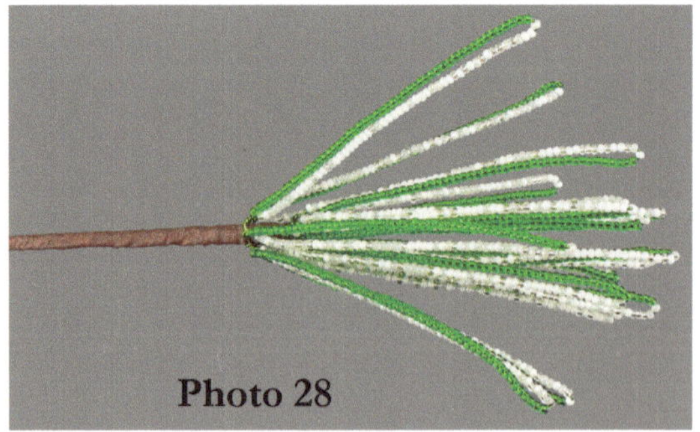

Photo 28

Spray:

1. Putting the sprays together is very simple. Cut a long length of 30g brown wire and use it to combine one pinecone with one of the needle sprays (**Photo 29**). Then cover the exposed wires with brown floral tape.

2. Use floral tape to add in the second needle spray. (**Photo 30**)

3. **Photo 31** shows a finished small branch with one pinecone. Repeat to make two more branches with one pinecone each.

4. For the two large branches that have two pinecones each, cut another long length of 30 gauge brown wire and attach a second pinecone under and slightly below the first one. Then cover with floral tape. (**Photo 32**)

5. Trim all stems to approximately 6 inches (15.2 cm) below the last pinecone.

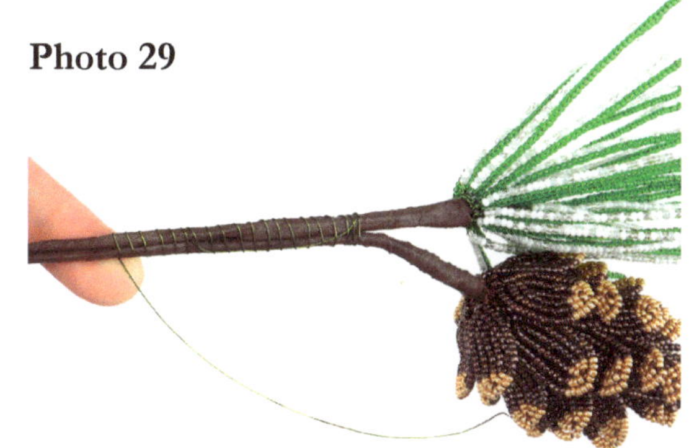

Photo 29

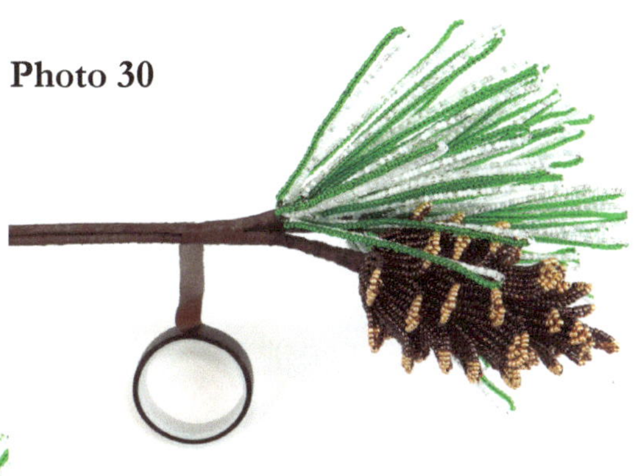

Photo 30

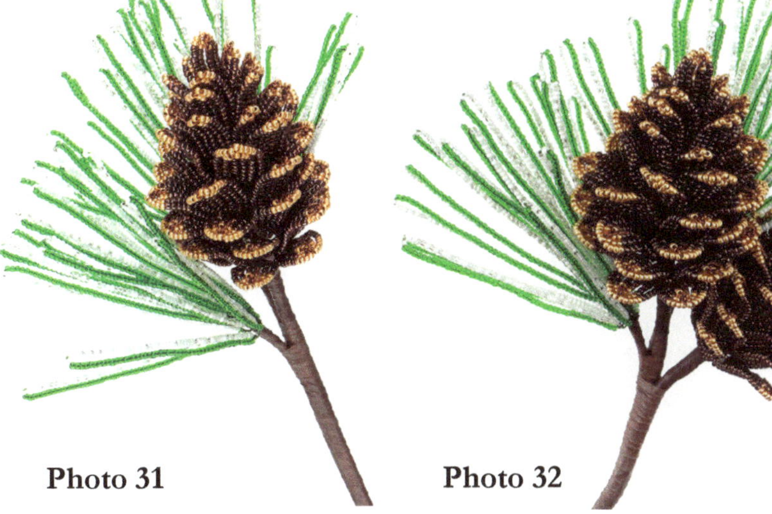

Photo 31   Photo 32

Alterations: This pattern can be modified to make larger branches for other arrangements. **Photo 33** shows a branch made by combining two small sprays and one large spray with floral tape. You will want to leave all the stem wires long until after you have combined the stems. Then trim them all to the same length.

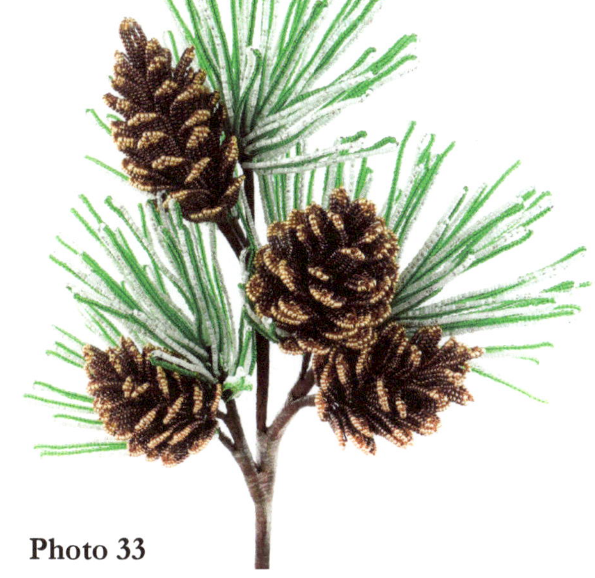

Photo 33

.....Fir Branches.....

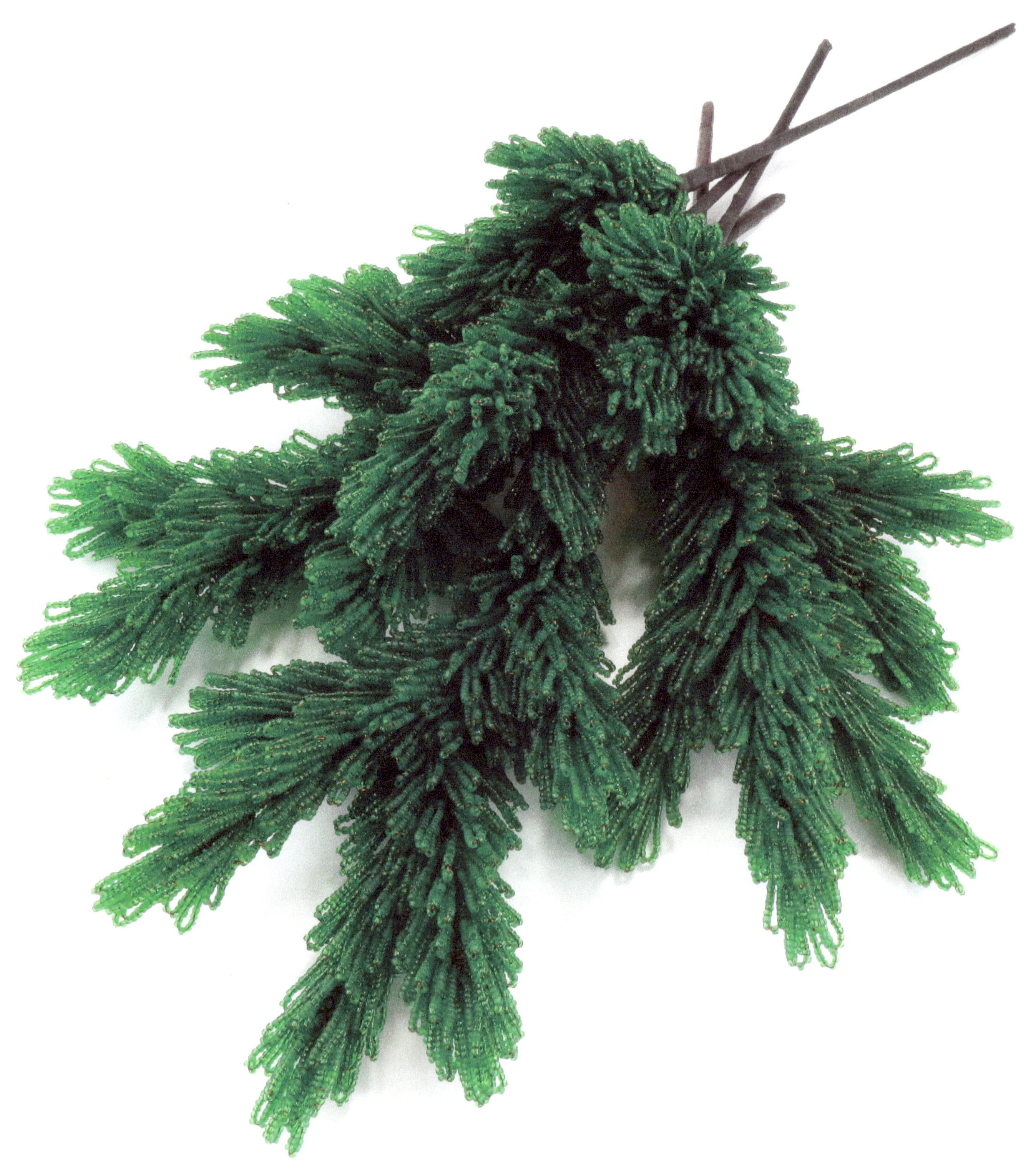

Materials

For the wreath, make nine Small Branches. As a bonus, I've included a pattern for a Large Branch, though it is not used in the wreath. The pattern instructions have the unit counts for the Bonus Large Branch listed separately.

BEADS:	FULL WREATH	1 SMALL BRANCH	1 LARGE BRANCH
Size 11/0 transparent green seed beads	450 grams	50 grams	85 grams
Size 11/0 transparent matte green seed beads	450 grams	50 grams	85 grams
WIRE:			
26 gauge (.4 mm) or 24 gauge (.5 mm) brown copper core wire *	540 ft (125 m)	60 ft (13.7 m)	93 ft (28.3 m)
16 gauge (1.3 mm) florist stem wire (galvanized steel)	27 pieces	3 pieces	5 pieces
OTHER:			
Brown floral tape	1 roll	< 1 roll	< 1 roll

NOTES:
*If you are making Fir Branches in a different color bead, match the 26 or 24 gauge wire to whatever color you are making the actual branch, not the needles. This will help disguise the component wire against the stem wires so it will be less visible between loops.

Prep: Mix the two colors of green together. Keep the wire attached to the spool. String as many beads as you need for one unit at a time, then work from the spool.

NEEDLES: *Each unit equals one day.*

Unit A:
Wreath: Make 27 (3 per small branch)
Bonus Large Branch: Make 4

Pattern: 60 x CL using 2 inches (5 cm) of beads per loop.

Instructions:

1. Leaving the wire attached to the spool, string approximately 10 feet (3.1 m) of beads onto the 26 or 24g wire.

2. Leave a 3 inch (5 cm) tail wire, then make the continuous loops according to the pattern above.

3. Leave a 3 inch (5 cm) ending tail wire and clip from the spool.

Photo 1 shows the finished Unit A.

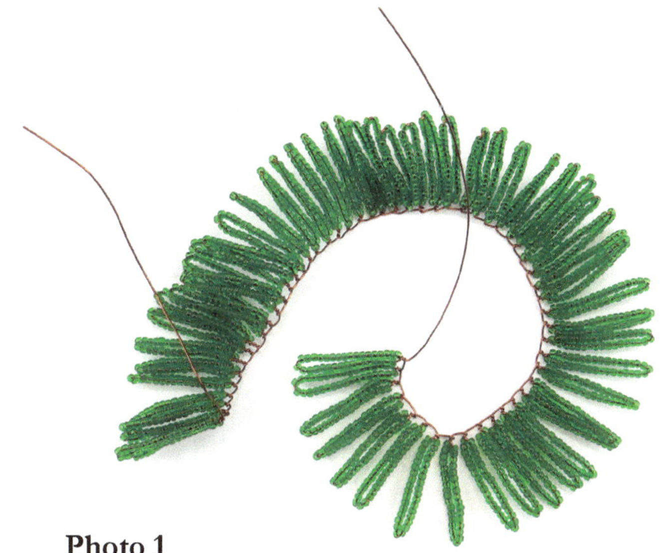

Photo 1

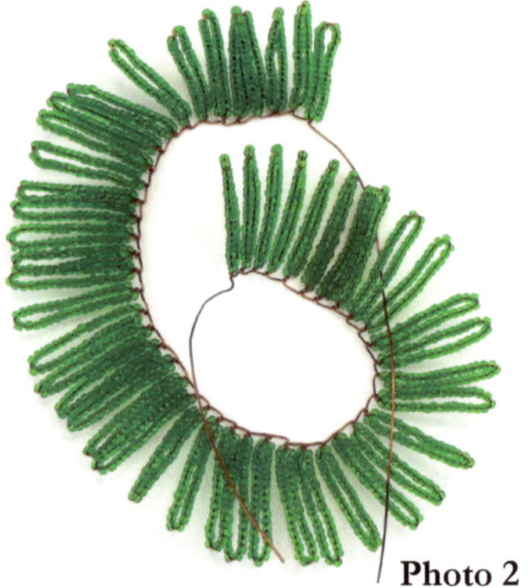

Photo 2

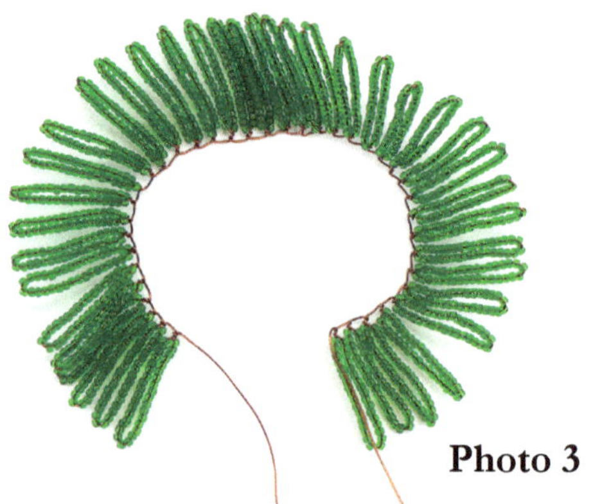

Photo 3

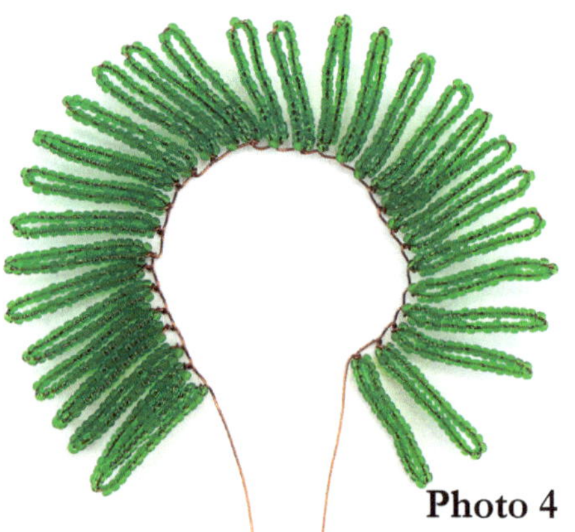

Photo 4

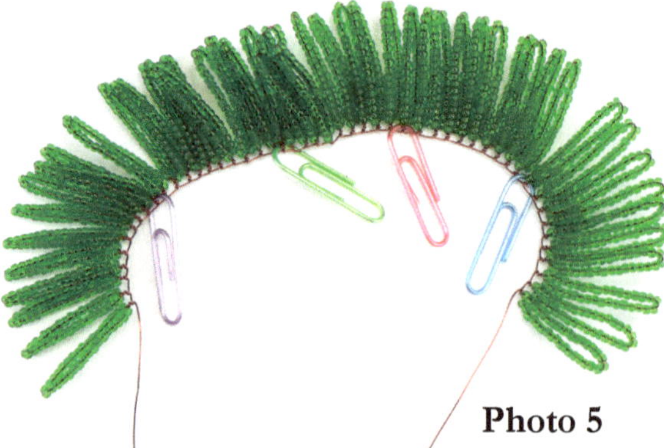

Photo 5

Unit B:

Wreath: Make 18 (2 per Small Branch)
Bonus Large Branch: Make 3

Pattern: 50 x CL using 2 inches (5 cm) of beads per loop.

Instructions:

1. Leaving the wire attached to the spool, string approximately 8 feet and 4 inches (2.6 m) of beads onto the 26 or 24g wire.

2. Leave a 2 inch (5 cm) tail wire, then make the continuous loops according to the pattern above.

3. Leave a 2 inch (5 cm) ending tail wire and clip from the spool.

Photo 2 shows the finished Unit B.

Unit C:

Wreath: Make 0 (0 per Small Branch)
Bonus Large Branch: Make 1

Pattern: 40 x CL using 2 inches (5 cm) of beads per loop.

Instructions:

1. Leaving the wire attached to the spool, string approximately 6 feet and 8 inches (2 m) of beads onto the 26 or 24g wire.

2. Leave a 2 inch (5 cm) tail wire, then make the loops according to the pattern above.

3. Leave a 2 inch (5 cm) ending tail wire and clip from the spool.

Photo 3 shows the finished Unit C.

Unit D:

Wreath: Make 0 (0 per Small Branch)
Bonus Large Branch: Make 1

Pattern: 30 x CL using 2 inches (5 cm) of beads per loop.

Instructions:

1. Leaving the wire attached to the spool, string approximately 5 feet (1.5 m) of beads onto the 26 or 24g wire.

2. Leave a 2 inch (5 cm) tail wire, then make the loops according to the pattern above.

3. Leave a 2 inch (5 cm) ending tail wire and clip from the spool.

Photo 4 shows the finished Unit D.

TIP: Use paper clips as markers while making loops to help keep count of how many loops you have made. **Photo 5**

ASSEMBLY:

Small Branches

1. Wrap 3x 16 gauge (1.3 mm) florist stem wires with brown floral tape.

2. Attach one Unit A to the end of one prepared stem wire by winding the wire around a few times. Position the first loop right at the tip of the stem wire. (**Photo 6**)

3. Wrap the full length of Unit A around the stem wire. Angle downward while wrapping, and visually estimate about 1/8 inch (3.2 mm) of space between each wrap. If you wrap too close together, your segment will be too short. The finished wrapped section of stem wire should be approximately 3 inches (7.6 cm) long. Wrap the ending tail wire around the stem below the last wrap of loops to secure the unit in place. (**Photos 7 & 8**)

4. Fold the loops down close to the stem wire. Check the stem to make sure all of the wire wraps underneath are covered by loops. If not, shift a few around to cover the wires. (**Photo 9**)

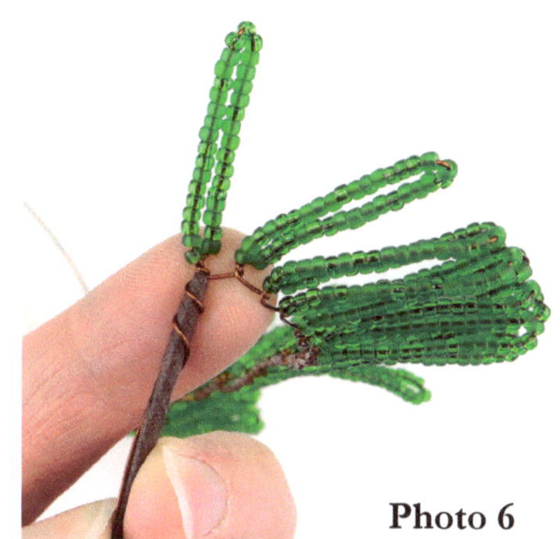

Photo 6

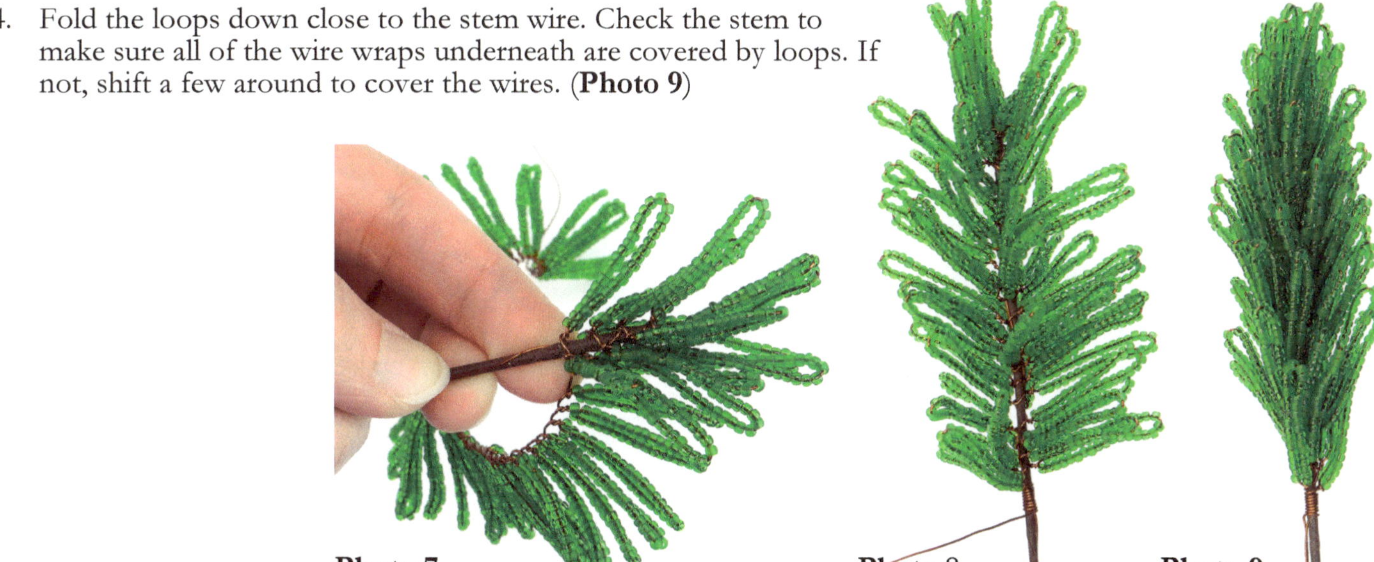

Photo 7   **Photo 8**   **Photo 9**

5. Repeat two more times to make three stem wires with Unit A's wrapped at the tips. Set one aside.

6. Use brown floral tape to combine two of the Unit A stems together just below the last wrap of loops. You may need to bend one or both of the 16 gauge stems to get the bare wire stems close together. (**Photo 10**)

7. Take one Unit B and position the first loop right where the two stem wires come together. Lay the starting tail wire flat against the combined stem wires. (**Photo 11**)

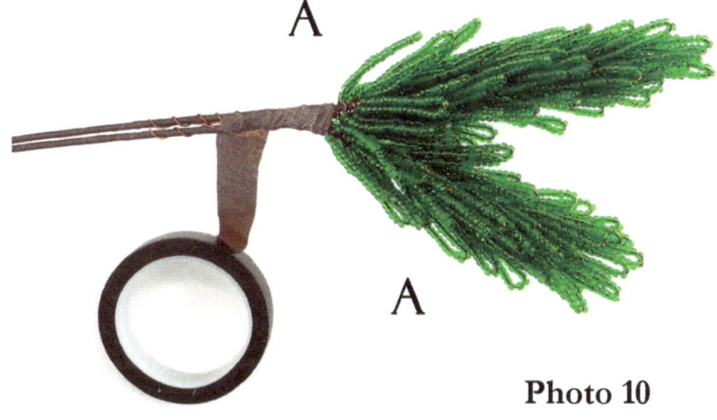

Photo 10

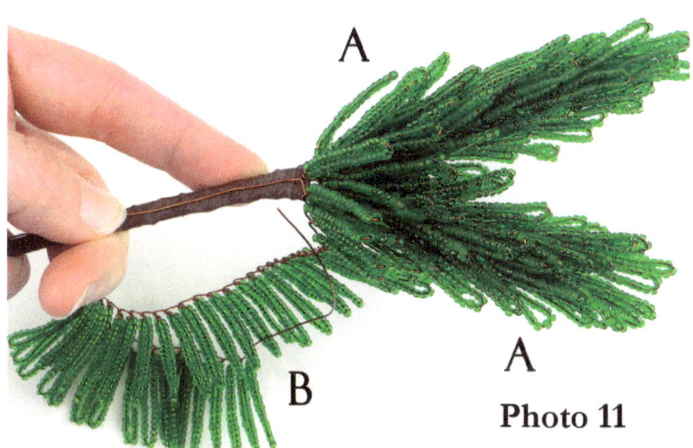

Photo 11

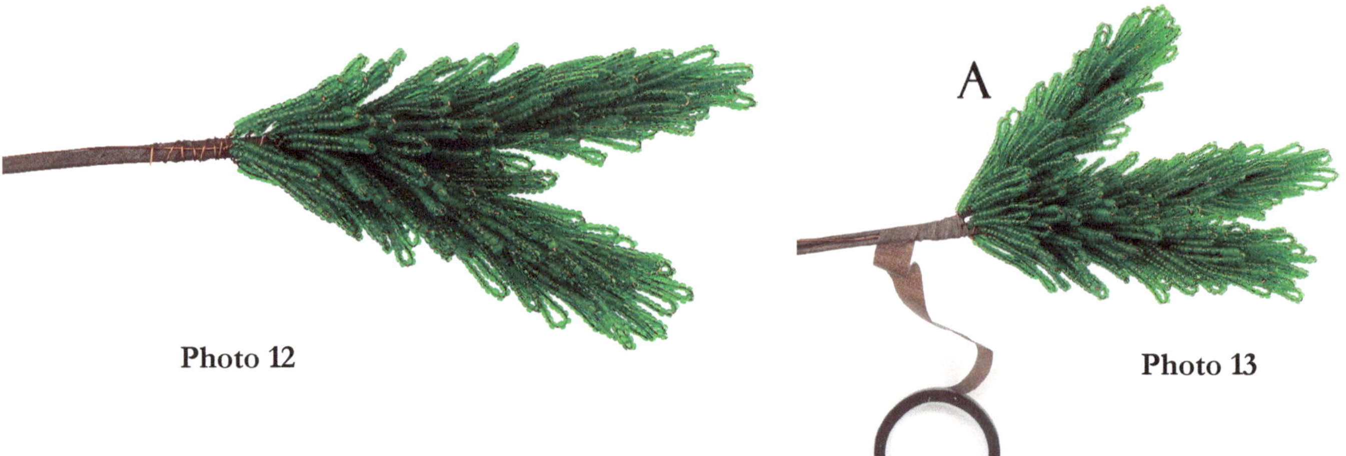

Photo 12

Photo 13

8. Wrap the Unit B around the combined stem, using the same spacing as you did for the Unit As. (**Photo 12**)

9. Take the Unit A stems that you set aside earlier. Bend the stem wire directly below the wrapped section of loops. Use floral tape to add it into the branch's stem wire. There should be no space between the last loops and the branch stem, and it should also be directly below the wrapped Unit B with no gaps. (**Photo 13**)

10. Take one Unit B and position the first loop where the previous Unit A stem joins the main stem. Lay the starting tail wire flat against the stem (**Photo 14**). Then wrap the Unit B around the stem. Cover the exposed wires with floral tape.

11. Trim the branch stem to approximately 6 inches (15.2 cm). **Photo 15** shows a completed Small Branch.

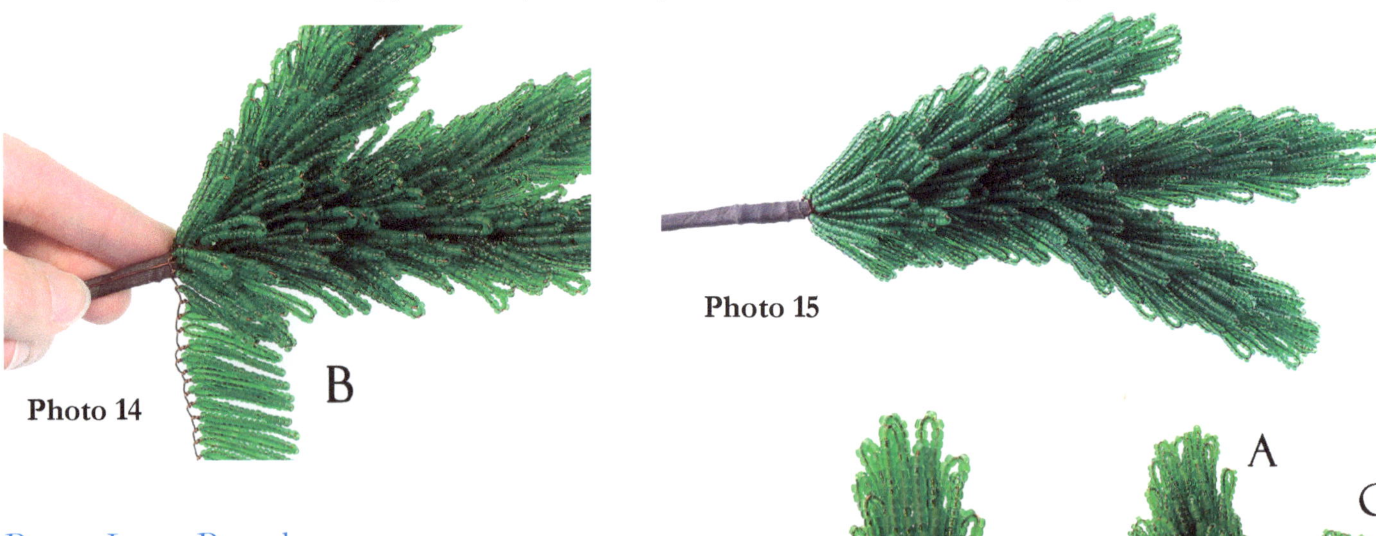

Photo 14

Photo 15

Bonus Large Branch

1. Prepare 5x 16 gauge stem wires by wrapping them with floral tape.

2. Wrap 4x Unit A's around four of the prepared stem wires.

3. Use 3x Unit A stems and 2x Unit B's to complete one Small Branch as described in the assembly instructions above. Set the branch aside while we make a side branch to add to it.

4. On the last prepared 16g stem wire, wrap the Unit C, the same way as you wrapped the Unit A's. (**Photo 16**)

5. Use floral tape to combine this Unit C stem with the fourth and final Unit A stem. Remember to bend the branches as necessary to get those bare stem wires close together. (**Photo 17**)

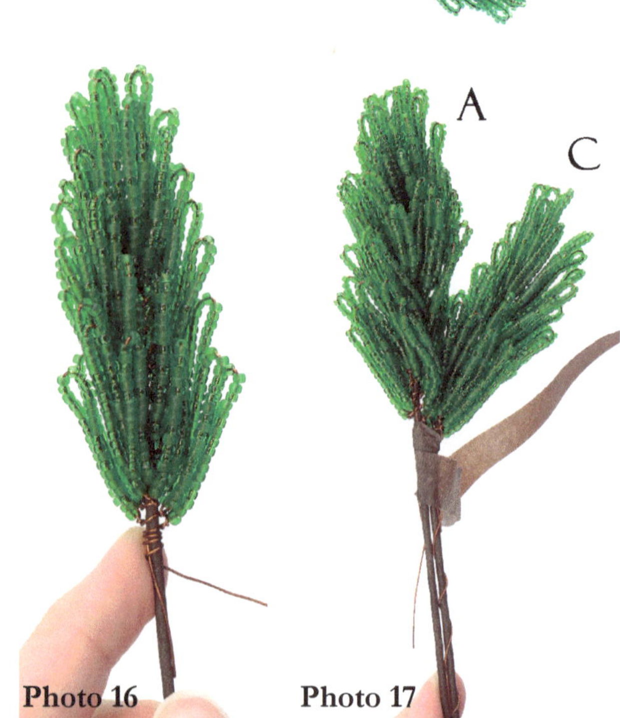

Photo 16

Photo 17

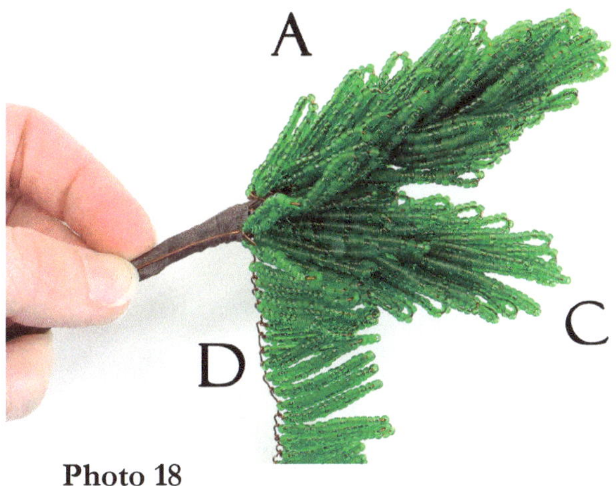

Photo 18

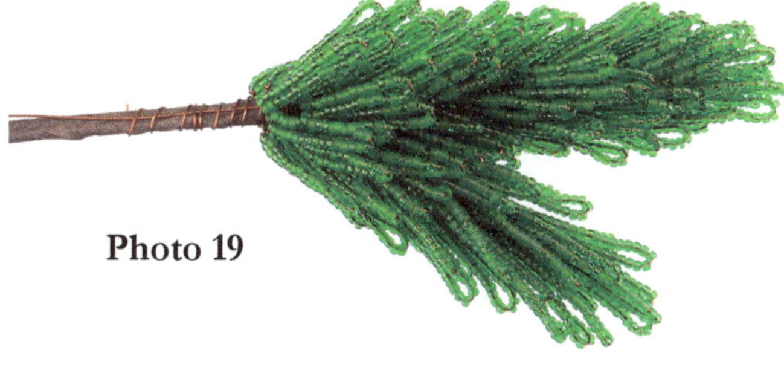

Photo 19

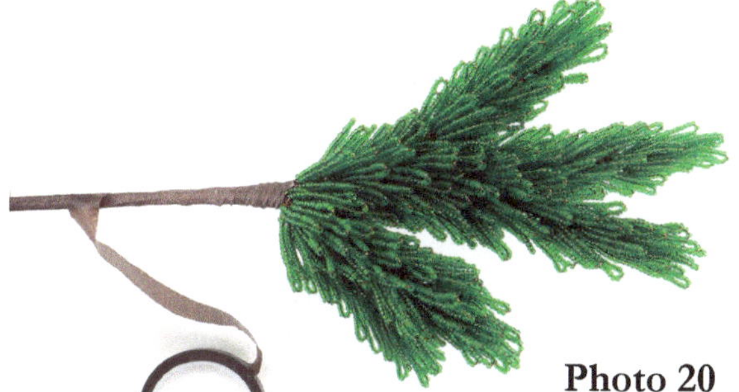

Photo 20

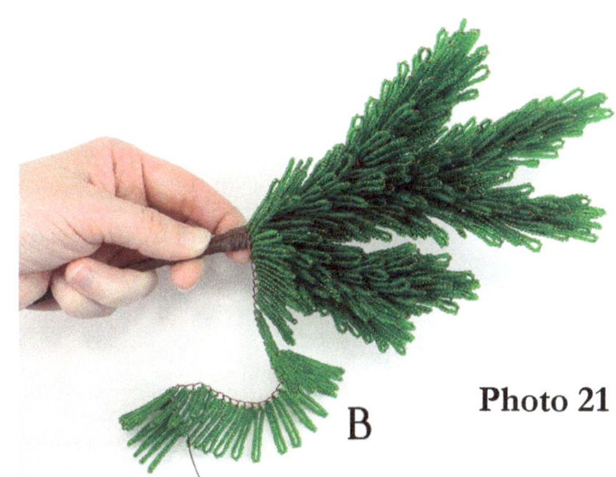

Photo 21

6. Take the Unit D and position the first loop directly below where the Units A & C join. Lay the beginning tail wire against the stem wire. (**Photo 18)**

7. Wrap Unit D around the combined stems (**Photo 19**). This completes the side branch.

8. Use floral tape to join the side branch together with the main stem. (**Photo 20**)

9. Add in the last Unit B directly below where the main branch and side branch join together (**Photo 21**).

10. Wrap the Unit B around the combined stem wire. Then cover the exposed wires with floral tape.

Photo 22 shows a finished Large Branch.

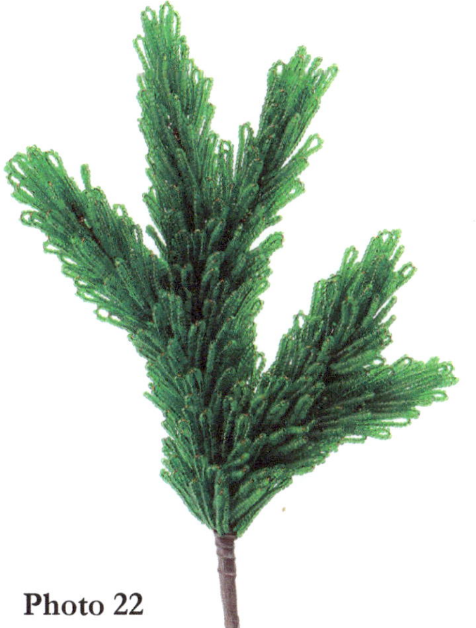

Photo 22

Alterations: Photo 23
shows a Large Branch with an alternate layout. I attached the side branch higher up in the middle of the branch rather than the bottom. You could make an even larger branch by joining multiple small and large branches together. Just be sure to make extra units (any size will work) to wrap around where the branches join.

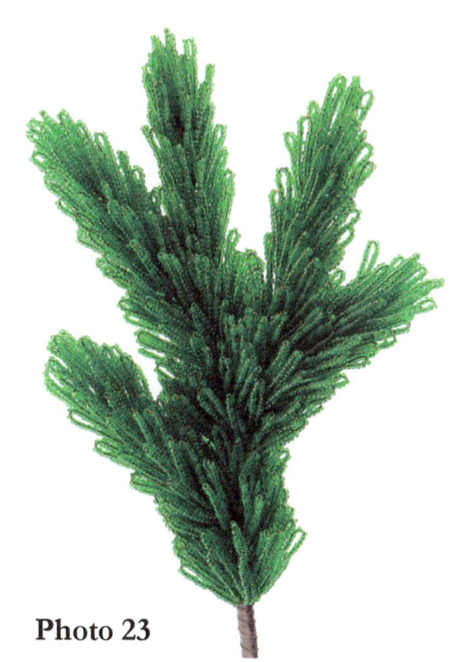

Photo 23

· · · · · Holly · · · · ·

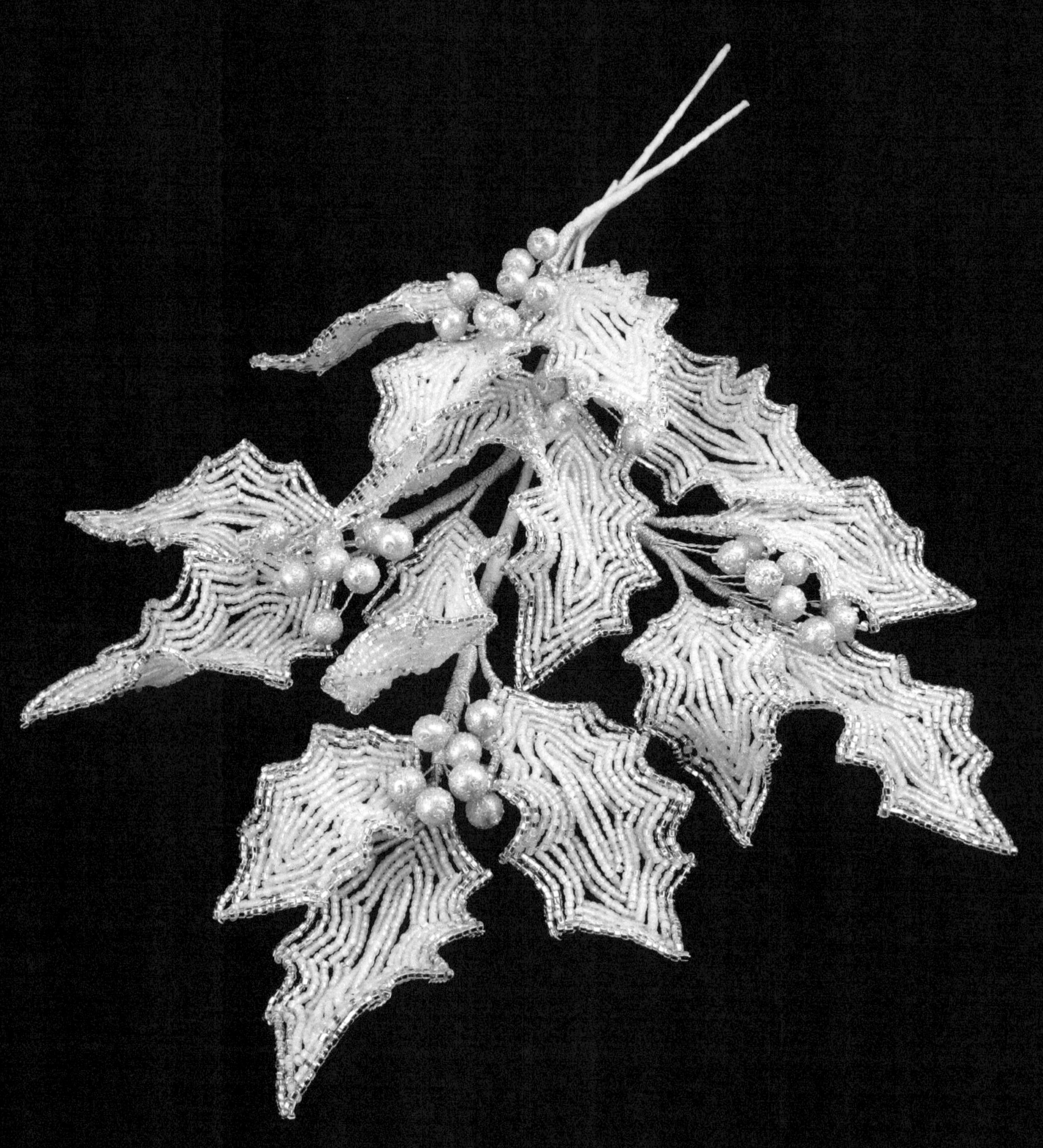

TECHNIQUES USED:
- Basic Frame (BF)
- Wire-back Fringe (WBF)
- Twisted Fringe (TF)
- Lacing
- Top Wire Extensions
- Spokes

FINISHED SIZE:
Large Leaf: 3 ¼ inches (8.3 cm) long
Small Leaf: 2 ½ inches (6.4 cm) long

ONE-A-DAY COUNTS:
Berry Bunches: 20 (4 per stem)
Leaves: 15 (3 per stem)
Total Days: 35 (7 per stem)

Materials

For the full wreath make five stems, each with three leaves and 8 berries.

BEADS:	FULL WREATH	1 STEM
Size 11/0 silver lined opal white seed beads	50 grams	10 grams
Size 11/0 transparent white matte AB seed beads	50 grams	10 grams
Size 11/0 silver lined clear seed beads	40 grams	8 grams
10 mm round metallic silver glass beads	40 pieces	8 pieces
WIRE:		
24 gauge (.5 mm) silver colored copper core wire	90 ft (27.5 m)	18 ft (5.5 m)
28 gauge (.315 mm) silver colored copper core wire	20 ft (6 m)	4 ft (1.5 m)
30 gauge (.25 mm) silver or white colored copper core wire	10 ft (3 m)	2 ft (< 1 m)
16 gauge (1.3 mm) florist stem wire (or galvanized steel)	5 pieces	1 piece
OTHER:		
White floral tape	< 1 roll	< 1 roll
Metallic silver embroidery floss	2 skeins	< 1 skein

BERRY BUNCHES: *Each bunch with two berries equals one day.*

Wire: *28g (.315 mm) silver*
Beads: *11/0 silver lined clear, 10 mm round silver*

Make 20 (4 per stem).

Pattern: 2x wire-back fringes using 1x 11/0, 1x 10 mm, 1x 11/0 on a ¾ - 1 inch (1.9-2.5 cm) twisted stem.

Instructions:

1. Cut approximately 10 inches (25.4 cm) of wire.

2. String 1x 11/0, 1x 10 mm, 1x 11/0. Position the beads approximately 3 inches (7.6 cm) from one end of the wire. Then take the long end of the wire and pass back down through just the 10 mm bead. Skip both the 11/0 beads on either side. (**Photo 1**)

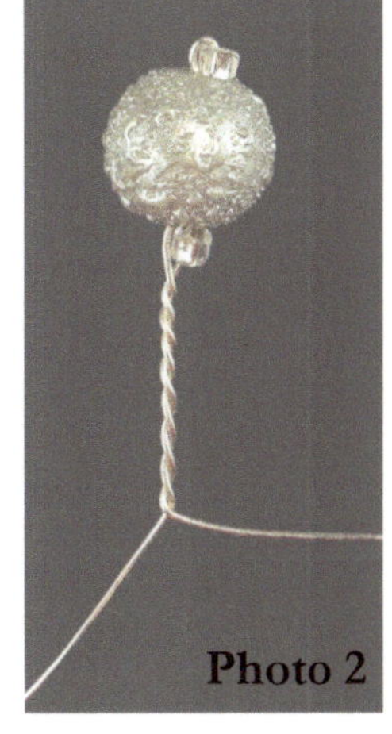

Photo 1

3. Pull the wire tight, then twist the two wires together below the bottom 11/0 bead approximately ¾ - 1 inch (1.9-2.5 cm) down. (**Photo 2**)

4. String 1x 11/0, 1x 10mm, 1x 11/0. Leave approximately ¾ - 1 inch (1.9-2.5 cm) of bare wire below the beads. *Use a different length than the previous berry so the finished berry stems will have a variety of lengths.* Insert the long end of the wire back down through just the 10mm bead and pull it all the way through. (**Photo 3**)

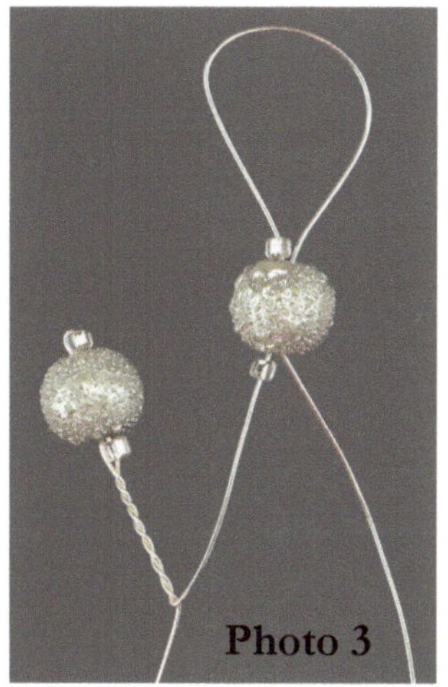

Photo 2

Photo 3

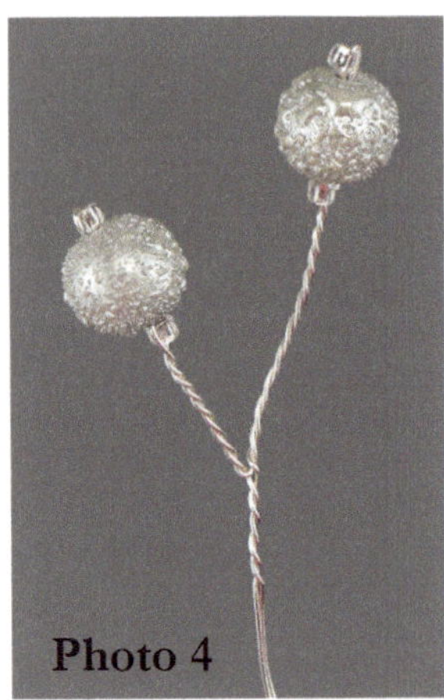

Photo 4

5. Twist the two wires below the 11/0 bead all the way down to the stem of the first berry, then twist the starting tail wire with the working wire below the two twisted berry stems just a few times. (**Photo 4**)

LEAVES: *Each leaf equals one day.*

Wire: *24g (.5 mm) silver, 30g (.25 mm) silver for lacing*
Beads: *11/0 silver lined opal white, transparent matte white AB, silver-lined clear*

Prep:

1. Mix all the silver-lined opal white and transparent matte white AB beads together in a bowl. This "Mix A" will be used for the main body of the leaves.

2. Divide out approximately 15 grams of the Mix A and add an equal amount of silver-lined clear beads to it. This "Mix B" will be used for the second-to-last rows on each leaf.

3. Reserve the rest of the silver-lined clear beads in a separate container. We will use these beads for the shading in the two outer rows on each leaf.

4. String all of Mix A onto the 24g silver wire.

Small Leaf:

Make 5 (1 per stem)

Pattern: 13 row BF, 1 inch (2.5 cm) BR, PB PT

- **EXTENSIONS: Add 1 bead to the top wire after rows 3, 5, 7, 9, and 11 (5 total)**
- **SPOKES:**
  - **Rows 4 & 5: Add 2 spokes each, 1 ½ inches long, spaced evenly.**
  - **Rows 8 & 9: 2 spokes each, 1 inch long, positioned between previous spokes and top/bottom wires.**
- **3 bottom wires**

Instructions:

1. Construct a Basic Frame using 1 inch (2.5 cm) plus 5 beads for the Basic Row.

2. Separate out the top 5 beads and slide them to the very end of the top wire. Bend a small section of the top wire back to hold the beads out of the way. (**Photo 5**)

3. Wrap rows 2 & 3 around the Basic Row.

4. In row 4, add two Spokes, dividing the row into thirds. Each spoke will need approximately 3 inches (7.6 cm) of wire folded in half. Slide one bead down from the top wire before wrapping row 4. (**Photo 6**)

5. Make row 5 a mirror image of row 4. (**Photo 7**)

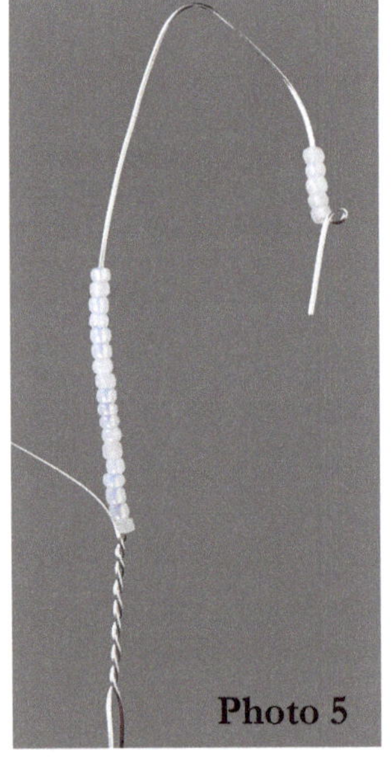

Photo 5

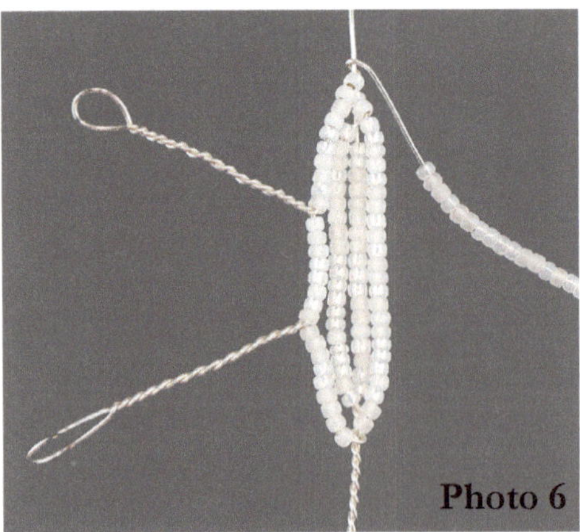

Photo 6

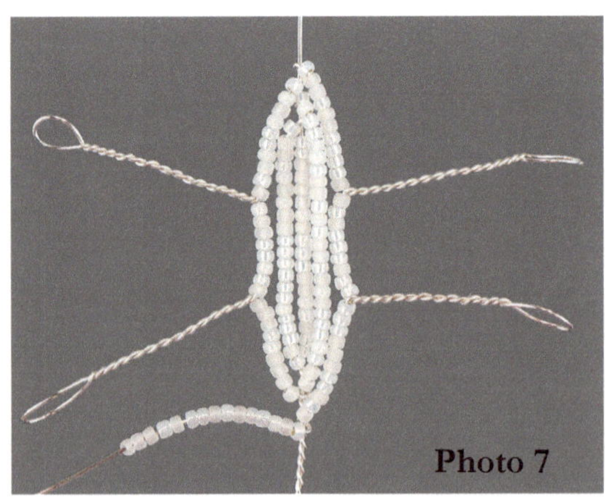

Photo 7

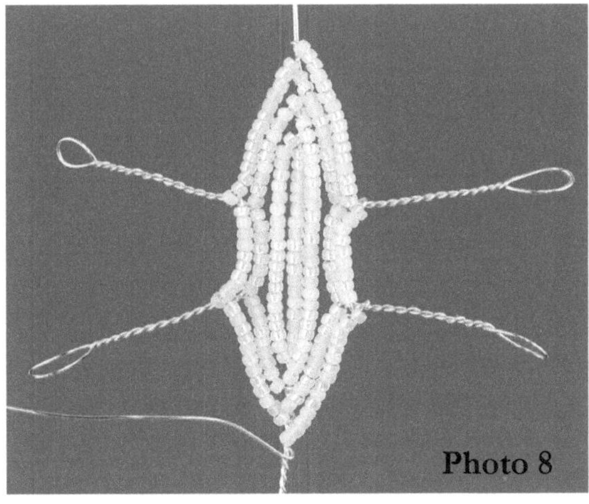

Photo 8

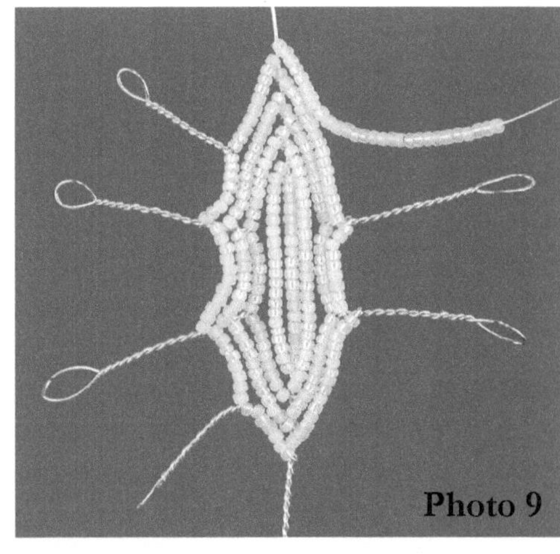

Photo 9

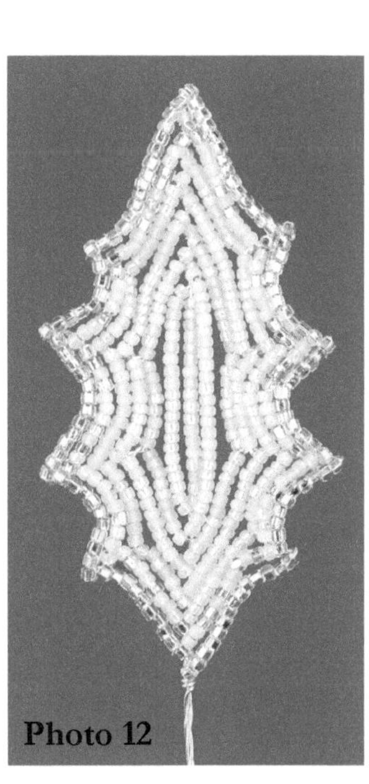

Photo 10

6. Slide down 1 bead from the top wire, then wrap rows 6 & 7 around all frame and spoke wires. (**Photo 8**)

7. In row 8, add two more spokes. Position the first half-way between the bottom wire and the first spoke. Position the second half-way between the second spoke and the top wire. Slide down one bead from the top wire, then wrap row 8. Make row 9 a mirror image of row 8. (**Photo 9**)

8. After row 9, measure and cut approximately 22 inches (56 cm) of bare working wire. String approximately 6 ½ inches (16.5 cm) of Mix B. Then slide one bead down from the top wire and wrap rows 10 & 11 around all frame and spoke wires. (**Photo 10**)

9. If there is any excess Mix B, remove it from the working wire. Then string approximately 7 ½ inches (19 cm) of silver-lined clear beads. Slide down the last bead on the top wire and wrap rows 12 & 13 around all frame and spoke wires. (**Photo 11**)

10. Twist the working wire into the bottom wire to make three bottom wires.

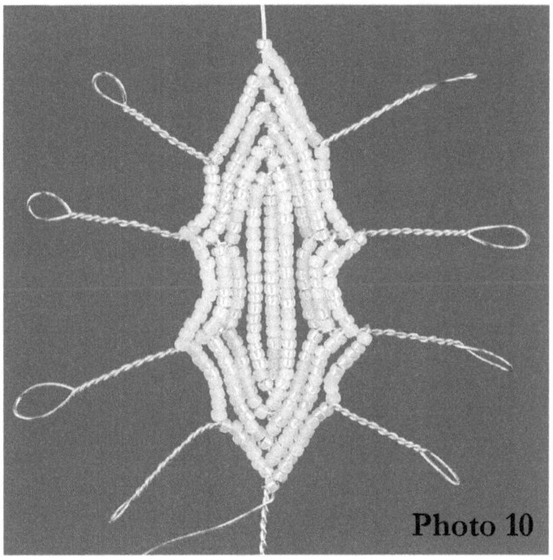

Photo 12 shows the finished Small Leaf.

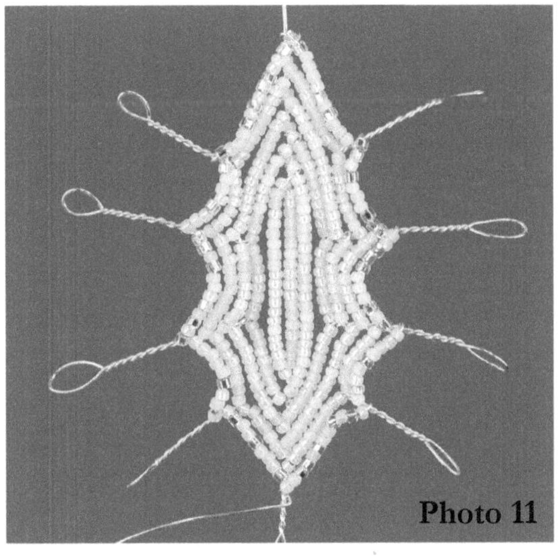

Photo 11

Photo 12

Large Leaf:

Make 10 (2 per stem)

Pattern: 15 row BF, 1 ¼ inch (3.2 cm) BR, PB PT
- **EXTENSIONS: Add 1 bead to the top wire after rows 3, 5, 7, 9, 11, and 13 (6 total)**
- **SPOKES: in Rows 4 & 5 and Rows 8 & 9.**
- **3 bottom wires**
- **Lace once across the center.**

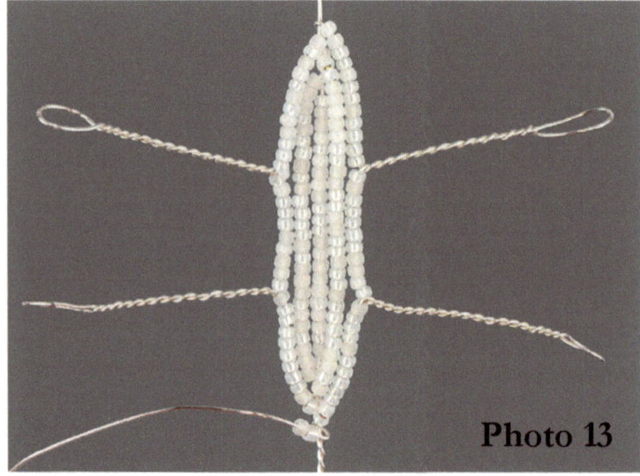

Photo 13

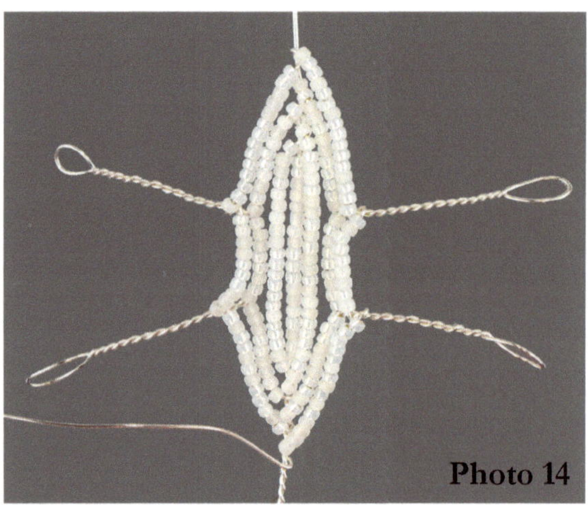

Photo 14

Instructions:

1. Construct a Basic Frame using 1 ¼ inch (3.2 cm) plus 6 beads for the Basic Row.

2. Separate out the top 6 beads and slide them to the very end of the top wire. Bend a small section of the top wire back to hold the beads out of the way.

3. Wrap rows 2 & 3 around the Basic Row.

4. In row 4, add two Spokes, dividing the row into thirds. Each spoke will need approximately 3 ½ inches (8.9 cm) of wire folded in half. Slide one bead down from the top wire before wrapping row 4. Make row 5 a mirror image of row 4. (**Photo 13**)

5. Slide down one bead from the top wire, then wrap rows 6 & 7 around all frame and spoke wires. (**Photo 14**)

6. In row 8, add two more spokes. Position the first half-way between the bottom wire and the first spoke. Position the second half-way between the second spoke and the top wire. Slide down one bead from the top wire, then wrap row 8. Make row 9 a mirror image of row 8. (**Photo 15**)

7. Slide down one bead from the top wire, then wrap rows 10 & 11 around all frame and spoke wires. (**Photo 16**)

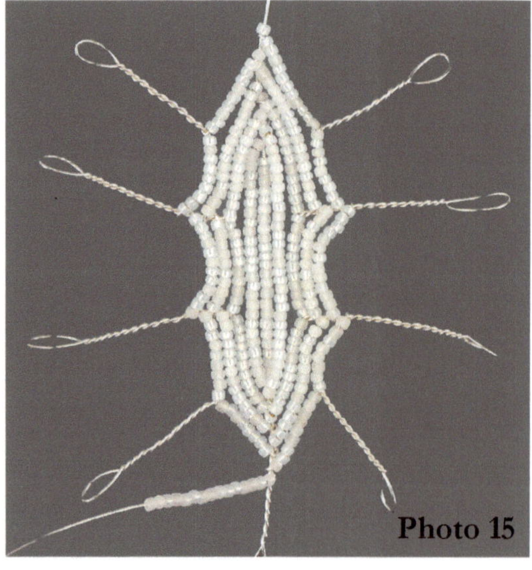

Photo 15

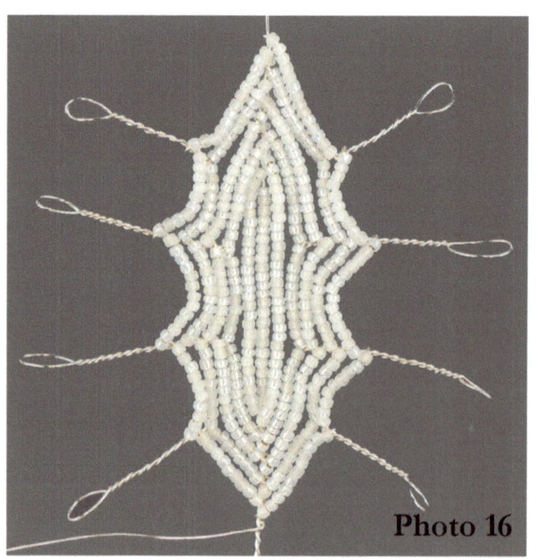

Photo 16

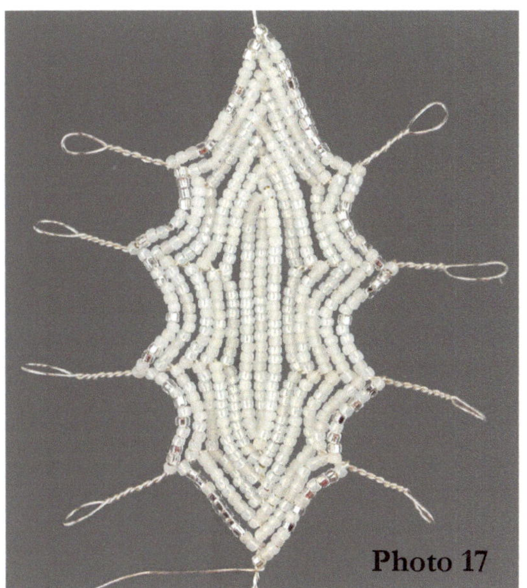
Photo 17

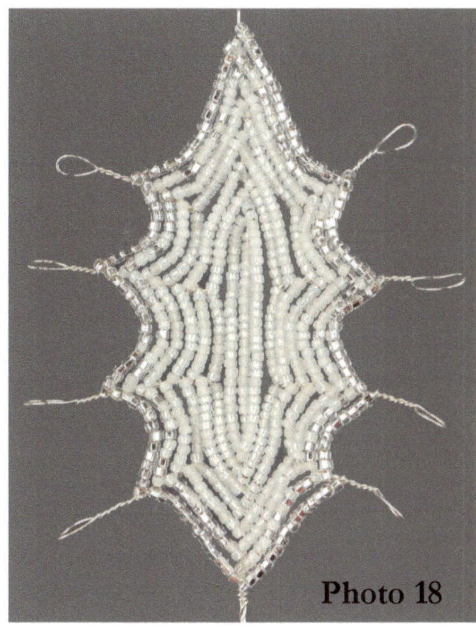
Photo 18

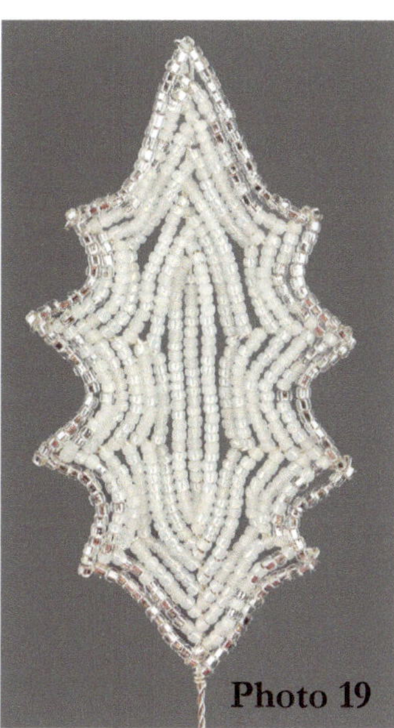
Photo 19

8. After row 11, measure and cut approximately 2 feet (61 cm) of bare working wire. String approximately 8 inches (20.3 cm) of Mix B. Slide down one bead from the top wire, then wrap rows 12 & 13 around all frame and spoke wires. (**Photo 17**)

9. If there is any excess Mix B, remove it from the working wire. String approximately 9 inches (23 cm) of silver-lined clear beads. Slide down the last bead on the top wire, then wrap rows 14 & 15 around all frame and spoke wires. (**Photo 18**)

10. Twist the working wire into the bottom wire to make three bottom wires.

11. Cut a 7 inch (17.8 cm) length of 30g wire and lace across the center.

Photo 19 shows the finished Large Leaf.

ASSEMBLY:

1. Wrap the stem wire with floral tape to prepare the surface. Cut a long length of white floral tape in half lengthwise to make thin tape. Use this tape to wrap the stem wires on each leaf.

2. Cut a foot of silver embroidery floss, and use it to wrap the stem wire on two leaves approximately ¾ inch (1.9 cm) down below the leaf. Leave the third leaf for each branch without floss.

3. Cut several feet of silver floss. Lay a small tail of the floss flat against the prepared 16g stem wire. Add 1 leaf of any size to the end of the stem, and wrap the floss tightly around it to secure it to the stem. Wrap the floss down about ½ inch (1.3 cm) below the leaf. (**Photo 20**)

4. Add in two berry sprigs, using the floss to attach them to the stem. Wrap the floss about ½ inch (1.3 cm) down. (**Photo 21**)

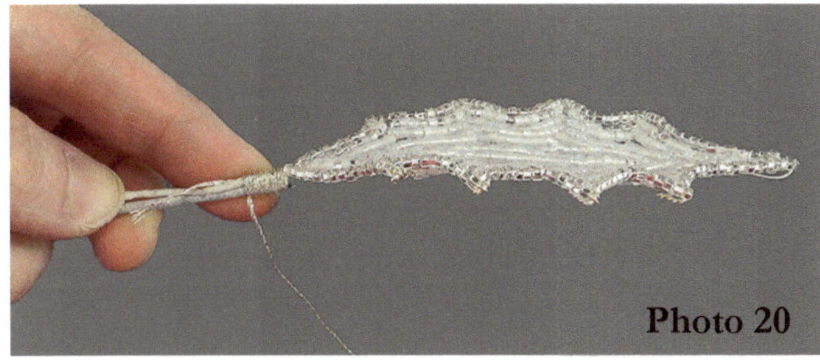
Photo 20

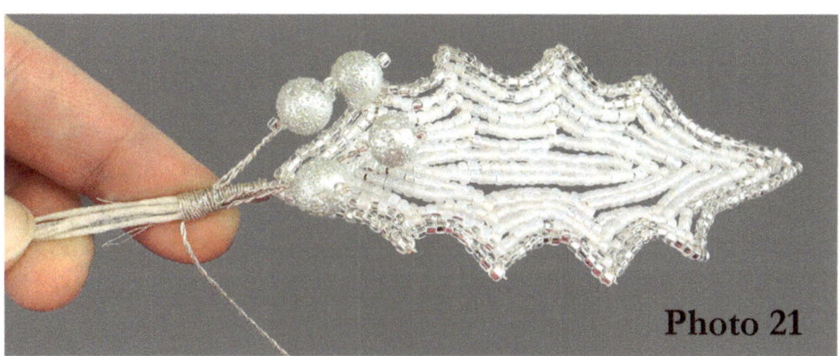
Photo 21

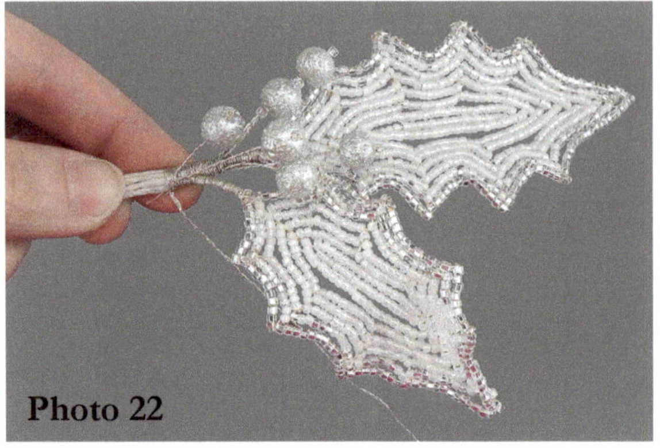

Photo 22

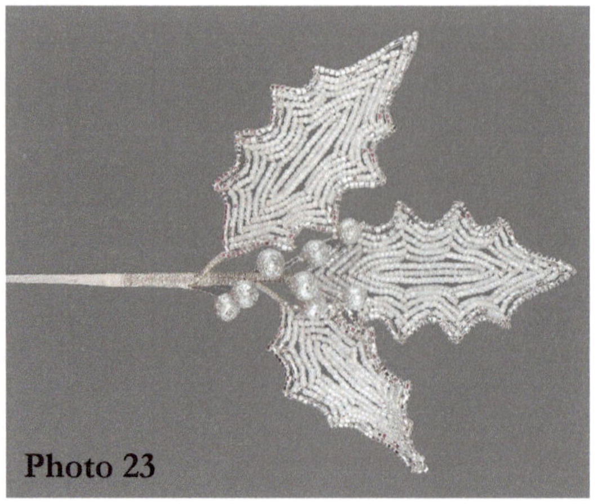

Photo 23

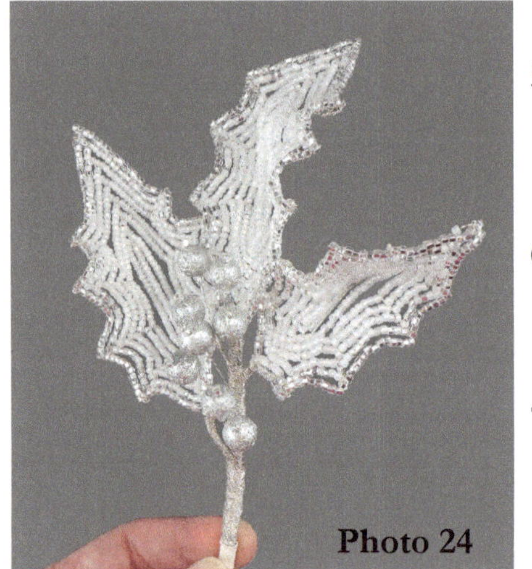

Photo 24

5. Add in one more leaf of either size on one side of the stem, leaving a ½ - ¾ inch (1.3-1.9 cm) stem between the leaf and the branch stem. Wrap the floss down another ¼ - ½ inch (6.4 mm- 1.3 cm) then add in another berry sprig. (**Photo 22**)

6. Wrap down another ½ inch (1.3 cm) then add the last leaf and the last berry sprig on the opposite side of the stem. Wrap the floss down another inch (2.5 cm) below the last leaf, then secure the end by wrapping over it with floral tape. (**Photo 23**)

7. Shape the leaves by grabbing the bottom of the leaf with one hand and the top of the leaf with the other and twisting in opposite directions. Bend and fold them, and pinch the edges like a pie crust to create extra ripples between spokes. (**Photo 24**)

Alterations: Photo 25 shows an example of a more traditionally colored holly branch with extra leaves and berries. For this branch I made 7 small leaves, 3 large leaves, and 20 pairs of berries. For a branch this size you will need ~60 grams of transparent green, ~10 grams of transparent lime green, < 1 gram of transparent brown, and 40x 8-10 mm opaque dark red Czech druks. I used green copper core wire for the leaves, and brown copper core wire for the berries. Add them into the branch following the same procedure as outlined in the instructions above. To create a more dimensional branch, attach leaves and berries to all sides of the stem, not just left and right.

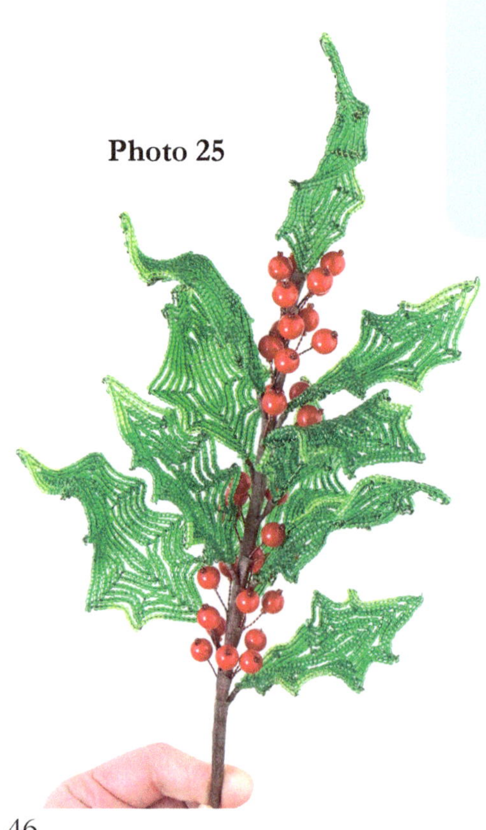

Photo 25

Photos 26 & 27 show some close-up examples of the shading on the leaves. The first leaf shows a lighter tip, which I made by adding a little lighter green in the outer four rows near the tip. The second leaf has small touches of lighter green in the outer two rows near just a few of the points. Use the same working wire lengths as the main pattern.

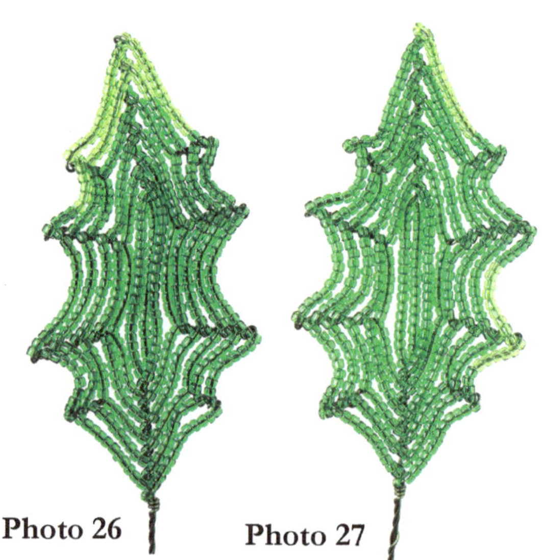

Photo 26   Photo 27

.....Berry Stems.....

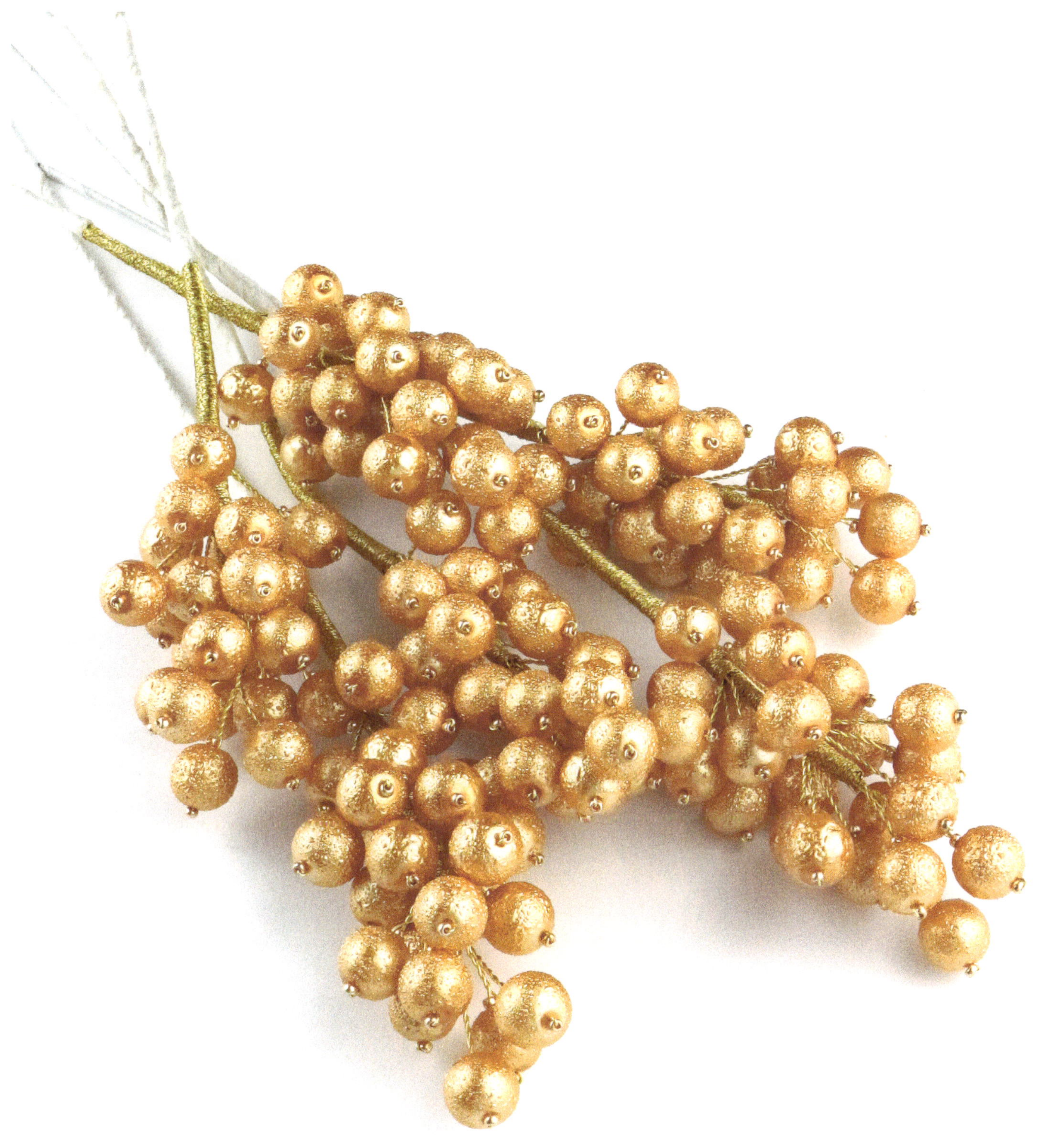

Materials

For the full wreath you will need seven of these loaded berry stems.

BEADS:	FULL WREATH	1 STEM
12 mm round glass beads in berry color	168 pieces	24 pieces
Size 11/0 seed beads in berry color	< 2 grams	< 1 gram
WIRE:		
26 gauge (.4 mm) gold colored copper core wire	56 ft (17 m)	8 ft (2.4 m)
16 gauge (1.3 mm) florist stem wire	7 pieces	1 piece
OTHER:		
floral tape in stem color (or white)	< 1 roll	< 1 roll
Embroidery floss in stem color	1-2 skeins	< 1 skein

These berry stems are made using a similar method as the berries in the Holly pattern, but with three berries instead of two.

BERRY BUNCHES: *Each bunch with three berries is one day.*

Make 56 (8 per stem)

Pattern: 3x WBF using 1x 11/0, 1x 12 mm, 1x 11/0 on a ¾ - 1 inch twisted stem.

Instructions:

1. Cut approximately 12 inches (30.5 cm) of 26 gauge gold copper core wire.

2. String 1x 11/0, 1x 12mm round, 1x 11/0 and position them approximately 3 inches (7.6 cm) from one end of the wire. (**Photo 1**)

3. Insert the long end of the wire back down through the 12mm round bead, skipping both of the 11/0 seed beads. (**Photo 2**)

4. Pull the wire all the way through, and slide the lower 11/0 seed bead all the way up against the berry bead. Twist the two wires below approximately ½ - 1 inch (1.3 - 2.5 cm) down. (**Photo 3**)

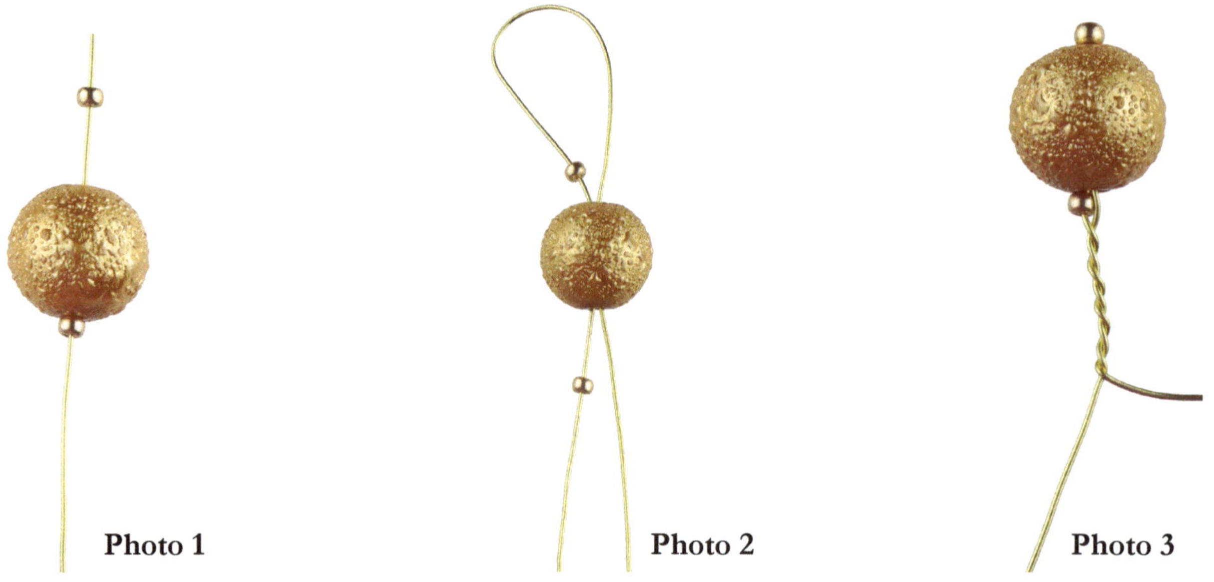

Photo 1   **Photo 2**   **Photo 3**

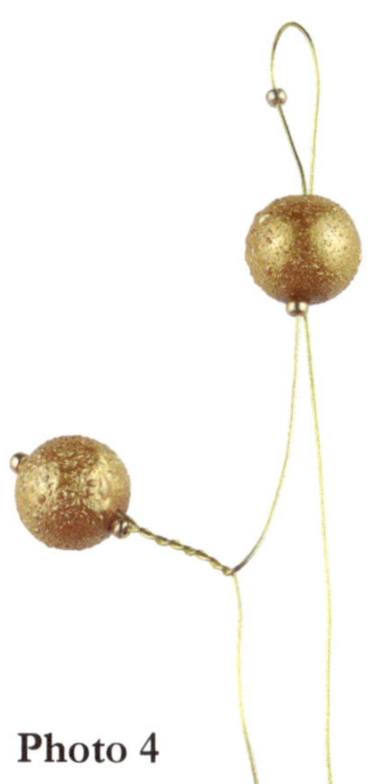

Photo 4

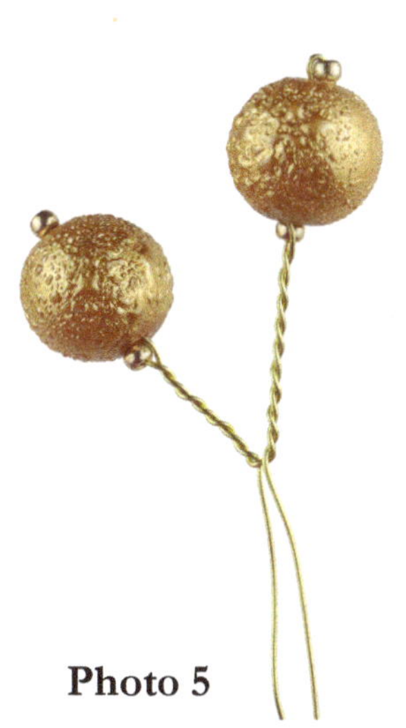

Photo 5

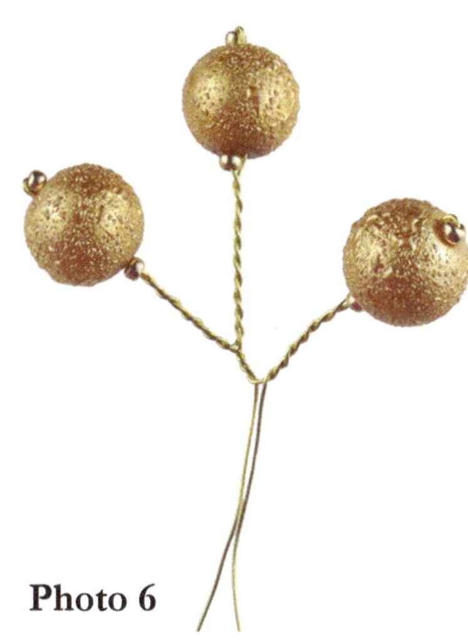

Photo 6

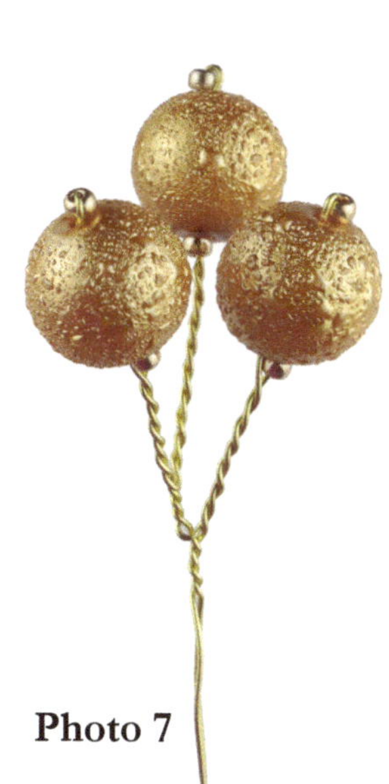

Photo 7

5. String another 1x 11/0, 1x 12mm, 1x 11/0 onto the working end of the wire. Just like before, insert the working wire back down into just the 12mm bead. Before pulling the wire tight, make sure there is 1/2 - 1 inch (1.3 - 2.5 cm) of bare wire between the new berry and the twisted stem of the previous berry. (**Photo 4**)

6. Pull the working wire tight, slide the lower 11/0 bead up against the bottom of the berry bead, then twist the two wires together all the way down to the bottom of the previous berry stem. (**Photo 5**)

7. Twist the two wires below the two berry stems down a few times, then repeat steps 5 and 6 to add a third berry. Make the individual twisted berry stems slightly different lengths between 1/2 and 1 inch (1.3 - 2.5 cm) long. (**Photo 6**)

8. Twist the two wires below together a few times, and squeeze the berries closer together. A finished berry bunch is shown in **Photo 7.**

ASSEMBLY:

1. Wrap the 16 gauge stem wires with floral tape to prepare the surface.

2. Cut a few feet of embroidery floss. Lay a tail of the floss against the stem wire, then add one berry bunch at the tip. Wrap the floss around tightly to secure the bunch to the stem. (**Photo 8**)

3. Wrap down about 1/2 inch (1/3 cm), then add in another berry bunch. (**Photo 9**)

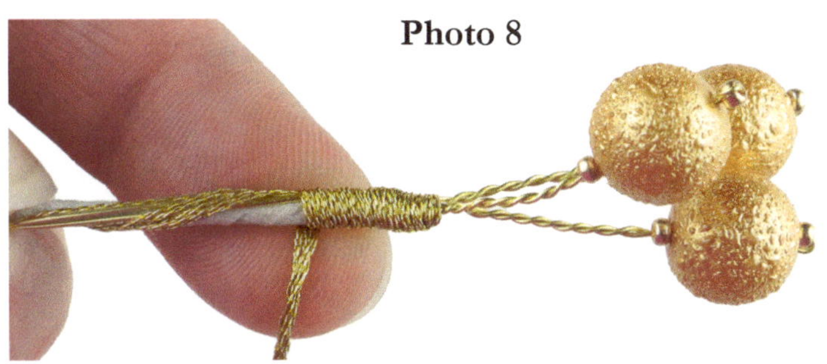

Photo 8

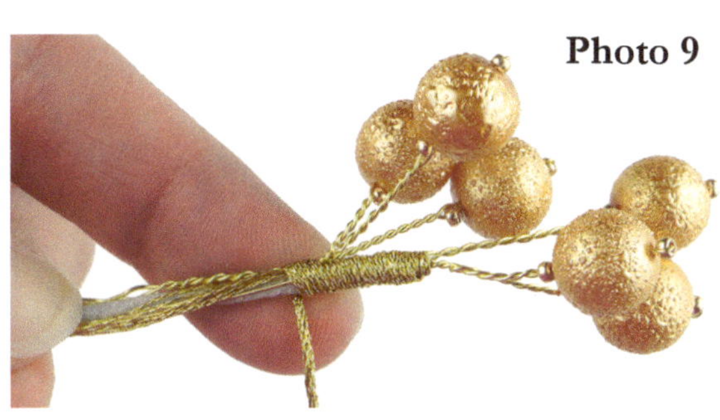

Photo 9

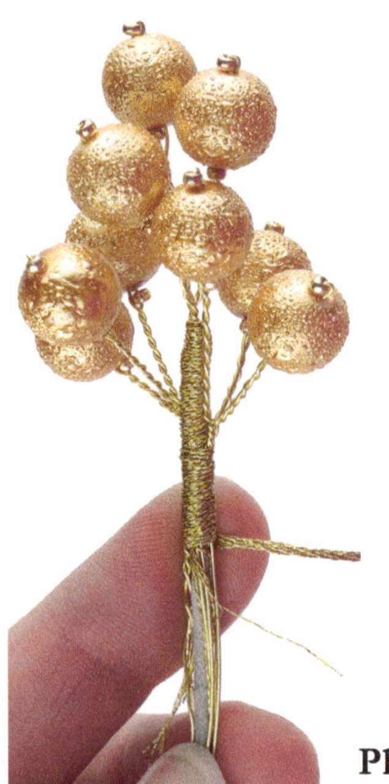
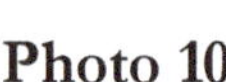
Photo 10

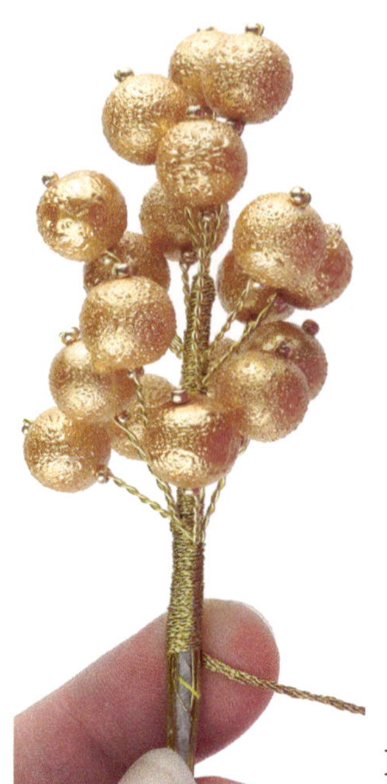
Photo 11

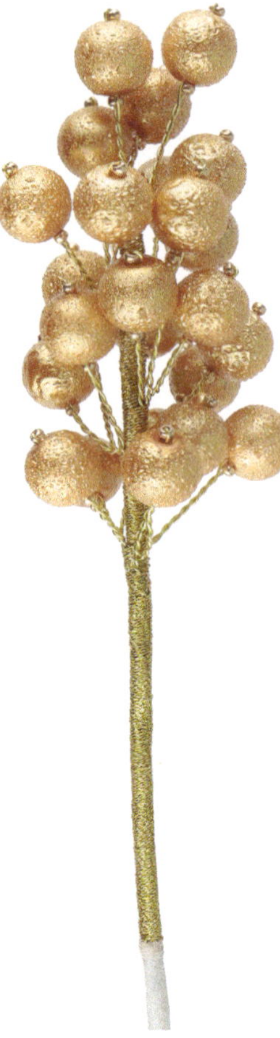

Photo 12

4. Wrap the floss around a couple times, then add in another berry bunch on the opposite side of the stem. (**Photo 10**)

5. Wrap the floss down about 1/2 inch (1.3 cm), then add in a berry bunch on the front of the stem. Wrap the floss a couple times, then add in a berry bunch on the back of the stem (**Photo 11**). This alternating left/right and front/back will ensure that the berries fully encircle the stem.

6. Continue wrapping down, adding in new berry bunch on all sides of the stem wire, and wrapping floss down a little bit between them until you have attached 8 total bunches. After the last berries, wrap the floss down at least 4 inches (10.2 cm). Secure the end of the floss with floral tape. (**Photo 12**)

.....Baby Eucalyptus.....

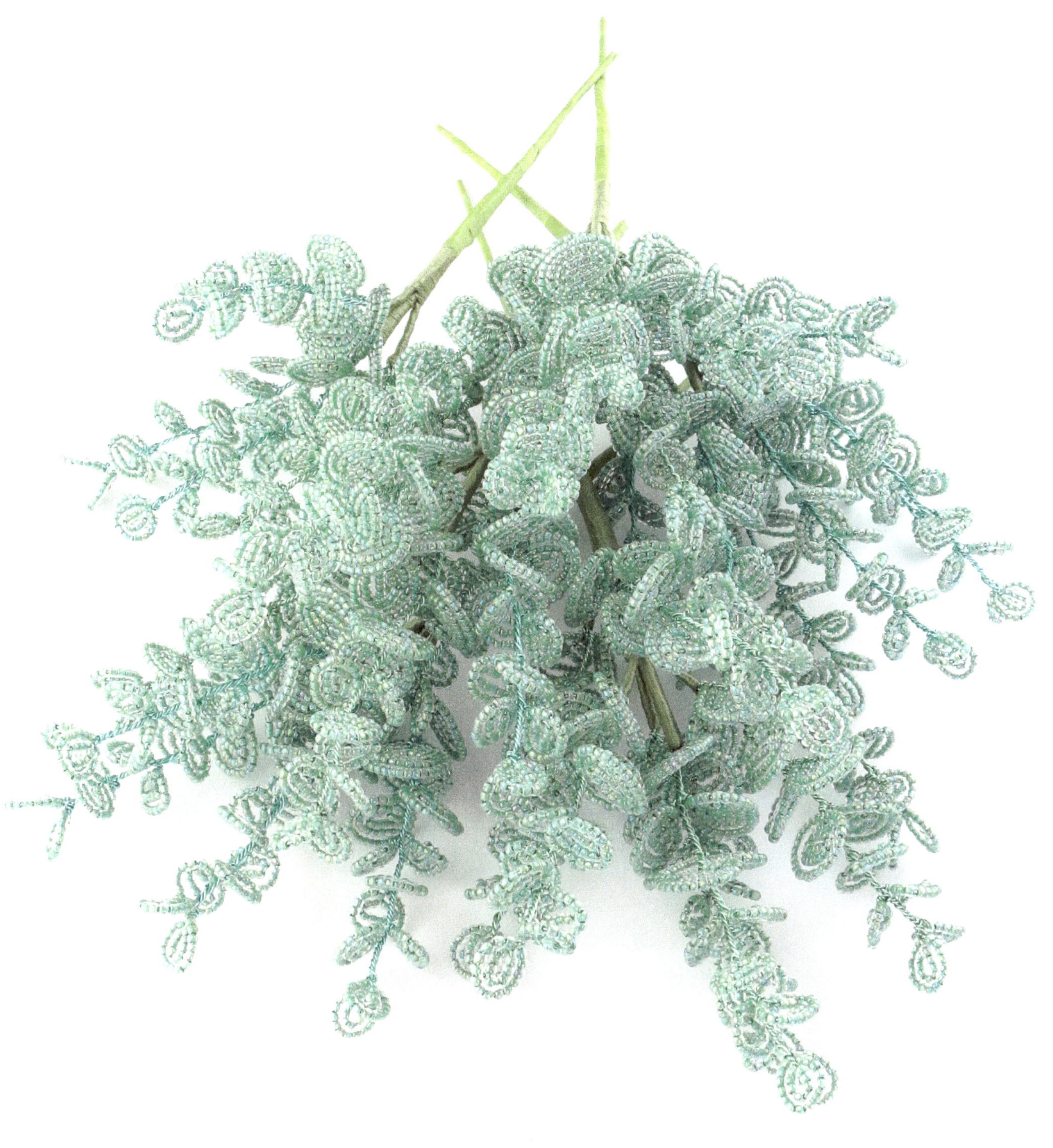

DIFFICULTY LEVEL: Beginner

TECHNIQUES USED:
- Continuous Wraparound Loops (CWL)

FINISHED SIZE:
4 inches (10.2 cm) tall, not including stem

ONE-A-DAY PIECES:
3x Large Sprays: 7 pieces each
2x Small Sprays: 4 pieces each
Total Days: 29

Materials

For the full wreath make three large spray and two small sprays.

BEADS:	FULL WREATH	1 SMALL SPRAY	1 LARGE SPRAY
Size 11/0 blue-green seed beads (Toho #699)	145 grams	20 grams	35 grams
WIRE:			
24 gauge (.5 mm) blue-green colored copper core wire (Parawire Seafoam)	145 ft (45 m)	20 ft (6 m)	35 ft (10.6 m)
16 gauge (1.3 mm) florist stem wire	5	1	1
OTHER:			
Light green floral tape	< 1 roll	< 1 roll	< 1 roll
Seafoam green embroidery floss	1 skein	< 1 skein	< 1 skein

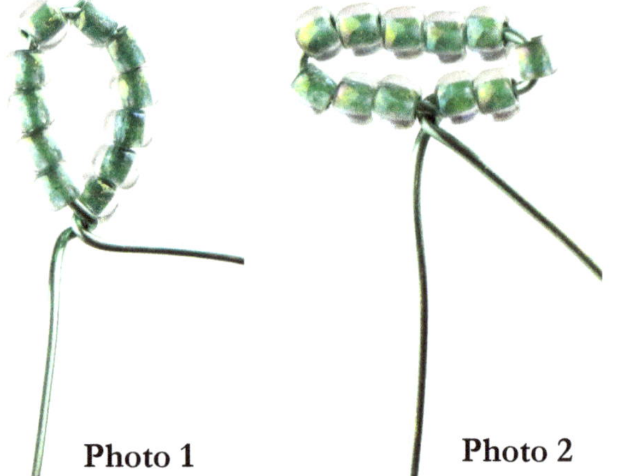

Photo 1   **Photo 2**

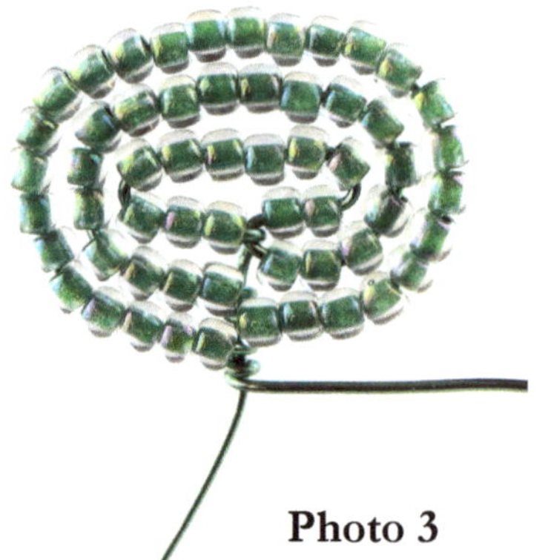

Photo 3

SPRIG: *Each sprig equals one day.*

Make 29 (4 per small spray, 7 per large spray)

On one wire, make 14 CWL leaves following the patterns below. Make leaves in this order: 2x Leaf A, 1x Leaf B, 3x Leaf C, 2x Leaf D, 3x Leaf C, 1x Leaf B, 2x Leaf A.

Patterns:
Leaf A: 3 row CWL, 11 bead Starting loop
Leaf B: 3 row CWL, 9 bead starting loop
Leaf C: 2 row CWL, 9 bead starting loop
Leaf D: 2 row CWL, 7 bead starting loop

Instructions:

1. String all the beads onto the 24 gauge wire.

2. Leave a 4 inch (10 cm) tail wire, and make an 11-bead starting loop for the first Leaf A. (**Photo 1**)

3. Flatten the loop so it is short and wide. (**Photo 2**)

4. Wrap rows 2 and 3 around the starting loop, then wrap the working wire twice below the last row of beads. (**Photo 3**)

TIP: If flattening the starting loops is hard on your fingertips, try pressing the top of the loop against a table. You can also use nylon jaw pliers.

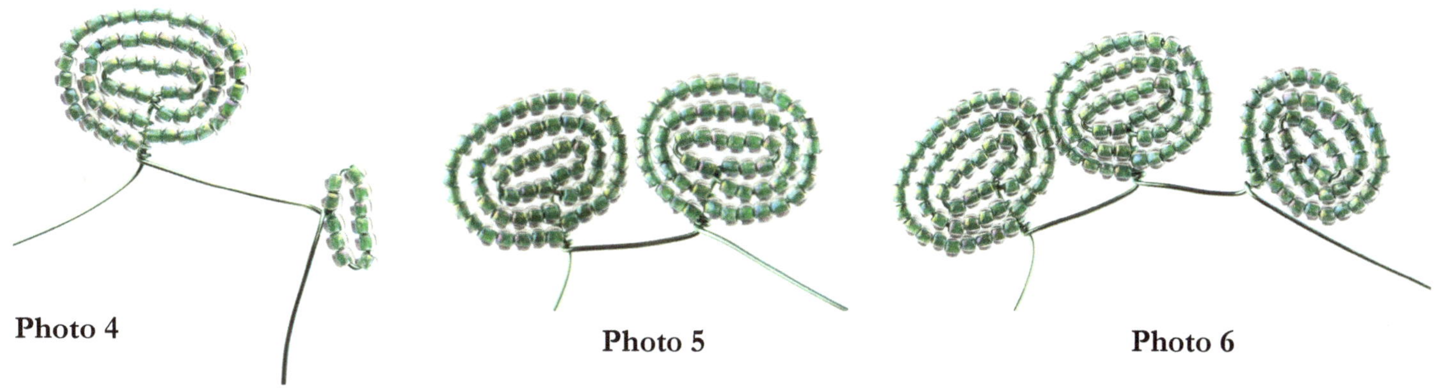

Photo 4   **Photo 5**   **Photo 6**

5. Leave a ¾ inch (1.9 cm) space in the wire, then make an 11-bead starting loop for the second Leaf A. *The space left over between leaves once completed needs to be ½ inch (1.3 cm), so leave a little extra space to allow room for the wraps.* Flatten the starting loop. (**Photo 4**)

6. Complete the second Leaf A by wrapping rows 2 & 3, then wrap the working wire twice. (**Photo 5**)

7. Leave another ¾ inch (1.9 cm) space in the wire, and make a 9-bead starting loop for the Leaf B. Flatten the starting loop, then wrap rows 2 & 3 around it. (**Photo 6**)

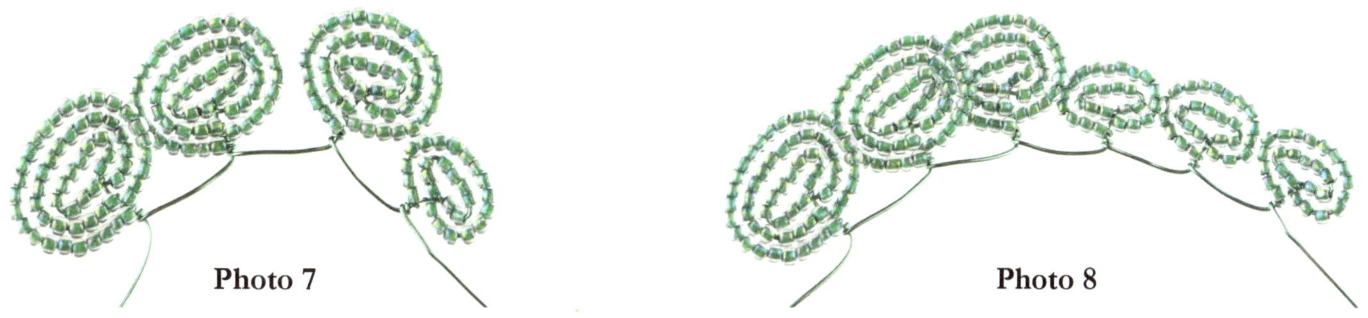

Photo 7   **Photo 8**

8. Leave a 5/8 inch (1.6 cm) space in the wire, then make a 9-bead starting loop for the first Leaf C. *The wire space between leaves does not need to be as long since there are fewer rows on Leaf C.* Flatten the starting loop, then wrap the second row of beads around it. (**Photo 7**)

9. Repeat step 8 to make two more Leaf Cs. (**Photo 8**)

10. Leave 5/8 inch (1.6 cm) space in the wire, then make a 7-bead starting loop for the first Leaf D. Do not flatten the starting loop. Wrap row 2 around it. (**Photo 9**)

11. The two Leaf Ds are the 7th and 8th leaves, and do not require any space between them. Leave just enough space for the wraps, then make a second Leaf D. (**Photo 10**)

12. Make 3x Leaf C, 1x Leaf B, and 2x Leaf A. Remember to leave a 5/8 inch (1.6 cm) space in the wire before leaves with two rows, and ¾ inch (1.9 cm) of space in the wire before leaves with three rows. The leaves on this second half of the unit need to match up as close as possible with their "mates" on the first half. (**Photo 11**)

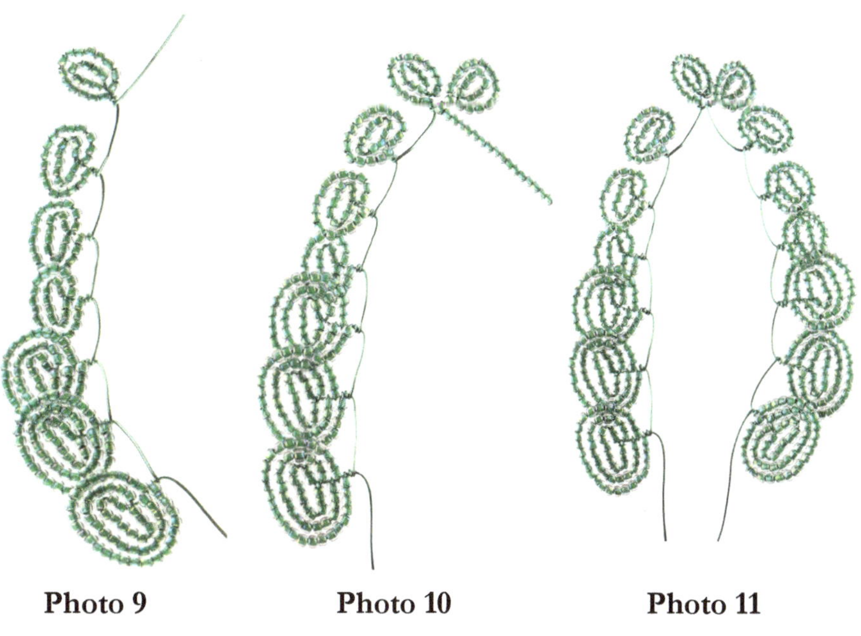

Photo 9   **Photo 10**   **Photo 11**

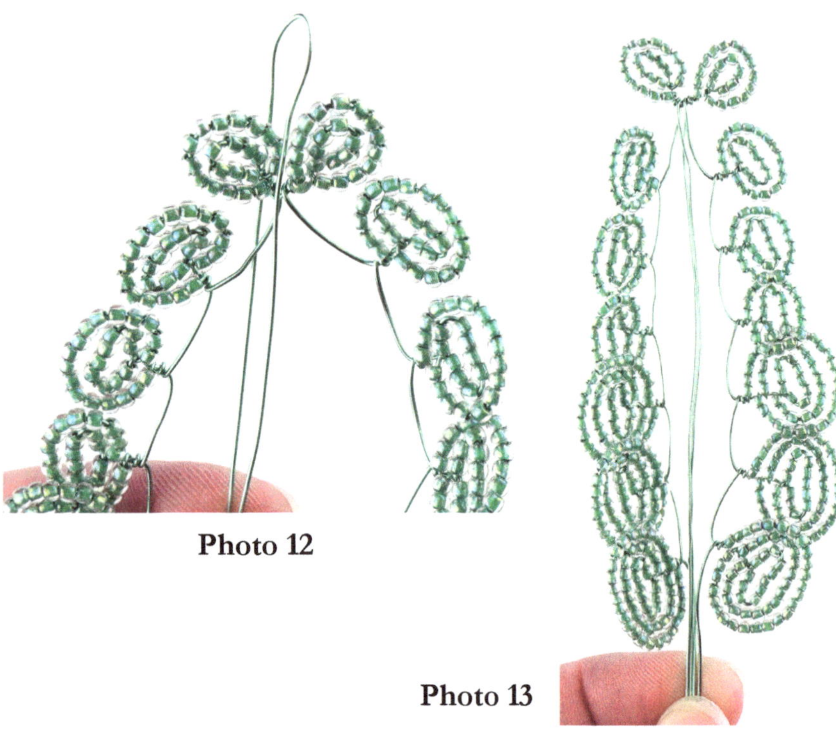

Photo 12

Photo 13

13. After the last leaf, measure a 4 inch (10 cm) ending tail wire and cut from the spool.

14. Slide the rest of the beads further down the spool, then measure and cut 12 inches (30.5 cm) of the bare 24 gauge wire. Fold it in half. This wire will provide extra support for the sprig.

15. Position the center fold of the support wire between the two Leaf Ds in the middle of the unit. (**Photos 12 & 13**)

16. Line up the support wires with the wires between pairs of leaves. Twist all four wires between the leaves tightly together, beginning at the top and working your way down in sections. (**Photos 14 & 15**)

17. After the last set of leaves, twist all four wires together approximately 1 ½ inches (3.8 cm) down. Leave the rest untwisted, but trim the wires to different lengths so the stem will taper down in width.

18. After twisting all the wires together, the sprig should be somewhat flat-looking, with leaves laying sideways along the twisted stem.

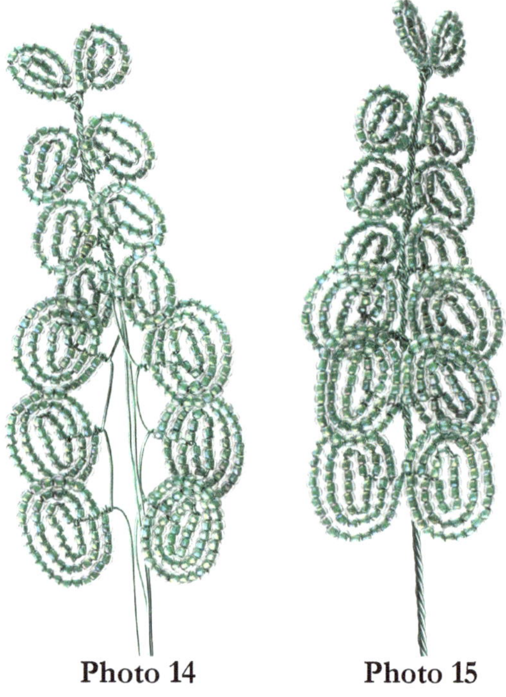

Photo 14   **Photo 15**

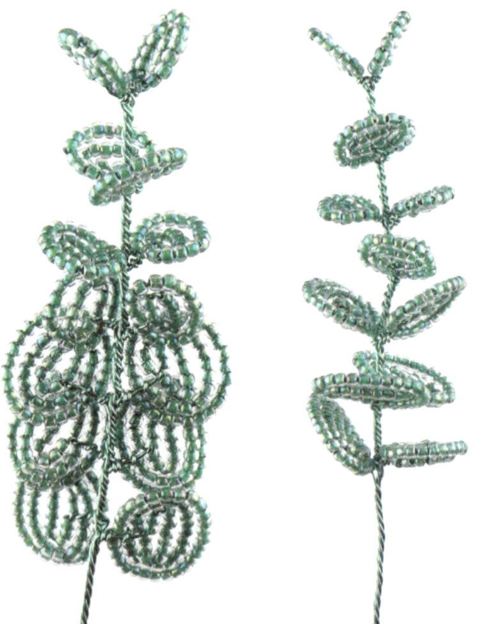

Photo 16   **Photo 17**

19. Twist and re-position the two Leaf Ds at the top of the sprig so the fronts of the leaves face upward, making a V-shape.

20. For the second set of leaves, twist and re-position them so they are sticking out between the previous set of leaves. The third set of leaves should mirror the first set. *The leaf pairs will end up in an alternating pattern of pointing left/right, and front/back, at a slight upward angle to make a V-shape.* (**Photo 16**)

21. Continue down the stem twisting and re-positioning leaves, alternating directions with every pair. (**Photo 17**)

ASSEMBLY:

1. Wrap the 16 gauge stem wire with floral tape to prepare the surface. Cut several feet of floral tape in half lengthwise to make thinner tape. Use this tape to cover the stems of each sprig below the last set of leaves.

2. Cut several feet of embroidery floss, then divide the thread into two 3-strand lengths. Wrap the stem on the sprig approximately 3/4 inch (1.9 cm) below the last leaf (**Photo 18**). Repeat for all but one of the sprigs for each spray.

3. Use another length of 3-strand floss to attach the sprig without floss to the end of the 16 gauge stem wire. (**Photo 19**)

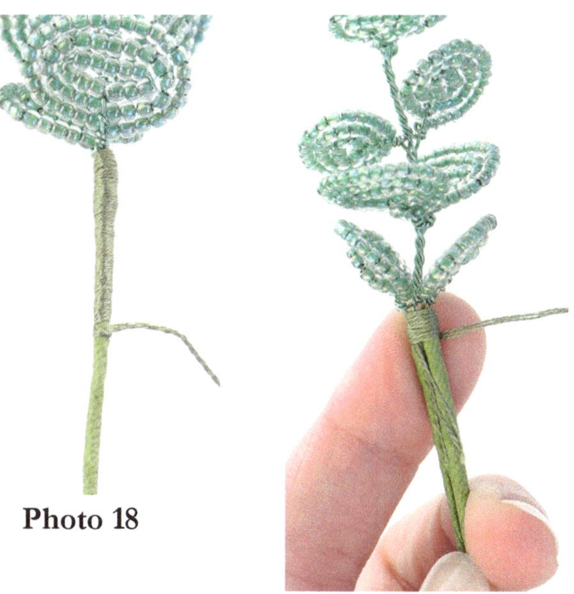

Photo 18

Photo 19

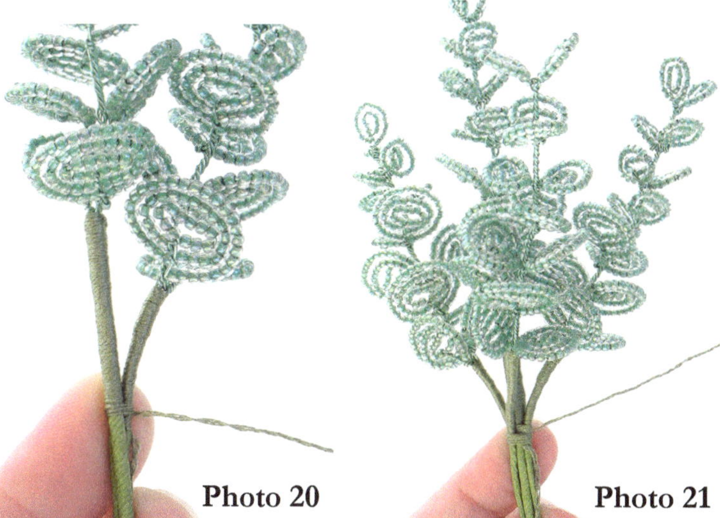

4. Continue wrapping the floss down the stem wire approximately 1 inch (2.5 cm), then add in one more sprig, lining up the bottom of the floss wrappings on both the stem wire and sprig stem. (**Photo 20**)

5. Wrap the floss a few times, then add in a third sprig on another side of the stem. Repeat to add a fourth sprig. The three lower sprigs should encircle the sprig at the tip of the stem wire. (**Photo 21**)

Photo 20

Photo 21

6. To make a Small Spray, wrap the floss down the stem wire another 1 inch (2.5 cm) below the last sprig. Cover the end of the floss with floral tape. For the wreath, make two Small Sprays. (**Photo 22**)

7. If you are making a Large Spray, repeat steps 4 & 5 to add in three more sprigs (**Photo 23**). Then wrap the floss down another 1 inch (2.5 cm) below the last sprig (**Photo 24**). For the full wreath, make three Large Sprays.

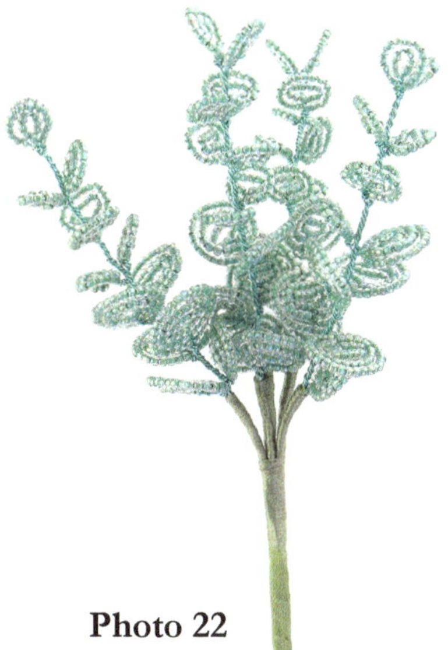

Photo 22

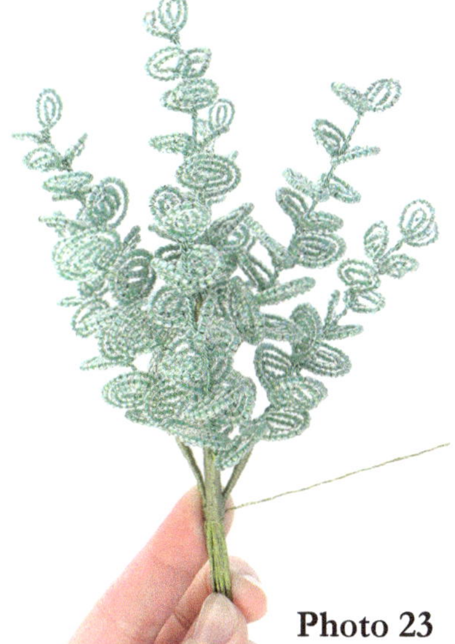

Photo 23

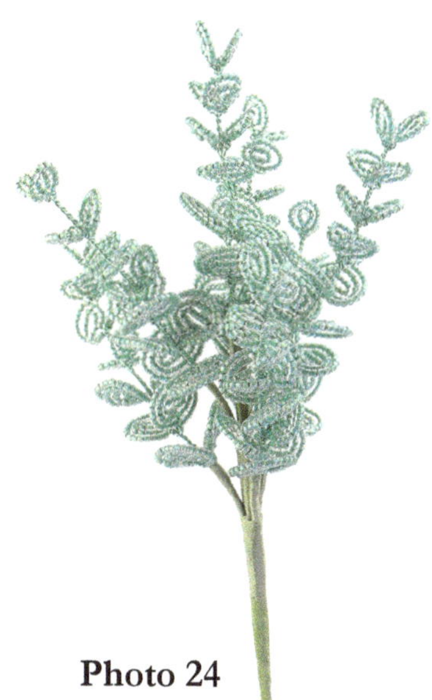

Photo 24

Amaryllis Flowers

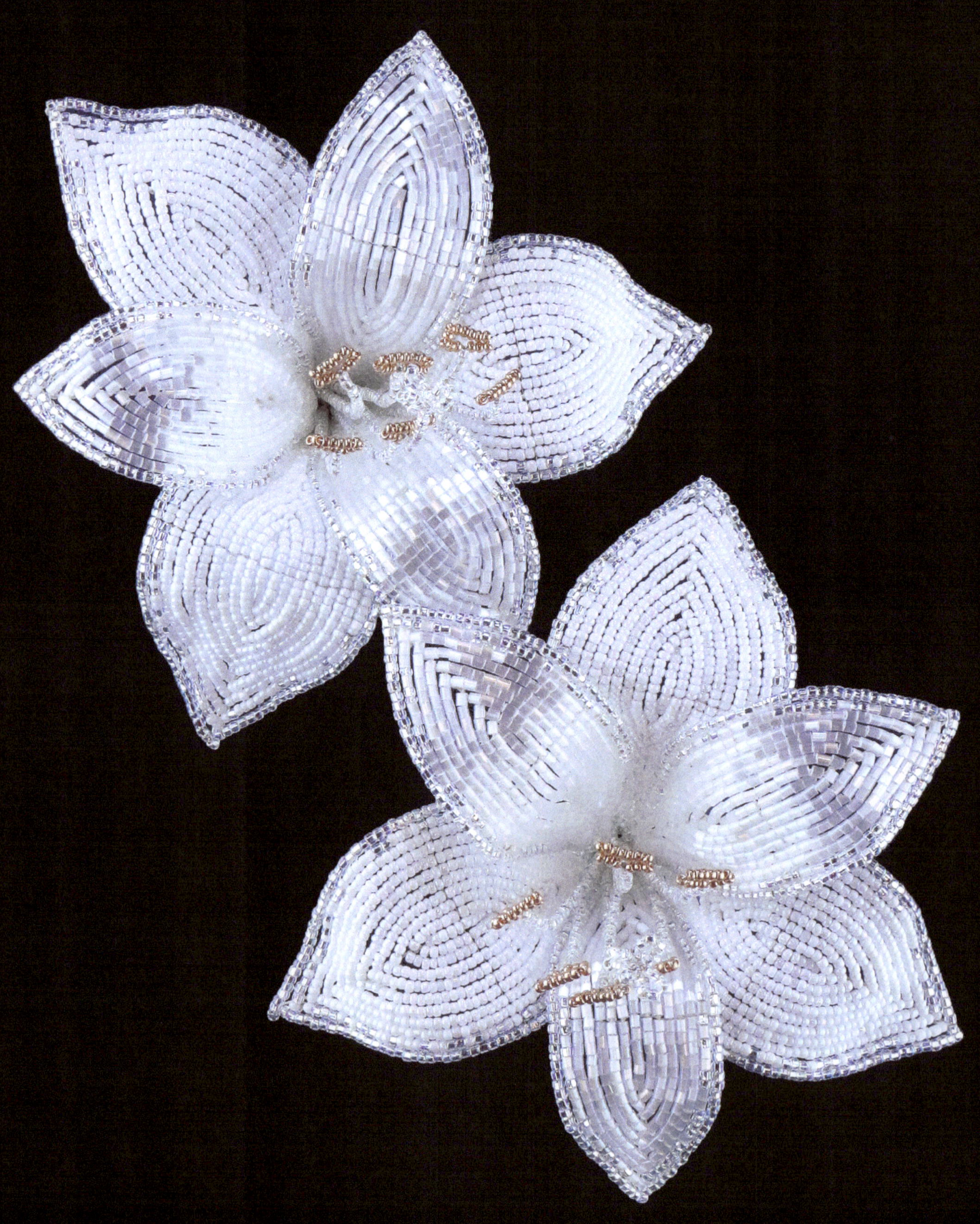

DIFFICULTY LEVEL: Intermediate

TECHNIQUES USED:
- Wire-Back Fringe (WBF)
- Basic Frame (BF)
- Bottom Wire Extensions
- Lacing

FINISHED SIZE:
Approximately 5 inches (12.7 cm) wide

ONE-A-DAY COUNTS:
2x Flowers: 8 pieces each
Total Days: 16

Materials

For the full wreath make two Amaryllis flowers.

BEADS:	FULL WREATH	1 FLOWER
11/0 Matsuno silky white rainbow seed beads (Color A)	40 grams	20 grams
11/0 Matsuno silver lined clear rainbow seed beads (Color B)	30 grams	15 grams
11/0 Matsuno opaque white rainbow seed beads (Color C)	40 grams	20 grams
11/0 metallic gold seed beads (Color D)	2 grams	1 gram
WIRE:		
24 gauge (.5 mm) white copper core wire*	60 ft (18.3 m)	30 ft (9.1 m)
32 gauge (.2 mm) white copper core wire**	6 ft (1.8 m)	3 ft (<1 m)
28 gauge (.315 mm) silver copper core wire	20 ft (6.1 m)	10 ft (3 m)
16 gauge (1.3 mm) florist stem wire	½ piece	1 piece
OTHER:		
Green floral tape	< 1 roll	< 1 roll

NOTES:

This flower was designed with a shorter trumpet than a typical Amaryllis flower. This was done intentionally so the flower wouldn't stick out of the wreath farther than any of the other wreath components. I also designed the coloring to be more decorative than realistic as I wanted it to match the style of the rest of the wreath.

* I used Artistic Wire's White wire for my flowers. Parawire's Ultra White wire tends to be very soft, and may not work well for this project. If you use Japanese brand beads, which tend to have larger holes, you could use Parawire Ultra White in 22 gauge instead of 24 gauge.

** Antique White is a color of wire made by Parawire that I use to lace white components. It is off-white, but it almost disappears against white beads.

FLOWER CENTER:

Pistil: *Each pistil equals one day.*
Wire: *28g (0.315 mm) silver*
Beads: *silver lined clear rainbow (B)*

Make 2 (1 per flower)
Pattern: 1x 2 ½ inch (6.35 cm) WBF with 3x 7 bead CL at the top

Instructions:
1. Leave the 28 gauge wire attached to the spool. String approximately 8 inches (20.3 cm) of beads onto the 28 gauge wire. This will be enough to make the pistils for both flowers.

2. Leave a 6 inch (15.2 cm) starting tail wire, then make three Continuous Loops using 7 beads each. (**Photo 1**)

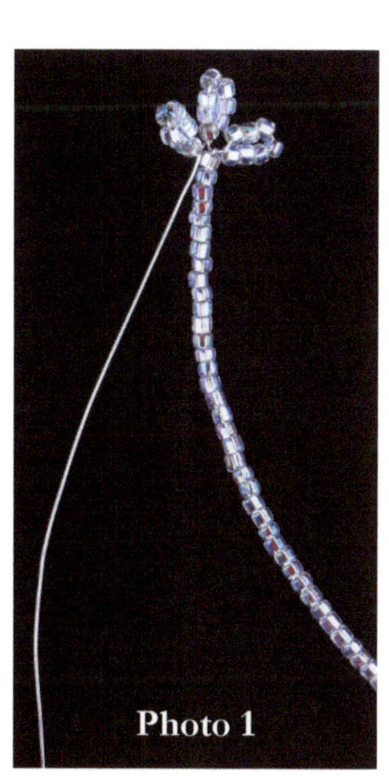

Photo 1

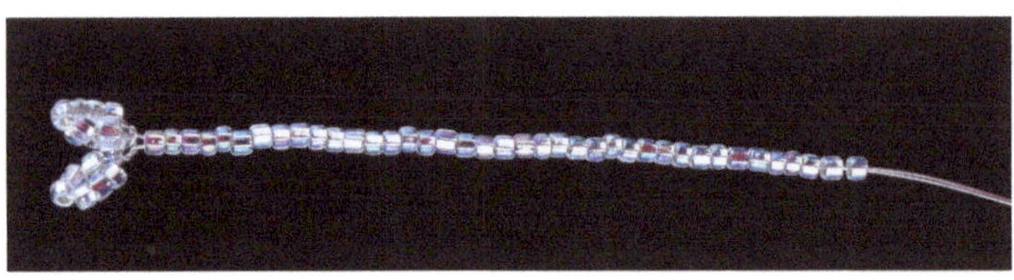

Photo 2

3. Measure 2 ½ inches (6.35 cm) of beads after the loops. Insert the starting tail wire down through the beads on the working wire, starting at the top near the loops and pushing the wire through to the bottom. (**Photo 2**)

4. Measure about 3 inches (7.6 cm) of bare working wire and cut from the spool.

5. Make small wire loops in the ends of the two tail wires to prevent beads from sliding off.

Stamen: *Each stamen equals one day.*
Wire: *28g (0.315 mm) silver*
Beads: *silver lined clear rainbow (B), metallic gold (D)*

Make 2 (1 per flower)
Pattern: 6x 2 inch (5 cm) WBF with 13 beads in a loop at the top

Instructions:

1. Cut approximately 3 feet (91.4 cm) of bare 28 gauge wire.

2. String 2 inches (5 cm) of color B, followed by 13 D. Position the beads approximately 3 inches (7.6 cm) from the starting end of the wire.

3. Skipping the 13 D beads, insert the long end of the wire (the working wire) back down through all of the B beads. (**Photo 3**)

4. Pull the working wire tight, which will form the D beads into a loop at the top of the fringe. Gently flatten the loop as shown in **Photo 4**.

5. String another 2 inches (5 cm) of B and 13 D.

6. Repeat steps 2-5 until there are six total fringes. (**Photo 5**)

7. Close the unit into a circle by wrapping the working wire around the base of the first fringe, then twisting the beginning and ending tail wires together. (**Photo 6**)

8. Insert the Pistil's stem wire into the center of the Stamen, then twist the stem wires together to make one Flower Center. (**Photo 7**)

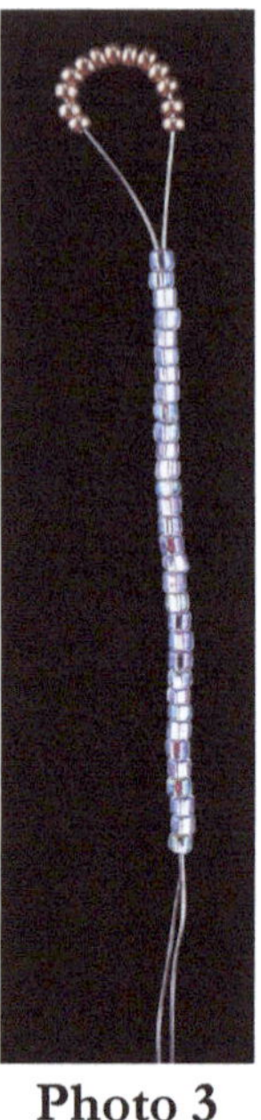 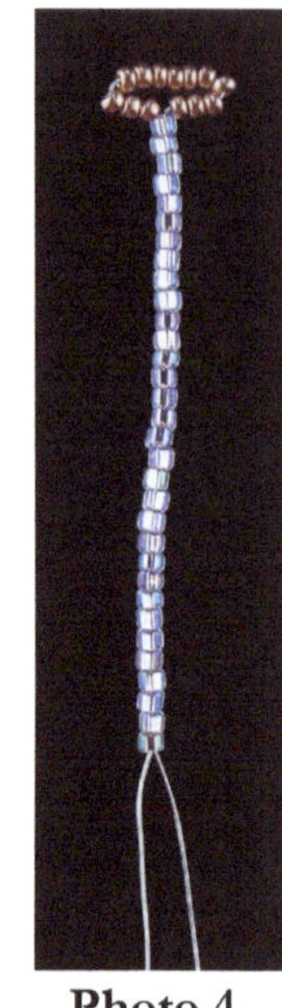

Photo 3   **Photo 4**

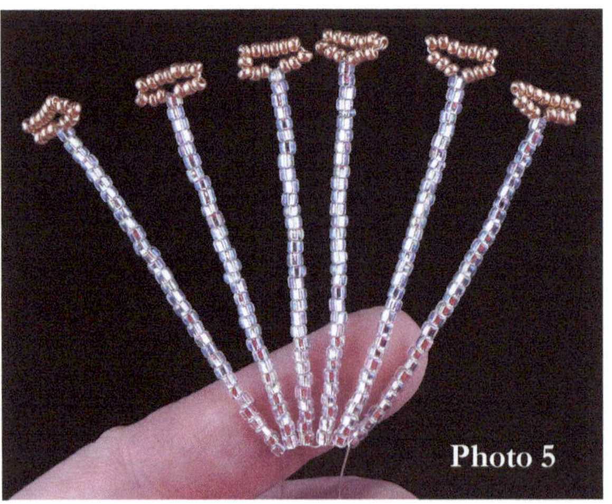

Photo 5

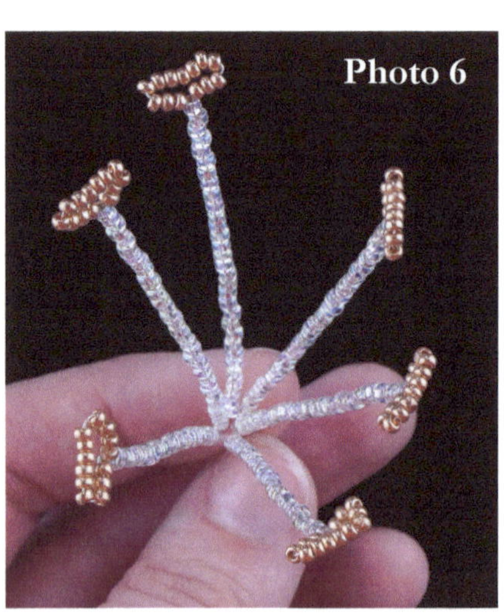

Photo 6

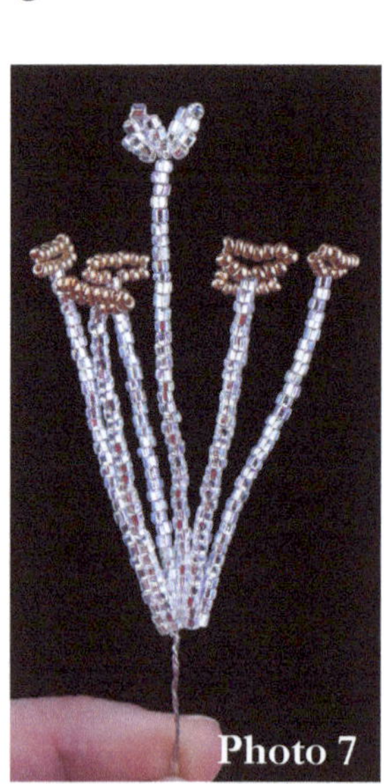

Photo 7

PETALS: *Each petal equals one day.*

Wire: *24g (0.5 mm) white, 32g antique white*
Beads: *silky white rainbow (A), silver lined clear rainbow (B), opaque white rainbow (C)*

Prepare two bead mixes. These bead mixes should be enough for both flowers.
For Mix 1, combine approximately 5 grams of A, and 5 grams of B.
For Mix 2, combine approximately 5 grams of B, and 5 grams of C.

Petal A

Make 2 (1 per flower)
Pattern: 15 row BF, 1 inch (2.5 cm) BR, PB PT
- **SUPPORT WIRE: Add a 10 inch (25.4 cm) 24 gauge support.**
- **EXTENSIONS: Add 2 beads to the bottom wire after rows 8 and 12 (4 beads total).**
- **5 bottom wires**
- **Lace once across the center.**

Instructions:
1. Cut two 10 inch (25.4 cm) lengths of 24g white wire to use later as Support Wires.

2. String the rest of color A onto the spool. Construct a Basic Frame with a 1 inch (2.5 cm) basic row, and with 4 beads in the bottom loop. (**Photo 8**)

3. Wrap rows 2-4.

4. Insert a support wire. Take one of the wires cut in step 1 and bend it in half. Insert it into the front of the petal, just above the last row of beads along the bottom wire. *Support wires are also used in the Poinsettia Bracts and leaves. Refer to the Bract C instructions on page 11 to see additional photos of the support process.*

5. Push the wire all the way through so the bend in the wire catches around the bottom wire between rows of beads. There will be two wire ends sticking out of the back of the petal. Fold them down with the petal's bottom wire. In **Photo 9** the support wire is shown in pink. As you add more rows wrap around all four bottom wires. Wrap rows 5-8.

6. If there are any twists in the bottom wire, untwist them. Move two beads in the bottom loop up directly below the last row of beads on the petal. Bring the second wire in the bottom loop behind the two beads, then twist the two wires together below the two bead extension. (**Photo 10**)

7. Wrap rows 9-11 (**Photo 11**), then measure approximately 20 inches (50.8 cm) of bare working wire, and cut the petal from the spool.

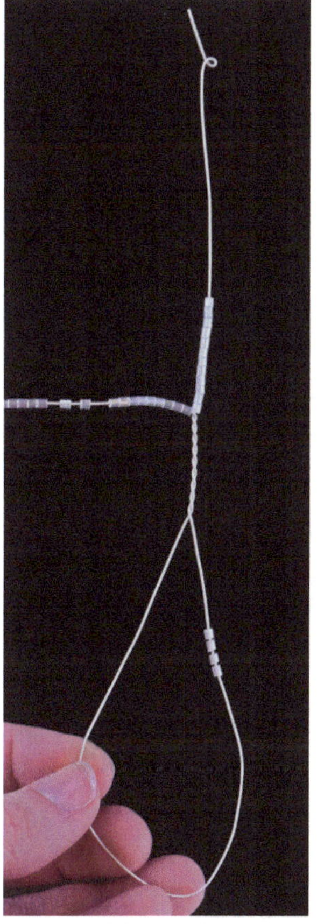
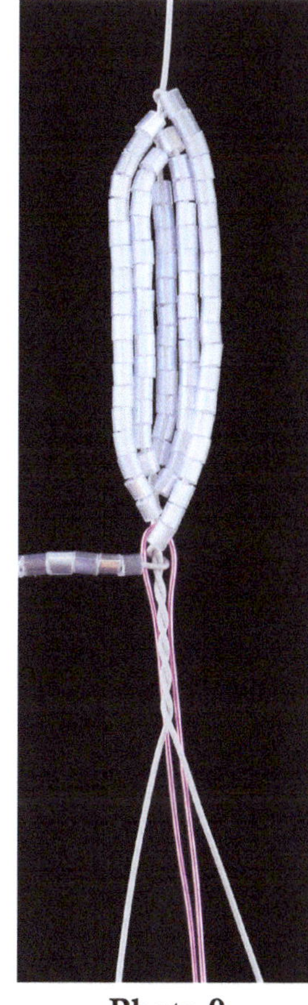

Photo 8   **Photo 9**

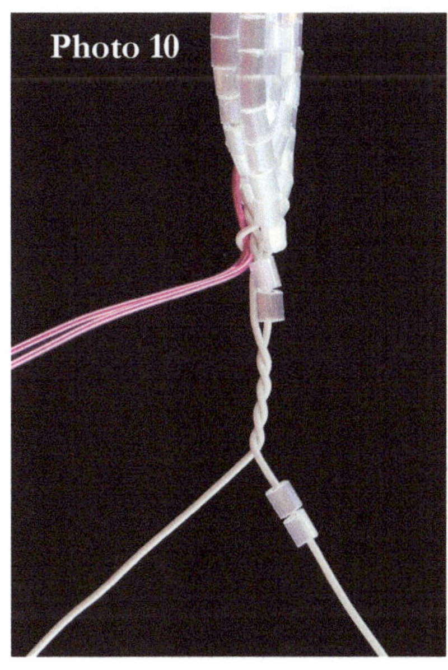

Photo 10

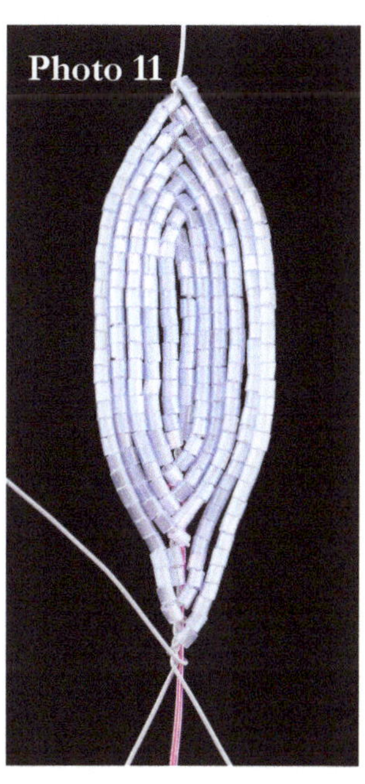

Photo 11

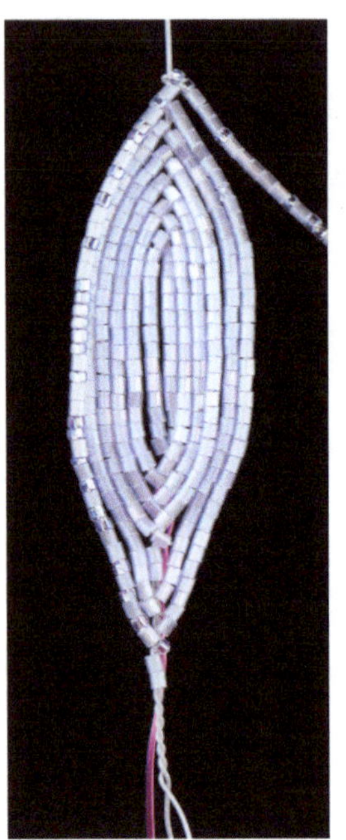

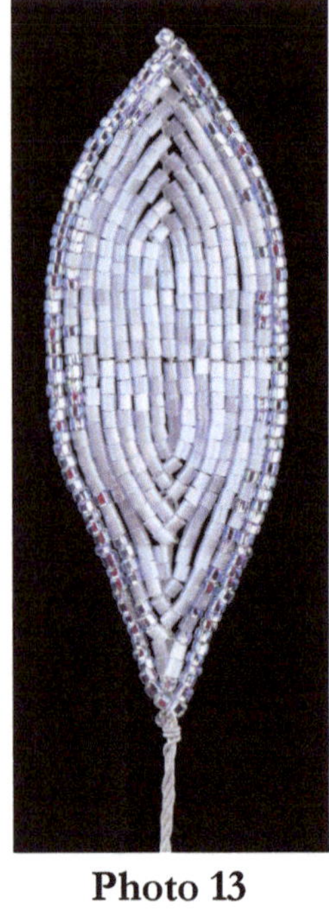

Photo 12   **Photo 13**

8. String 7 inches (17.8 cm) of Mix 1 onto the working wire and wrap row 12.

9. If there are any twists in the bottom wires, untwist them. Slide the last two beads in the loop up and make them into a second bottom wire extension. (**Photo 12**)

10. Wrap row 13.

11. Remove any excess Mix 1 from the working wire and put it back in your bowl for the next petal. String 8 inches (20.3 cm) of color B. Wrap rows 14 & 15.

12. Twist the working wire into the four bottom wires to make five bottom wires. Cut approximately 5 inches (12.7 cm) of 32 gauge wire and lace across the center. Clip and fold the top wire.

A finished Petal A is shown in **Photo 13**.

Petal B

Make 4 (2 per flower)
Pattern: 17 row BF, ¾ inch (1.9 cm) BR, PB PT
- **SUPPORT WIRE: Add a 10 inch (25.4 cm) 24 gauge support.**
- **EXTENSIONS: Add 2 beads to the bottom wire after rows 10 and 14 (4 beads total).**
- **5 bottom wires**
- **Lace once across the center.**

Petal B will be made with the same basic procedure as Petal A, but with different measurements.

Instructions:
1. Cut four 10 inch (25.4 cm) lengths of 24g white wire to use later as Support Wires.

2. Construct a Basic Frame with a ¾ inch (1.9 cm) basic row, and with 4 beads in the bottom loop.

Photo 14   **Photo 15**

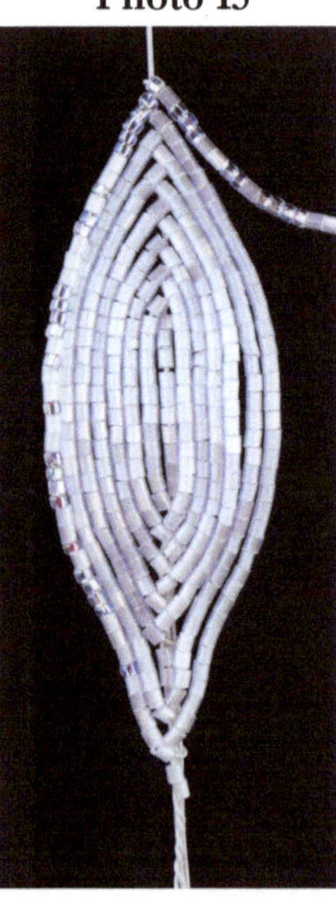

3. Wrap rows 2-4.

4. Bend one Support wire in half and insert it into the petal, just as you did with Petal A.

5. Wrap rows 5-10.

6. Untwist the bottom wire, move two of the beads in the bottom loop up, and make them into a bottom wire extension. (**Photo 14**)

7. Wrap rows 11-13, then measure approximately 20 inches (50.8 cm) of bare working wire and cut the petal from the spool.

8. String 7 ½ inches (19.1 cm) of Mix 1, then wrap row 14.

9. Move the last two beads in the bottom wire up and make them into a second bottom wire extension. Wrap row 15. (**Photo 15**)

10. Remove any extra Mix 1 from the working wire and put it back in your bowl for the next petal. String 8 inches (20.3 cm) of color B. Wrap rows 16 & 17.

11. Twist the working wire into the four bottom wires to make five bottom wires. Lace across the center with 32 gauge wire. Clip and fold the top wire back.

A finished Petal B is shown in **Photo 16**.

Petal C

Make 6 (3 per flower)
Pattern: 21 row BF, ½ inch (1.3 cm) BR, PB PT
- **SUPPORT WIRE: Add a 10 inch (25.4 cm) 24 gauge support.**
- **BOTTOM WIRE EXTENSIONS: Add 2 beads to the bottom wire after rows 10 and 16 (4 beads total).**
- **5 bottom wires**
- **Lace once across the center.**

Petal C will be made with the same basic procedure as Petal A, but with different measurements.

Instructions:
1. Cut six 10 inch (25.4 cm) lengths of 24g white wire to use later as Support Wires.

2. String all of Color C onto the 24 gauge white wire spool.

3. Construct a Basic Frame with a ½ inch (1.3 cm) basic row, and with 4 beads in the bottom loop.

4. Wrap rows 2-4.

5. Insert a support wire. Take one wire from step 1, bend it in half, and insert it into the petal just as you did with Petal A.

6. Wrap rows 5-10.

7. Untwist the bottom wire, move two of the beads in the bottom loop up, making them into a bottom wire extension. See Petal A instructions. (**Photo 17**)

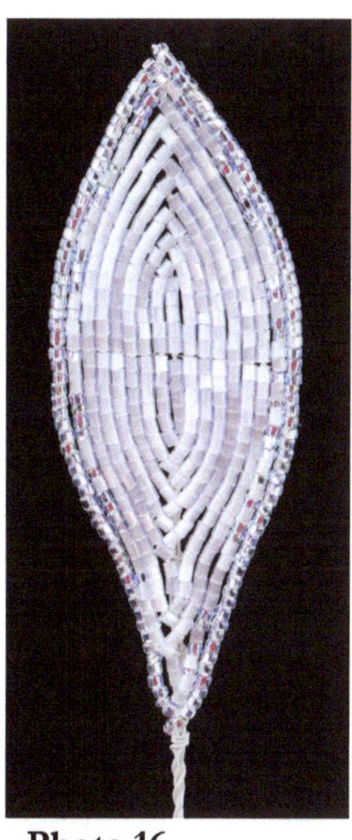

Photo 16

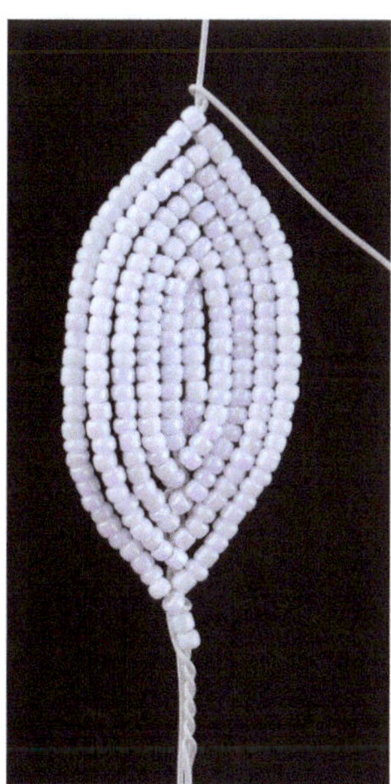

Photo 17

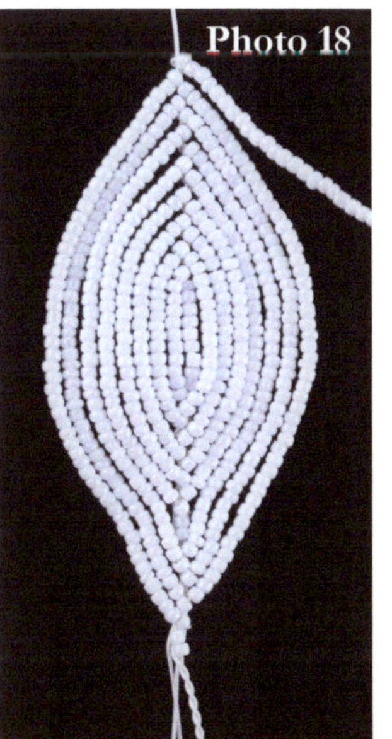

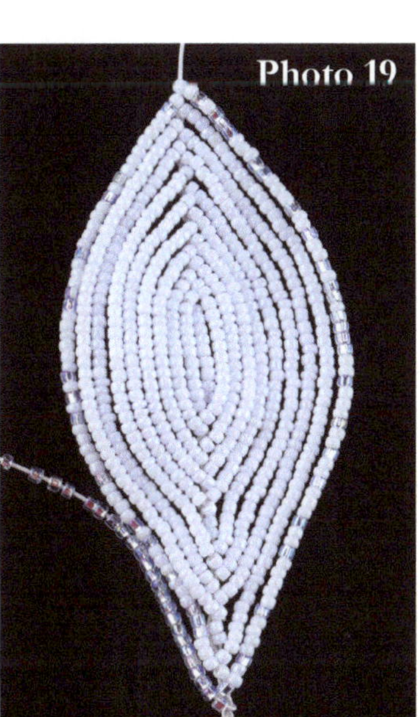

8. Wrap rows 11-16.

9. Move the last two beads in the bottom wire up and make them into a second bottom wire extension. (**Photo 18**)

10. Wrap row 17.

11. Measure out approximately 2 feet (61 cm) of bare working wire and cut the petal from the spool. String 7 ½ inches (19 cm) of Mix 2, then wrap rows 18 & 19. (**Photo 19**)

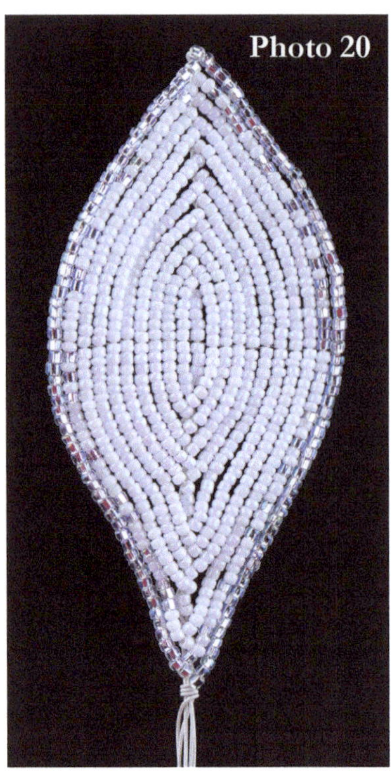

Photo 20

12. Remove any excess Mix 2 from the working wire and put it back in your bowl for the next petal. String 8 inches (20.3 cm) of color B. Wrap rows 20 & 21.

13. Twist the working wire into the four bottom wires to make five bottom wires. Lace across the center with 32 gauge wire. Clip and fold the top wire back.

14. A finished Petal C is shown in **Photo 20**.

ASSEMBLY:

1. Cut a long length of green floral tape in half length-wise to make thinner tape. Use this tape to wrap the stem wires on the flower centers and each petal.

2. Cut a 16 gauge florist stem in half to make two stems. Wrap the stem wire with a layer of floral tape to prepare the surface for assembly.

3. Use half-width floral tape to attach one Flower Center to the end of the prepared stem wire (**Photo 21**). Wrap the tape to the end of the flower center's stem wire.

4. Cut a few feet of 30 gauge wire in any color to use as assembly wire. Lay a tail of this wire against the flower stem. Add in one Petal A, then tightly wind the assembly wire around directly at the base of the petal 3-4 times. (**Photo 22**)

5. Add in two Petal Bs, wrapping the assembly wire around each one individually. The Petal Bs and Petal A should form a triangle around the Flower Center. (**Photo 23**)

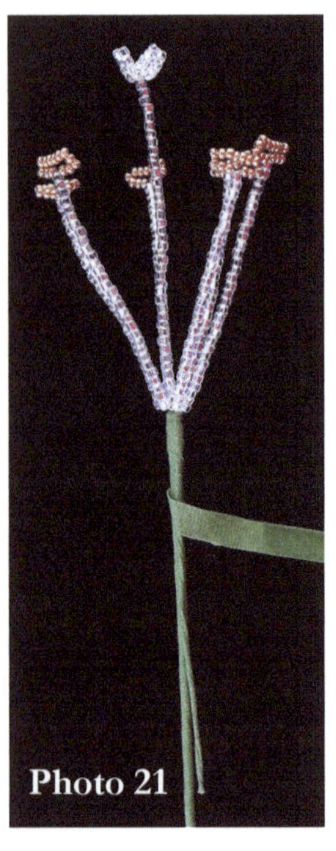

Photo 21

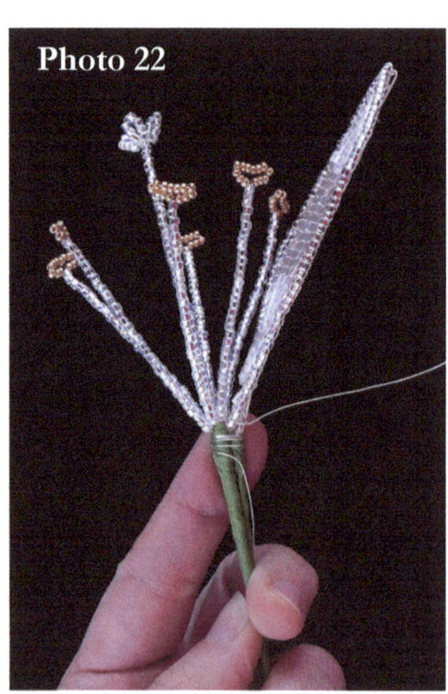

Photo 22

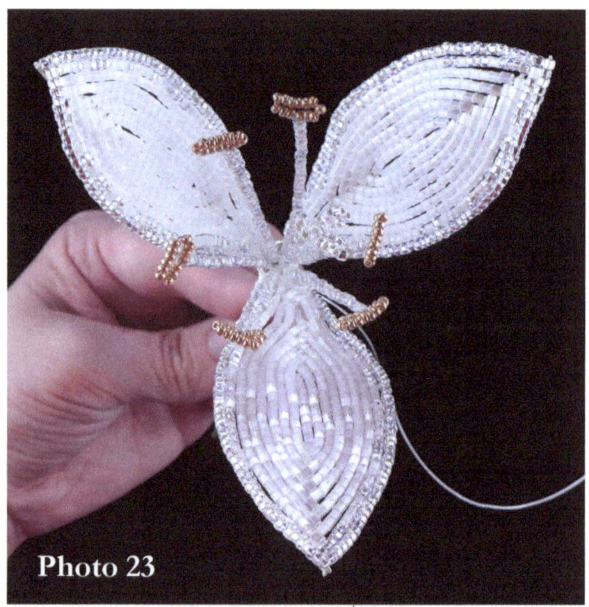

Photo 23

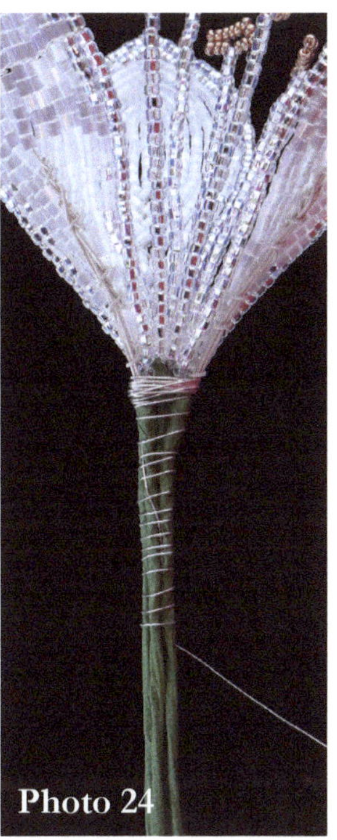

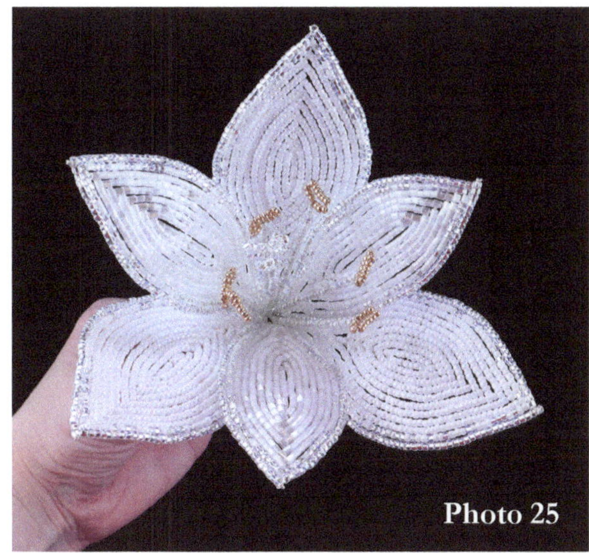

Photo 25

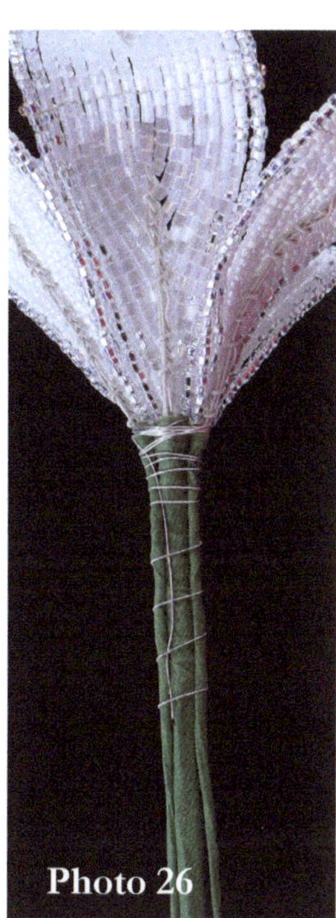

Photo 26

Photo 24

6. Wind the assembly wire down the stem. Make sure the petal stem wires remain straight so they don't form lumps on the flower stem (**Photo 24**). Clip the assembly wire and cover the exposed wires with a layer of floral tape to prepare the surface for the next layer of petals.

7. Cut a few more feet of 30 gauge wire and use it to add in the three Petal Cs, wrapping each one on individually with 3-4 wraps before adding in the next. Position the petals between the three petals in the previous layer. (**Photo 25**)

8. Wind the assembly wire down the stem to secure the petal stem wires to the flower stem. Clip the assembly wire and cover the exposed wires with floral tape. (**Photos 26 & 27**)

9. After assembling the flower, gently curl back the tops of the petals. Curl the Stamen and Pistils so they curve down toward Petal A, then bend back up at the very ends (**Photo 28**).

10. Repeat to assemble the second flower.

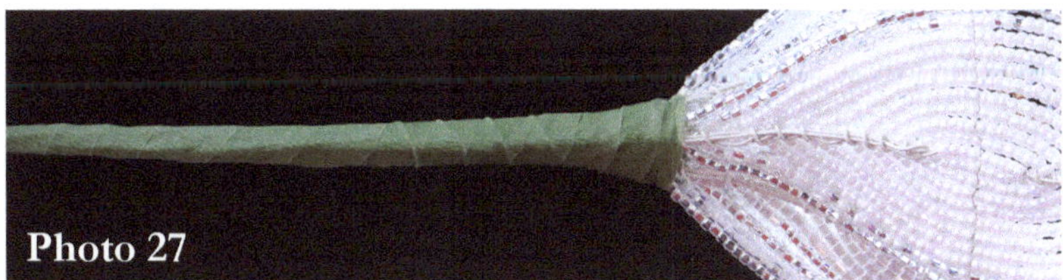

Photo 27

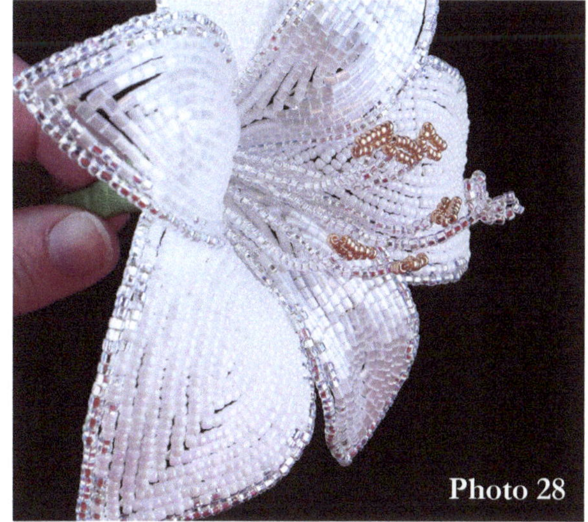

Photo 28

Gigantic Bow

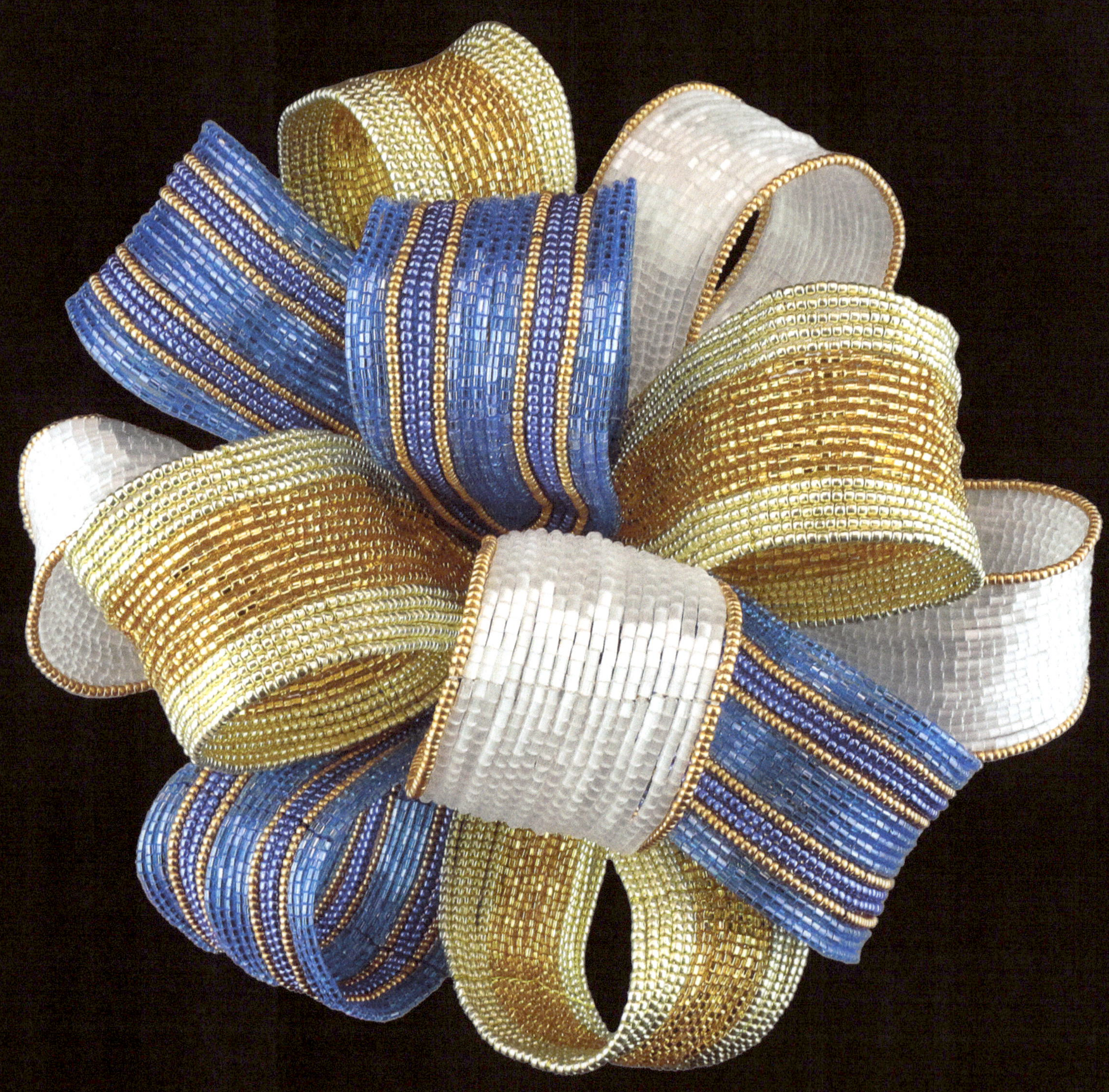

Materials

Make 1 bow for the wreath. The materials listed will make 12 bow loops and 3 bow tails.

	BEADS:	1 BOW
Ribbon A	11/0 Matsuno silky white (or 2 cut white satin Czech) (A)	85 grams
	11/0 Preciosa metallic gold (Color B)	20 grams
Ribbon B	11/0 Matsuno silver lined gold - square hole (C)	50 grams
	11/0 Toho PF559 metallic yellow gold (D)	75 grams
Ribbon C	11/0 Preciosa 2-cut transparent aqua luster seed beads (Color E)	55 grams
	11/0 Toho PF586 metallic cobalt (Color F)	30 grams
	11/0 Preciosa metallic gold (Color B, same as Ribbon A)	30 grams
	WIRE:	
Ribbon A	22 gauge (.6 mm) White copper core wire (Parawire)	70 ft (22 m)
	32 gauge (.2 mm) Antique white copper core wire (Parawire)	12 ft (3.7 m)
Ribbon B	22 gauge (.6 mm) Gold copper core wire (Parawire)	70 ft (22 m)
	30 gauge (.25 mm) Gold copper core wire (Parawire)	12 ft (3.7 m)
Ribbon C	22 gauge (.6 mm) Blue Flag copper core wire (Parawire)	70 ft (22 m)
	30 gauge (.25 mm) Baby Blue copper core wire (Parawire)	12 ft (3.7 m)
	14 gauge (1.6 mm) galvanized steel wire (for bow stem)	1x 10 inch length
	16 gauge (1.29 mm) florist stem wire (for tail stems)	3x 10 inch lengths
	OTHER:	
	white floral tape	< 1 roll

NOTES:

The bow uses three different color patterns to create the look of a bow made with mixed ribbons. I've separated the materials chart by ribbon type to allow for greater customization. To make a bow using only one of the color patterns, triple the materials listed for that ribbon type.

This pattern is best worked with 22 gauge wire for optimal support, but this thicker wire size can be harder to work with. It can also be a problem with *some* Czech seed beads as hole size is not consistent from one bead lot or color to the next. They may string a little more slowly, or sometimes not at all, especially if you string beads directly from a hank. A bead spinner will help load the beads a little more easily. If you encounter any difficulties switch to size 10/0 Czech beads, or a Japanese brand of 11/0 beads, which tend to have larger holes. Another option is to move down to a 24 gauge wire, but you will need to add additional support wires in a higher gauge than called for in the pattern to prevent drooping loops.

Remember that when working with a pattern that requires you to cut a specific length of wire, always cut a little bit extra the first couple times you make the component. This will help you gauge how much wire you use, because the exact amount of wire required will depend on your personal wrapping technique.

If you don't like working with long working wires, or if you just want to simplify the project, you can make all the ribbons in one solid color. To do this you will leave the wire attached to the spool and string all the beads. Then you can work from the spool and ignore the color changes and working wire lengths.

Ribbon A

Wire: *22g white, 32g antique white for lacing*
Beads: *silky white (A), metallic gold (B)*

Loops: *Each loop equals one day.*
Make 4

Pattern: 19 row BF, 5 inch (12.7 cm) BR, PB PT
- **Lace-as-you-go five times.**
- **SUPPORT WIRE: After row 5, insert a 10 inch (25.4 cm) 22g support wire at the Top Wire.**
- **3 bottom wires**
- **Do not clip the Top Wires; they are needed for assembly.**
- **Color Pattern:**
  Rows 1-17 = Color A
  Rows 18-19 = Color B

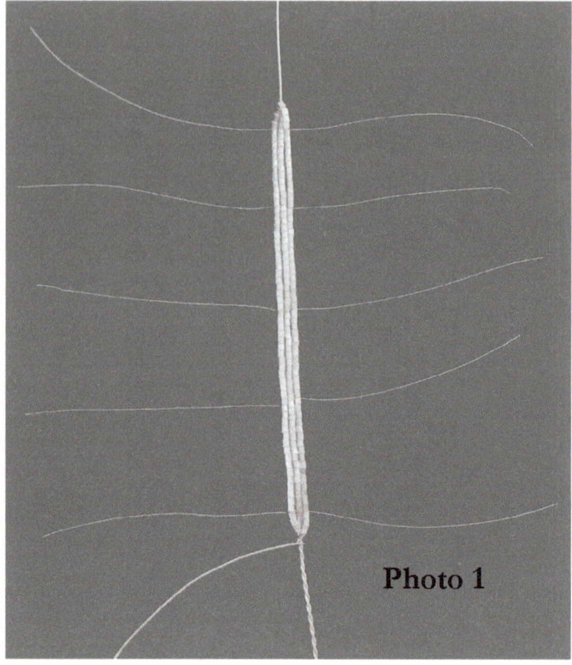

Photo 1

1. Cut a 10 inch (25.4 cm) length of 22 gauge wire and fold it in half. Set it aside to use later as a support wire.

2. String all of color A onto the 22g wire. Construct the Basic Frame according to the pattern, making the top wire approximately 6 inches (15.3 cm) long.

3. Carefully wrap rows 2 & 3, making sure the rows are straight. Cut five 6 inch (15.3 cm) long 32 gauge wires for lacing as you go. Attach one lacing wire in the middle of the Basic Row and lace the first three rows. Add two more lacing wires dividing the halves into fourths. Add the last two lacing wires two beads from the bottom of the BR and two beads from the top of the BR (**Photo 1**). From this point on, loop each lacing wire around a new row as you add it to the frame.

4. Wrap rows 4 & 5.

5. Insert the 22g support wire made in step 1 into the front of the ribbon, with one wire end on either side of the **top wire** below rows 4 & 5 (**Photo 2**). Push the wires all the way through so the fold in the center "catches" around the top wire between rows of beads. Fold the wires up in line with the top wire (**Photo 3**). Wrap all remaining rows around all three top wires.

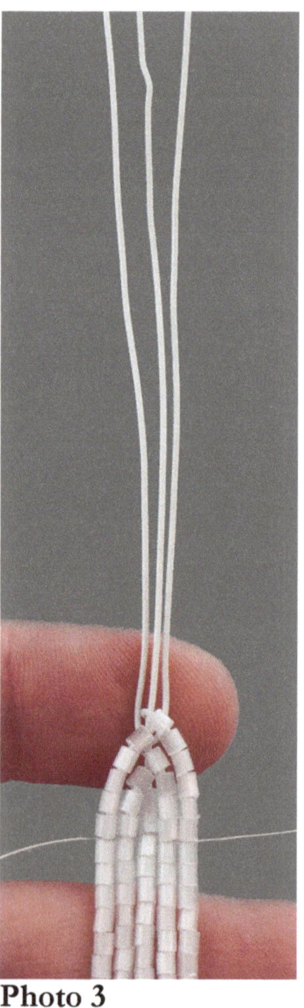

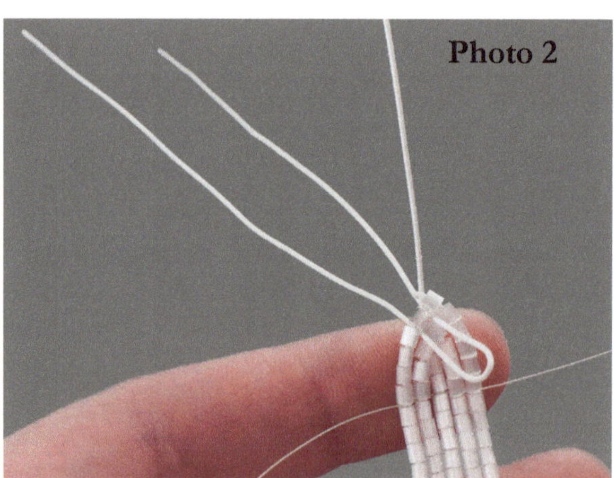

Photo 2

Photo 3

6. Wrap rows 6-17, then move any excess beads on the working wire further down the spool to use for the next loop. Measure and cut approximately 2 ½ feet (76 cm) of bare working wire.

7. String approximately 20 inches (50.8 cm) of Color B and wrap rows 18 & 19.

The finished Ribbon A Loop is shown in **Photo 4**.

Tail: *Each tail equals one day.*
Make 1

Pattern: 19 row BF, 3 ½ inch (8.9 cm) BR, PB PT
- **Lace-as-you-go three times.**
- **3 bottom wires**
- **Color Pattern:**
  Rows 1-17 = Color A
  Rows 18-19 = Color B

1. Work from the same spool of 22 gauge wire that is strung with Color A. Construct the Basic Frame according to the pattern. Make the top wire approximately 2 inches (5 cm) long.

2. Carefully wrap rows 2 & 3, making sure the rows are straight. Cut three 6 inch (15.3 cm) long 32 gauge wires for lacing as you go. Attach one lacing wire in the middle of the BR and lace the first three rows. Add two more lacing wires, one 4 beads from the bottom of the BR and one 4 beads from the top of the BR. From this point on, loop each lacing wire around a new row as you add it to the frame.

3. Wrap rows 4-17.

4. Move any excess Color F further down onto the spool so you can use it for the next ribbon. Measure and cut approximately 2 feet (61 cm) of bare working wire.

5. String approximately 16 inches (40.6 cm) of Color B and wrap rows 18 & 19.

The finished Ribbon A Tail is shown in **Photo 5**.

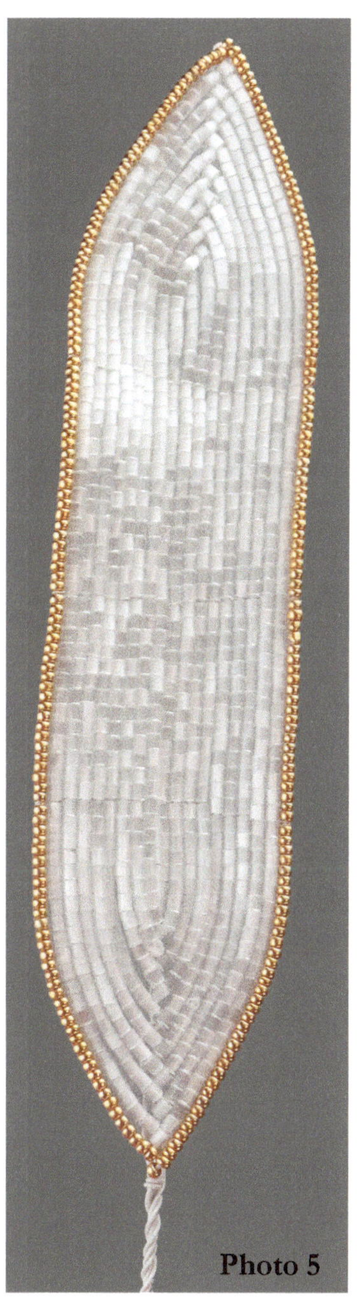

Photo 5

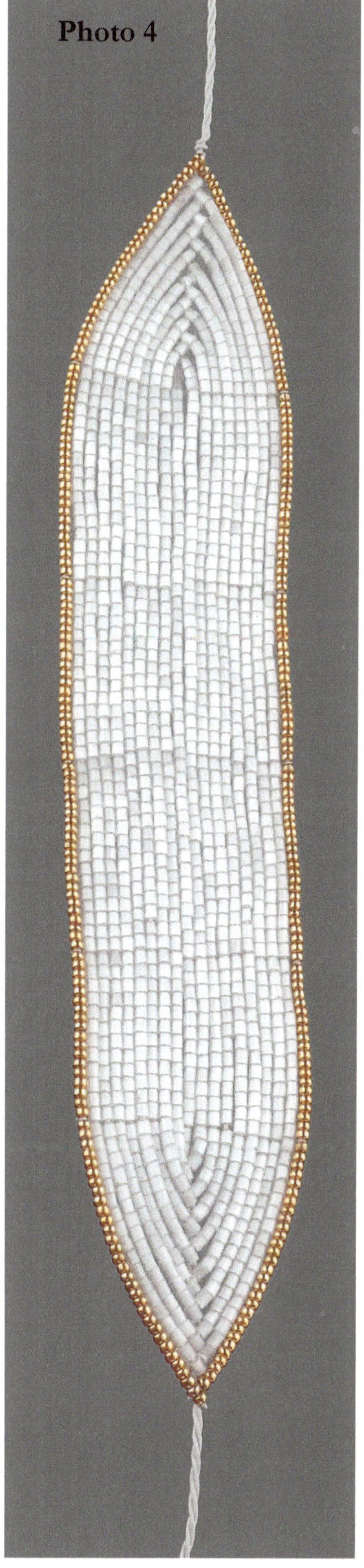

Photo 4

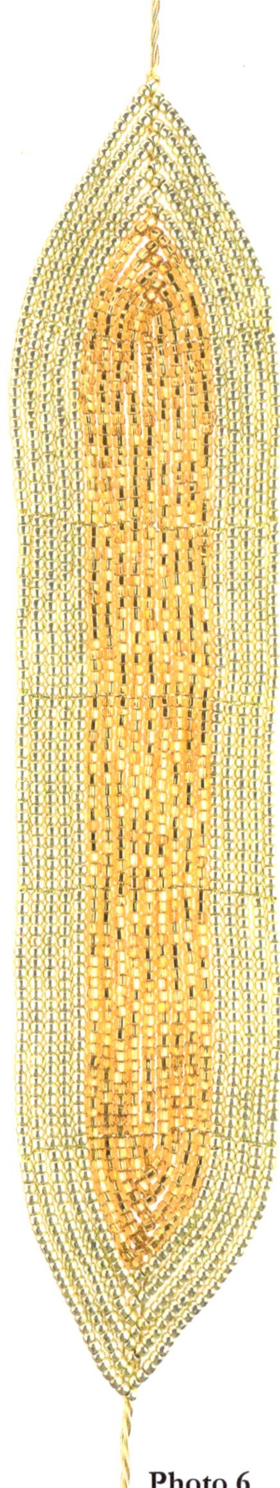

Photo 6

Ribbon B

Wire: *22g gold, 30g gold for lacing*
Beads: *Colors C, D*

Loops: *Each loop equals one day.*
Make 4

Pattern: 19 row BF, 5 inch (12.7 cm) BR, PB PT
- **Lace-as-you-go five times.**
- **SUPPORT WIRE: After row 5, insert a 10 inch (25.4 cm) 22g unit support wire at the Top Wire.**
- **3 bottom wires**
- **Do not clip the top wires; they are needed for assembly.**
- **Color Pattern:**
  Rows 1-9 = Color C
  Rows 10-19 = Color D

1. Cut a 10 inch (25.4 cm) length of 22 gauge wire and fold it in half. Set it aside to use later as a support wire.

2. String all of color C onto the 22g wire. Construct the Basic Frame according to the pattern, making the top wire approximately 6 inches (15.3 cm) long.

3. Carefully wrap rows 2 & 3, making sure the rows are straight. Cut five 6 inch (15.3 cm) long 32 gauge wires to lace-as-you-go. Attach them as shown in Step 3 of the Ribbon A Loop instructions.

4. Wrap rows 4 & 5.

5. Insert the support wire cut in step 1 into the front of the ribbon, with one wire end on either side of the top wire below rows 4/5. See **Photos 2 & 3** of the Ribbon A Loop instructions.

6. Wrap rows 6-9, then move any excess Color C further down the working wire onto the spool so you can use it for the next ribbon. Measure and cut approximately 8 feet (2.4 m) of bare working wire.

7. String approximately 7 feet (2.1 m) of Color D, and wrap rows 10-19.

The finished Ribbon B Loop is shown in **Photo 6**.

Tail: *Each tail equals one day.*
Make 1

Pattern: 19 row BF, 4 inch (10.2 cm) BR, PB PT
- **Lace-as-you-go three times**
- **3 bottom wires**
- **Color Pattern:**
  Rows 1-9 = Color C
  Rows 10-19 = Color D

1. Work from the same spool of 22 gauge wire that is strung with Color C. Construct the Basic Frame according to the pattern, making the top wire approximately 2 inches (5 cm) long.

2. Carefully wrap rows 2 & 3, making sure the rows are straight. Cut three 6 inch (15.3 cm) long 32 gauge wires for lacing as you go. Attach one lacing wire in the middle of the BR and lace the first three rows. Then add two more lacing wires, one 2 beads from the bottom of the BR and one 2 beads from the top of the BR. From this point on, loop each lacing wire around a new row as you add it to the frame.

3. Wrap rows 4-9.

4. Move any excess Color C further down onto the spool so you can use it for the next ribbon. Measure and cut approximately 7 feet (2.1 m) of bare working wire.

5. String approximately 6 ¼ feet (1.9 m) of Color D and wrap rows 10-19.

6. Twist the working wire into the bottom wires. Clip and fold the top wire.

The finished Ribbon B Tail is shown in **Photo 7**.

Ribbon C

Wire: *22g Blue, 32g baby blue for lacing*
Beads: *Colors E, F, B*

Loops: *Each loop equals one day.*
Make 4

Pattern: 19 row BF, 5 inch (12.7 cm) BR, PB PT
- **Lace-as-you-go x5.**
- **SUPPORT WIRE: After row 5, insert a 10 inch (25.4 cm) 22g unit support wire at the Top Wire.**
- **3 bottom wires**
- **Do not clip the Top Wires; they are needed for assembly.**
- **Color Pattern:**
  Rows 1-5 = Color E
  Rows 6-7 = Color B
  Rows 8-11 = Color F
  Rows 12-13 = Color B
  Rows 14-19 = Color E

1. Cut a 10 inch (25.4 cm) length of 22 gauge wire and fold it in half. Set it aside to use as a support wire later.

2. String approximately 2 ½ feet (76.2 cm) color E onto the 22g wire. Construct the Basic Frame according to the pattern. Make the top wire approximately 6 inches (15.3 cm) long.

3. Carefully wrap rows 2 & 3, making sure the rows are straight. Cut five 6 inch (15.3 cm) 30-32 gauge lacing wires and add them in, spacing them evenly.

4. Wrap rows 4 & 5.

5. Insert the support wire cut in step 1 into the front of the ribbon, with one wire end on either side of the top wire below rows 4/5. See **Photo 2** in the Ribbon A instructions.

6. Move any excess Color E further down onto the spool. Measure and cut approximately 9 feet (2.7 m) of bare working wire. String approximately 13 inches (33 cm) of Color B, and wrap rows 6 & 7.

7. Remove any excess color B. String approximately 2 ½ feet (76.2 cm) of Color F and wrap rows 8-11.

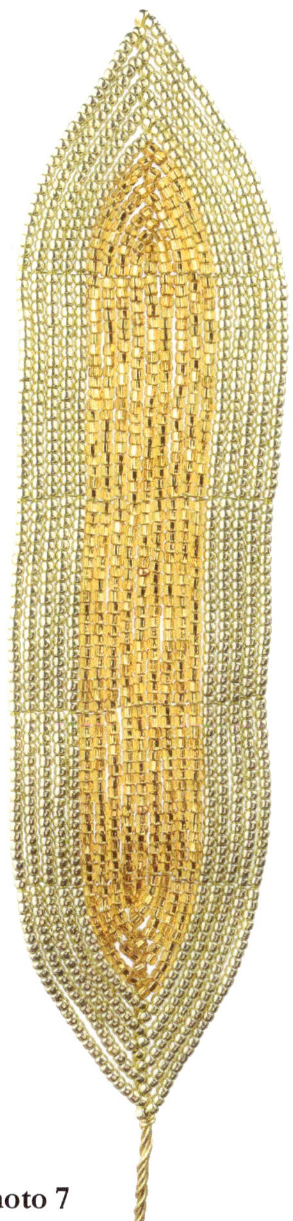

Photo 7

Photo 8

8. Remove any excess color F. String approximately 1 ½ feet (45.7 cm) of Color C and wrap rows 12 & 13.

9. Remove excess color C, then string approximately 4 ½ feet (1.4 m) Color E and wrap rows 14-19.

The finished Ribbon C Loop is shown in **Photo 8**.

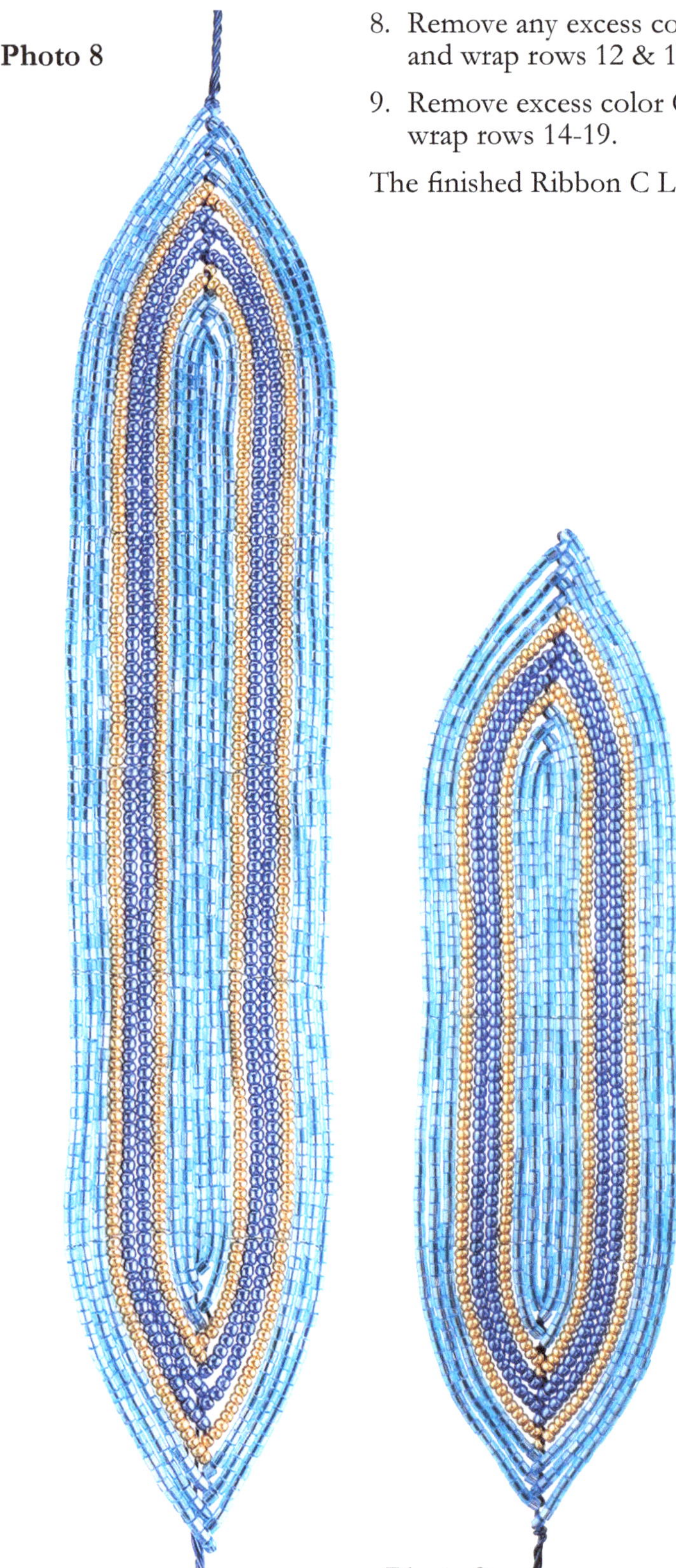

Photo 9

Tail: *Each tail equals one day.*

Make 1

Pattern: 19 row BF, 3 inch (7.6 cm) BR, PB PT
- **Lace-as-you-go three times.**
- **3 bottom wires**
- **Color Pattern:**
  Rows 1-5 = Color E
  Rows 6-7 = Color B
  Rows 8-11 = Color F
  Rows 12-13 = Color B
  Rows 14-19 = Color E

1. String approximately 1 ½ feet (45.7 cm) color E onto the 22g wire. Construct the Basic Frame according to the pattern, making the top wire approximately 2 inches (5 cm) long.

2. Carefully wrap rows 2 & 3, making sure the rows are straight. Cut three 6 inch (15.3 cm) long 32 gauge wires to lace-as-you-go. Attach them to the tail just like the previous ribbon tails, then lace-as-you-go for the remaining rows.

3. Wrap rows 4 & 5.

4. Move any excess Color E further down onto the spool. Measure and cut 8 feet (2.4 m) of bare working wire. String approximately 9 inches (22.8 cm) of Color B, and wrap rows 6 & 7.

5. Remove any excess color B. String approximately 21 inches (53.3 cm) of Color F, and wrap rows 8-11.

6. Remove any excess color F. String approximately 1 foot (30.5 cm) of Color B, and wrap rows 12 & 13.

7. Remove excess color B, then string approximately 3 ½ feet (1.1 m) Color E, and wrap rows 14-19.

The finished Ribbon C Tail is shown in **Photo 9**.

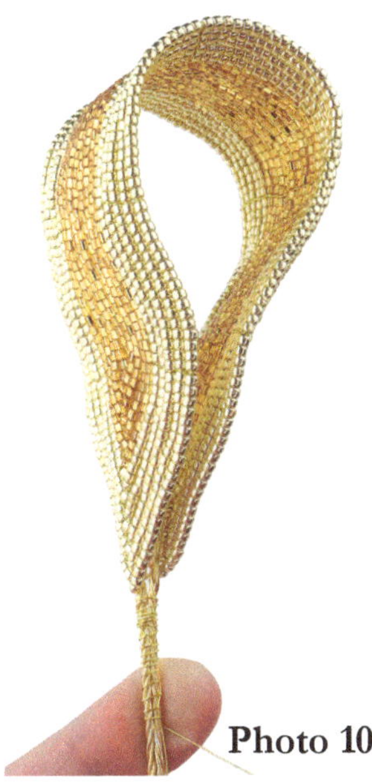

Photo 10

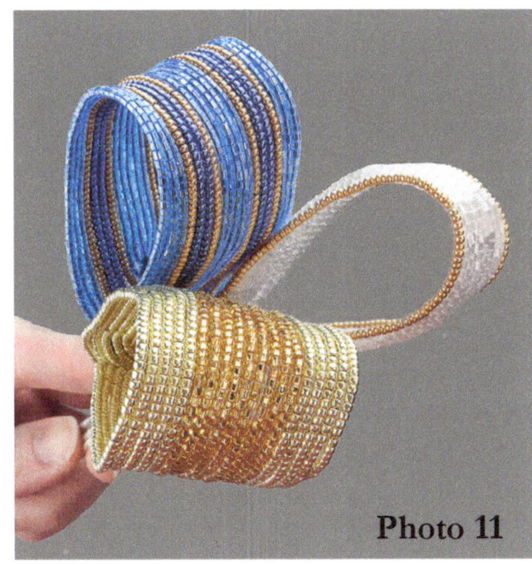

Photo 11

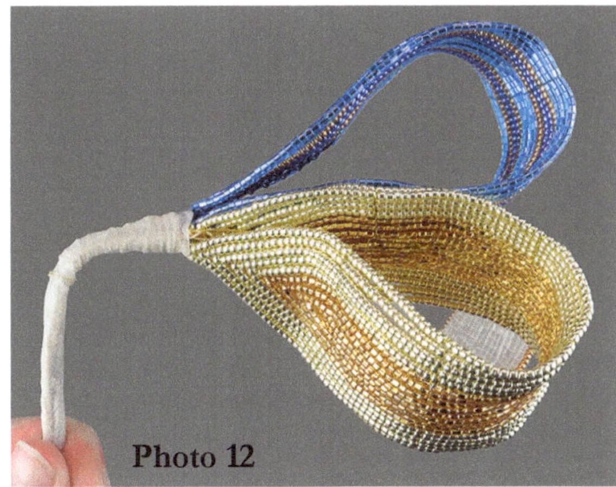

Photo 12

ASSEMBLY

1. Prepare the 14 gauge galvanized steel wire by wrapping it with a layer of floral tape.

2. Fold each of the twelve ribbon loops in half to form the loops, then use a length of 30 gauge wire to attach the top and bottom wires together. (**Photo 10**)

3. Wrap each of the loop stem wires with floral tape.

4. Gather one of each type of ribbon into a bundle around the prepared 14 gauge stem wire (**Photo 11**). Cut approximately 3 feet (91 cm) of 30 gauge wire in any color to use as an assembly wire. Beginning at the top just below the loops, tightly wind the 30 gauge wire around many times. Move down while winding to secure the ends of the loop stems.

5. Cover the exposed wire wraps with floral tape to prepare the surface for the next layer. Bend the stem wire 90 degrees about 1 ½ inches (3.8 cm) below the loops. You may need pliers for this. This bend is needed for wreath assembly. If you are using the bow in a different arrangement, you may or may not need a bent stem. (**Photo 12**)

6. Cut a few more feet of 30 gauge wire. Add in four more loops, one at a time. Just below the loop, wind the assembly wire a few times around the stems before adding in the next loop. Try to position the loops so that the same type of ribbons don't touch. Also, attach some of the loops sideways so they aren't all turned the same direction. This will help the bow look more realistic. (**Photos 13 & 14**) Once all four loops have been added, wind further down the stem to secure the ends. Cover the exposed wires with floral tape.

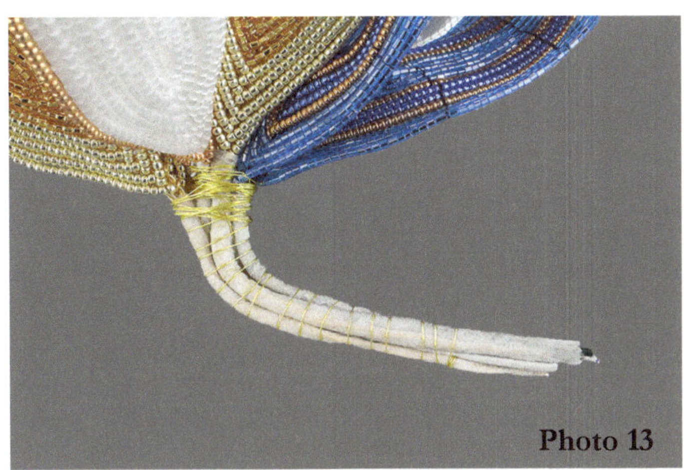

Photo 13

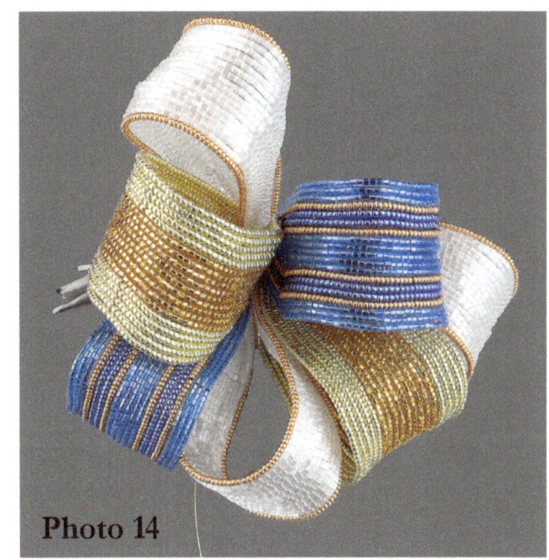

Photo 14

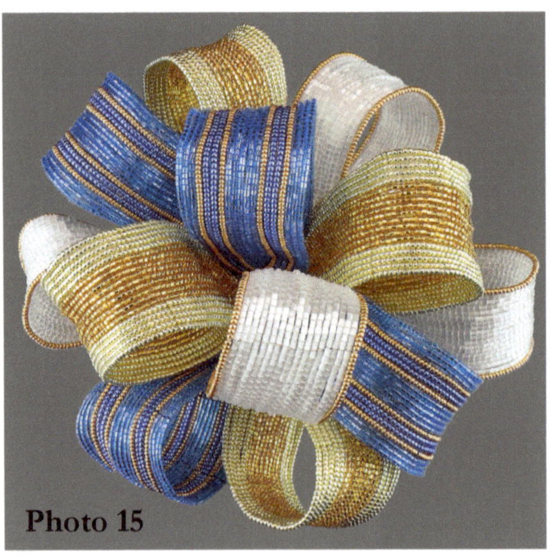

Photo 15

7. Cut a few more feet of 30 gauge wire. Add in the last five loops, one at a time, following the same procedure as the previous layer. Again cover the stem with a final layer of floral tape. When finished, the bow should look similar to **Photo 15**.

Assembling the Tails

Tails will be attached separately for the wreath. For other types of arrangements you may want to attach the tails to the bow stem directly underneath the loops, but either way, you will want to put them on separate stem wires for support.

1. Prepare the three 16 gauge stem wires by wrapping them with floral tape.

2. Cut about a foot (30.5 cm) of 30 gauge wire matching the ribbon tail. Attach the end of the 30 gauge wire to one 16g stem by winding it around several times.

3. Lay the 16g stem wire against the back of the ribbon tail, with the tip of the wire just below the bottom of the Basic Row.

4. Use the 30 gauge wire to sew the wire to the back of the tail. Insert the wire into one side of the tail, between two rows along the bottom wire. Pull it through to the front, cross it over the front, then insert it down into the opposite side of the bottom wire between two rows (**Photo 16**). Pull it tight and make sure the wire goes all the way down between two rows of beads along the bottom wire.

5. Repeat, moving down the stem until you reach the bottom of the tail. Wind the 30 gauge wire tightly several times around the tail stem wire and the 16g stem wire (**Photo 17**). Trim the 30g wire and cover the stem with floral tape.

6. Repeat for the two remaining tails.

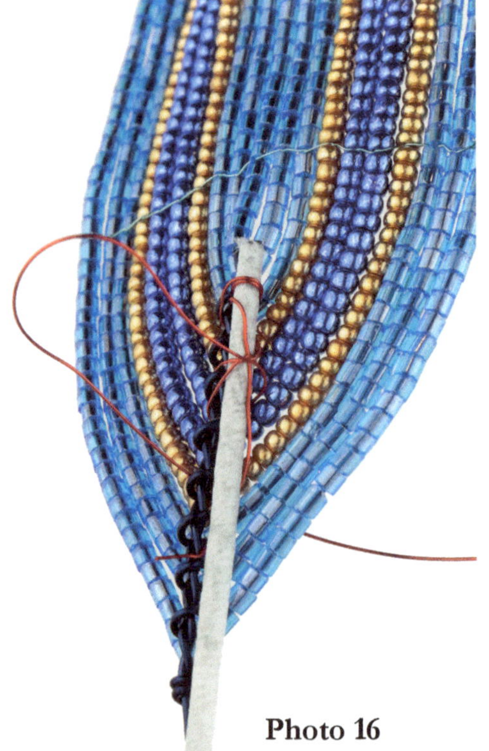

Photo 16

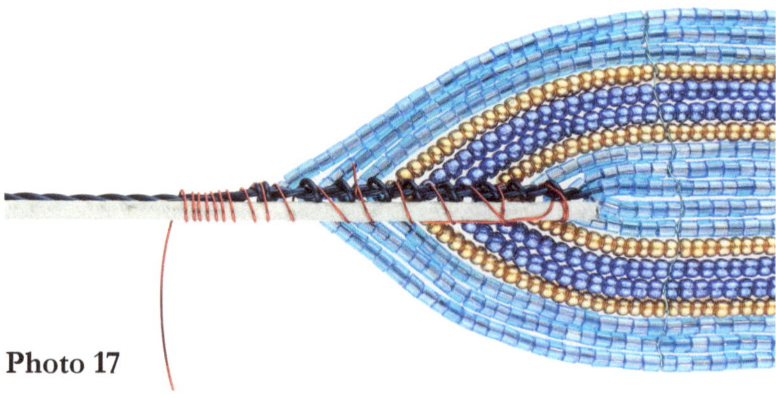

Photo 17

····· ASSEMBLING THE WREATH ·····

In addition to all of the components made from the patterns, you will also need the materials listed below.

- 14 inch (35.5 cm) diameter wreath frame*
- 26 -24 gauge (.4 - .5 mm) paddle wire or copper core wire
- Green floral tape
- ~ 20 Yards (18.3 m) 1 ½ inch (3.8 cm) wide medium or dark green ribbon
- 4-5 sheets of green felt
- Lighter
- Pliers
- Scissors
- Hot glue gun

The wreath frame should be the raised frame type with four rails, <u>not a flat frame</u>. The inside and outside rails will be flat against the wall, while the two inner rails are raised up. The domed shape made by the raised rails makes it possible to hide stems underneath

**If you have substituted any of the branches or flowers in the wreath, you may or may not need a different size of wreath frame.*

The finished wreath is approximately 19 inches (48 cm) wide and will weigh close to 9 pounds.

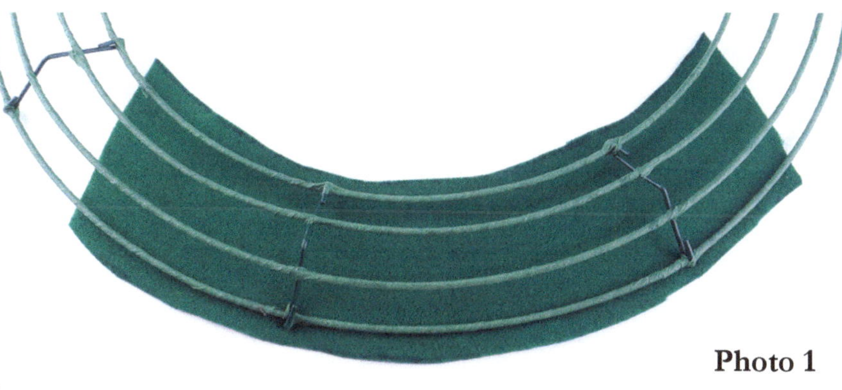

Photo 1

1. Wrap the each rail on the frame with a layer of floral tape to give the smooth metal surface more grip. This makes it easier to attach flowers without them slipping around or wiggling back and forth on the frame.

2. Lay the wreath frame on top of a sheet of felt. Trace on the felt around the frame, adding approximately 1/2 inch (1.3 mm) on each side of the frame. Use scissors to cut out the felt shape. Repeat until you have enough pieces of felt to cover the entire back of the frame. I needed 4 pieces, but you might need more depending on how you measure them. Set them aside for later. (**Photo 1**)

3. Before attaching pieces to the wreath, make a mock layout of your wreath by laying the stems on top of the frame. **Photo 2** shows my layout. See my suggestions for arranging the wreath on the next page. Take pictures, either with a camera or a phone, so you can reference them while assembling the wreath.

TIP: To make arranging easier, lift the wreath frame off the table using several tall cups of the same height.

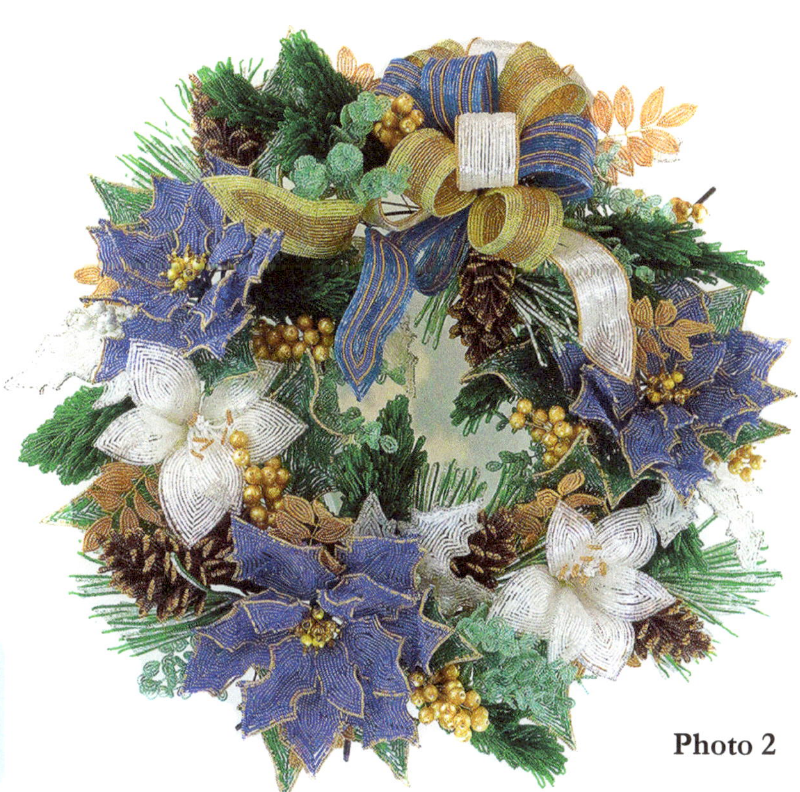

Photo 2

Tips for Arranging the Wreath:

Your wreath may look similar to mine, or you may choose to arrange it to your own personal tastes. But I would like to share some tips on how I placed all my pieces.

- The goal for me was even distribution of different types of branches and stems, and color. For example, I did not want too much gold in one place, with no gold in other places. Or several Holly stems on one side of the wreath, with very few on the other.

- You also want even coverage. You do not want large gaps between branches anywhere. Some gaps are inevitable, but they should be even throughout the wreath. This will feel a lot like building a puzzle, trying to get all the pieces to fit together nicely.

- Avoid having the same type of branches in the same position around the wreath. For example, I did not want all of my pinecones to point toward the inside of the wreath, leaving none on the outer edges. I would not want all the pinecones themselves to point up or down, but rather a mix of both. This should also be applied to all of the branches and stems.

- There are certain types of branches and stems, like the pinecones or berries, that I did not want covered up by other branches. Be certain that these are on the top layer wherever you have components stacked on top of each other.

- Other types of branches are okay to have partially covered. Like the fir branches, or poinsettia leaves. These branches make up the background canvas, while the others are more like the decorations on top. I used poinsettia leaves underneath other components in many places to fill in holes.

- Remember that the wreath won't be viewed only from the front, but the sides as well, so they should be interesting. The top edge of the wreath will receive the least attention, since you would have to be very tall or hang it very low to see it. Try not to put anything too important there unless it is visible from the front.

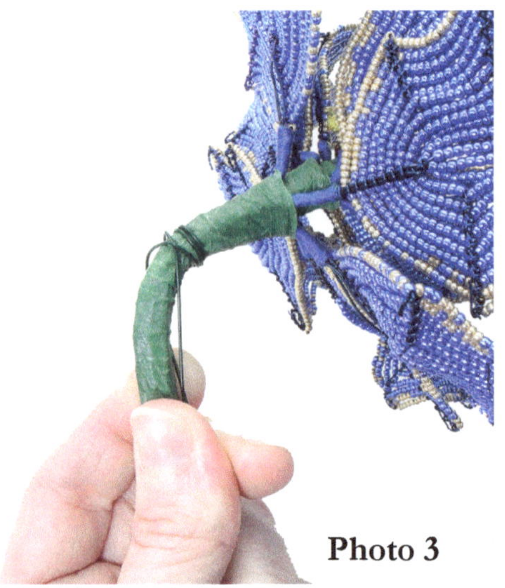

Photo 3

4. Remove all the pieces from the frame. *Place the bow back on the frame, making sure one of the crossbars in the frame is directly under the bow. This crossbar will provide extra stability during assembly.* Place the Poinsettias and Amaryllis on the frame and space them evenly. If you can put any Poinsettias near a crossbar without ruining the spacing, do so. This step is just to re-check the positioning before attaching them. You may want to mark on the frame where they go.

5. Start the assembly by attaching the three Poinsettias and the two Amaryllis. Attaching these pieces first will provide an easy visual to help you space the other components. Cut a few feet of 26 or 24 gauge wire. Bend the flower stems at a 90 degree angle about 1- 1 ½ inches (2.5-3.8 cm) below the flowers. Attach the cut wire right at the bend by laying a tail against the stem, then winding over it a few times. (**Photo 3**)

6. Insert the flower stem <u>underneath</u> the wreath frame along one of the raised center rails. The flower should not be flat against the front of the wreath. You want a little space between the wreath and the flower so all the other filler stems can fit underneath it. Use the attached assembly wire to wind it very tightly around one of the rails on the frame. Use pliers to pull the wire tight with every wrap. You can make multiple passes up and down the stem if needed. If the stem intersects a crossbar on the wreath frame, wind the assembly wire tightly around it in an "X" for extra support and security. If attached properly, the flower should not move around if you shake the frame. (**Photo 4**)

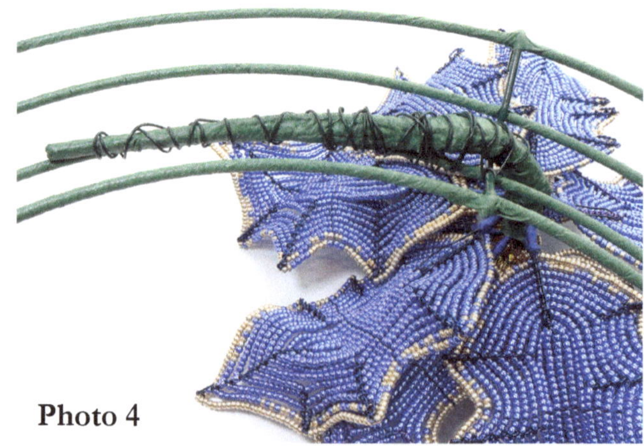

Photo 4

7. Cut a separate length of wire to attach each flower. Insert each of the larger flower stems *underneath* one of the two raised central rails. Do not attach the bow yet. It's weight will make it difficult to work on the rest of the wreath. (**Photo 5**)

8. Pick a spot near one of the flowers and work around the wreath, adding in branches and stems. Refer to the photos of your layout to determine placement. The pinecone sprays and fir branches will need to be attached with a separate length of wire to ensure their weight is properly secured. But the other components are light weight enough that the stems can be combined into bundles using the assembly wire, then attached to the frame as a group. (**Photo 6**)

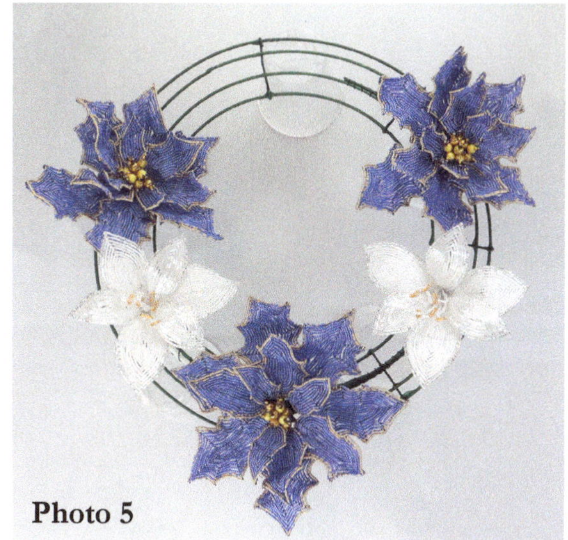
Photo 5

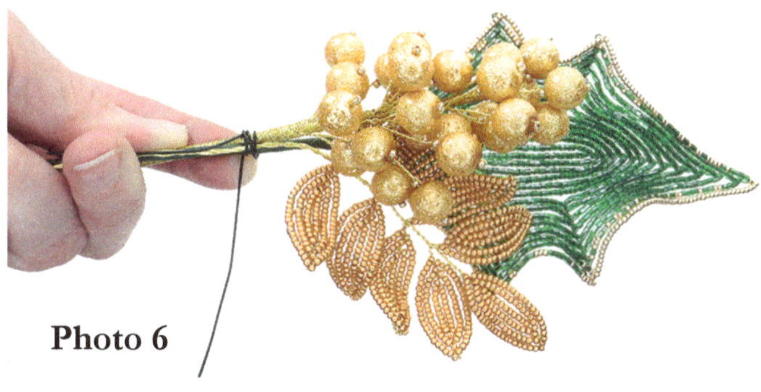
Photo 6

9. Continue moving around the wreath, paying careful attention to the spacing of pieces between the larger flowers to ensure proper coverage. Stem wires can be inserted into the frame in either direction. Choose the direction that provides the easiest way to position the component where it needs to be. *The inside and outside rails on these raised wreath frames need to lay flat against a wall. If you need to attach branches to these two rails to maintain their position, do so by laying the branches either on top or beside the rails, not underneath where they will cause uneven bulk on the back.* (**Photos 7 & 8**)

TIP: To make assembly a little easier, work at a table. Allow the section of the wreath you are currently working on to hang off the edge. This gives you open space underneath to wrap wires, while keeping the majority of the wreath on the table to support the weight. Place a cloth underneath the wreath so you don't scratch your table.

TIP: Use pliers to help grab the assembly wires between all the branches and frame wires.

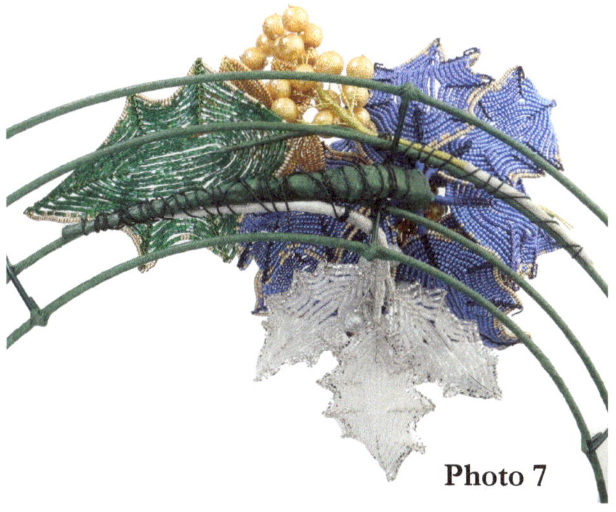
Photo 7

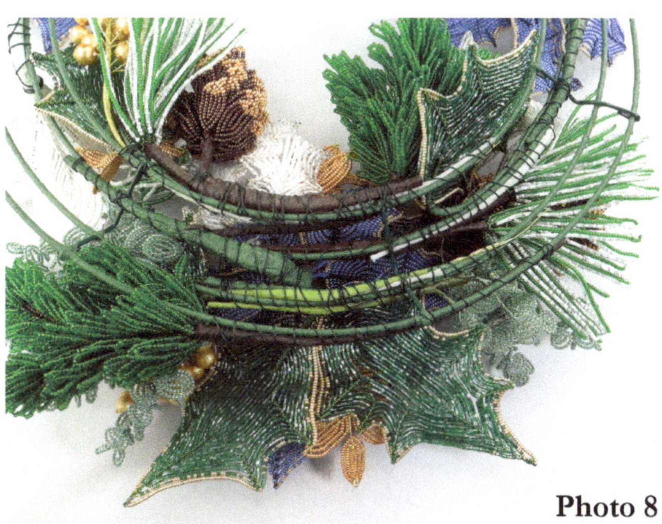
Photo 8

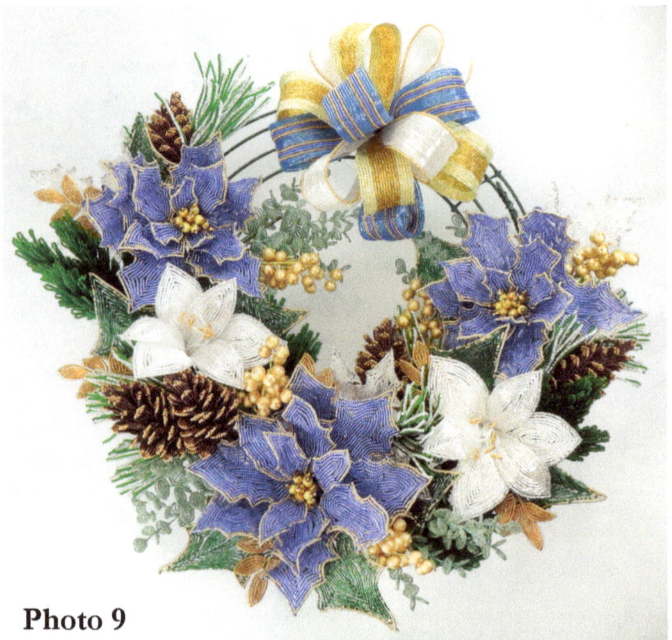

Photo 9

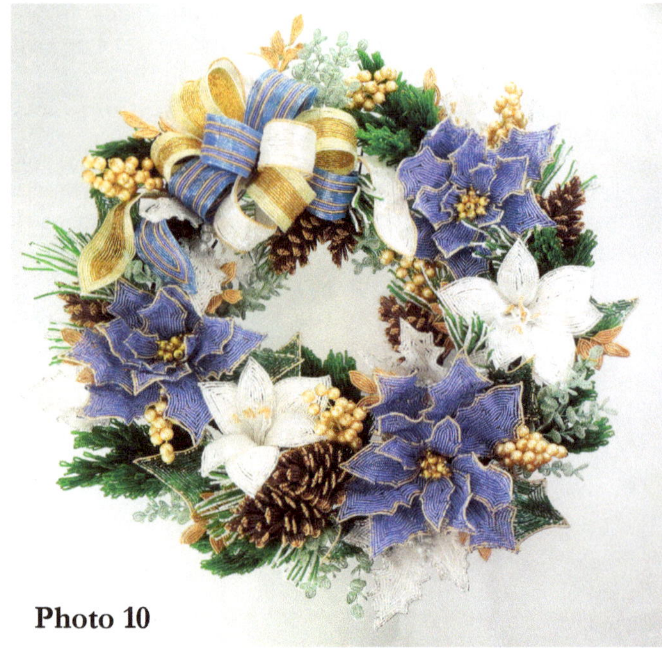

Photo 10

10. Once you get close to the bow's location, attach it. Just like the flowers, be sure to insert the stem so it is underneath the rails. This keeps the bow from sticking out too far. You do want some space between the bow and rails so you can fit the last of the other branches and stems underneath. Inserting the stem underneath also hides the thicker stem inside the dome made by the raised central rails, rather than causing extra lumps on top of the rails. Due to the bow's weight, you may need to use more than one assembly wire. If the bow's stem intersects any crossbars, wind the assembly wire in an X around it and the bow stem for extra security. (**Photo 9**)

11. Once the bow is securely mounted, attach the remaining branches and stems and the bow tails around the bow. (**Photo 10**)

Adding the Ribbon Backing

The next part of assembly involves wrapping the frame with ribbon. This serves multiple purposes in a beaded flower wreath. First, no matter how well you spaced your stems, there will probably still be some gaps between pieces where the wall will show through. Beaded flowers just don't squish together quite as well as fresh or silk flowers. Having a ribbon that matches the base greenery will fill in those gaps to give the illusion of fuller coverage. It also looks more attractive and finished. The felt underneath the ribbon prevents the assembly wires from poking through the ribbon and scratching your walls.

TIP: Place the wreath backwards on a wreath display easel while adding the ribbons. This makes it easy to access the back of the wreath without mangling the front.

12. Lay one of the cut pieces of felt on the back of the wreath. Tack it down to the frame with hot glue. Be careful not to get any glue on the beads.

13. Cut a few feet of ribbon. It's easier to work with a shorter length at a time and add in new lengths as needed. Run a flame from a lighter carefully along the two cut edges of the ribbon to seal the ends so they don't fray.

14. Insert the end of the ribbon between the branches and the wreath frame and pull it through. Use hot glue to attach the ribbon to itself to secure it around the frame. If you glue the ribbon to the felt or to the frame, it may cause damage if you ever need to remove and replace the ribbon.

15. Continue wrapping around the frame between branches. Be careful as you pull the ribbon through under the branches so you do not snag the ribbon on any wires. (**Photos 11 - 12**)

- The felt should be a little wider than the frame. Allow the edges of the felt to wrap around the sides of the inside and outside frame rails.

- Make sure the ribbon doesn't twist.

- The ribbon wraps should overlap a little bit. Because of the spacing of the branches in the wreath, you probably won't have exactly the same amount of overlap each time.

- Every few wraps, use a couple dots of glue to tack the ribbon to itself to help keep tension while you work.

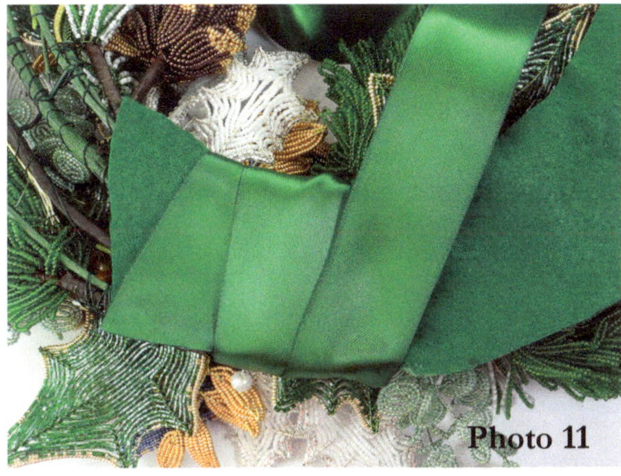

Photo 11

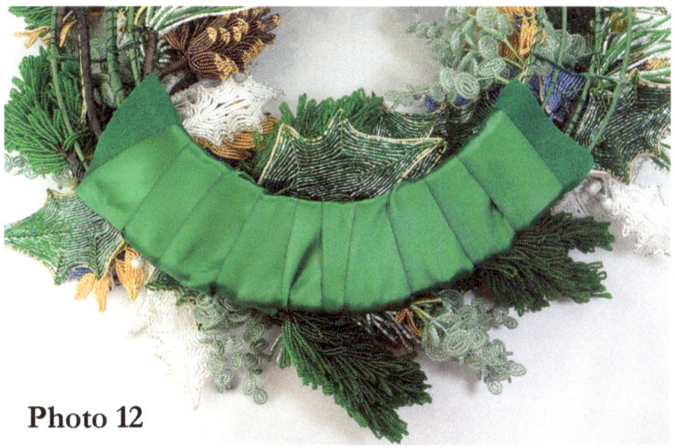

Photo 12

16. When you finish the first length of ribbon, attach it to itself with glue to secure the end - preferably under the branches, not on the back.

17. When you reach the end of the felt, glue a second piece of felt to the frame. Cut another few feet of ribbon and seal the ends with the lighter. Glue the end to the previous ribbon length, then continue wrapping. Make sure you are wrapping in the same direction around.

18. Repeat until the entire frame is covered. (**Photo 13**)

To hang the wreath securely, make sure you either screw into a stud, or use a wall anchor. Hang the wreath by the inside edge of the frame.

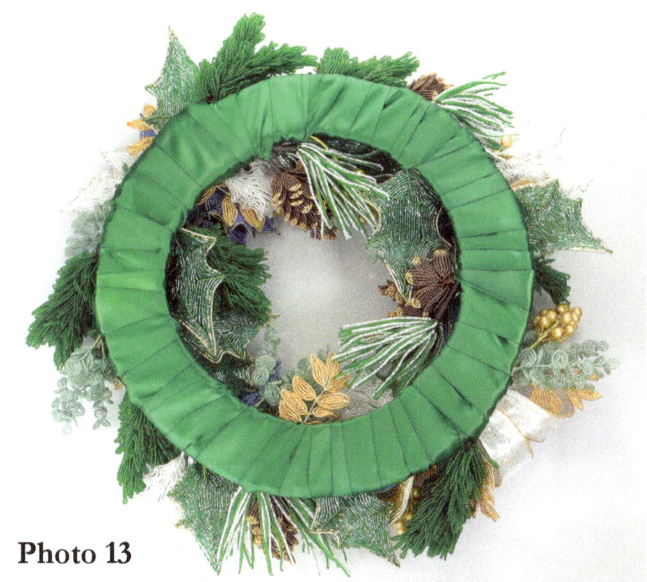

Photo 13

I do not recommend displaying any beaded flowers outside. Not only can they get very dirty, but sunshine, rain, or hot and cold weather can ruin some bead finishes and floral tape. Also, something so lovely will definitely tempt thieves. It would be much more worthy of your time and efforts in making such a piece to keep it inside where you can enjoy it.

Quick Technique Reference

The techniques in this section are listed in alphabetical order. These are quick, abbreviated tutorials intened to be a reference for people who already have some familiarity with the techniques.

If you require more in-depth technique tutorials, they are taught for free on my website - BeadandBlossom.com. Some techniques also have videos on my YouTube channel. Individual links to the videos can be found in each technique lesson on my website.

Basic Frame:

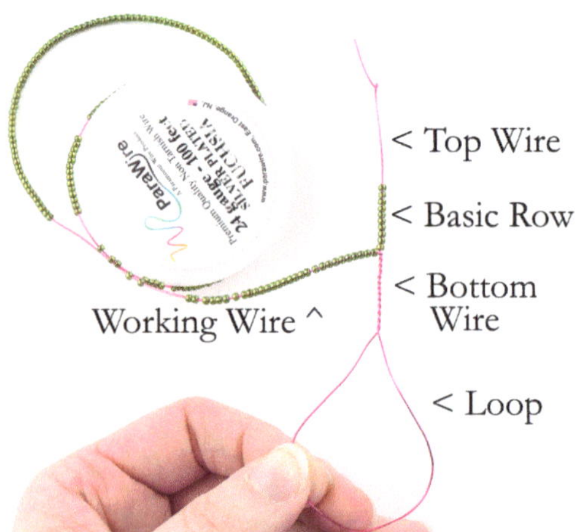

Basic Frame Construction

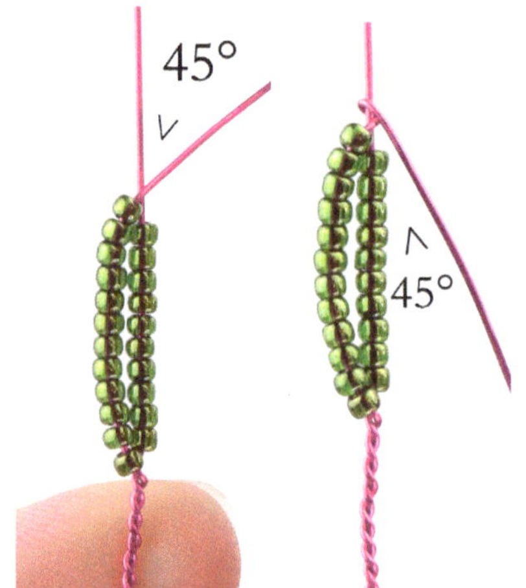

Pointed: 45 degree wrap at top or bottom wire.

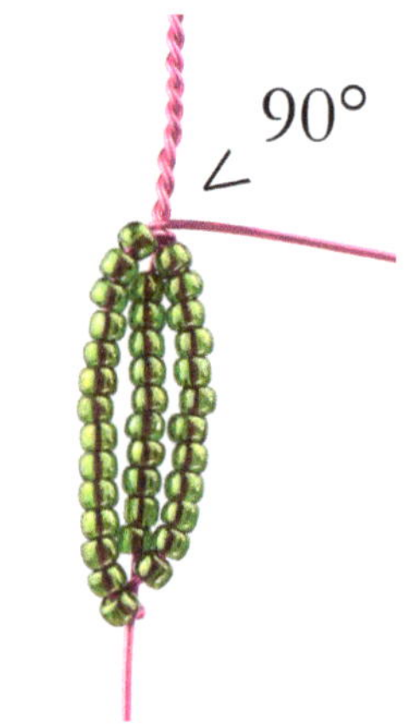

Round: 90 degree wrap at top or bottom wire.

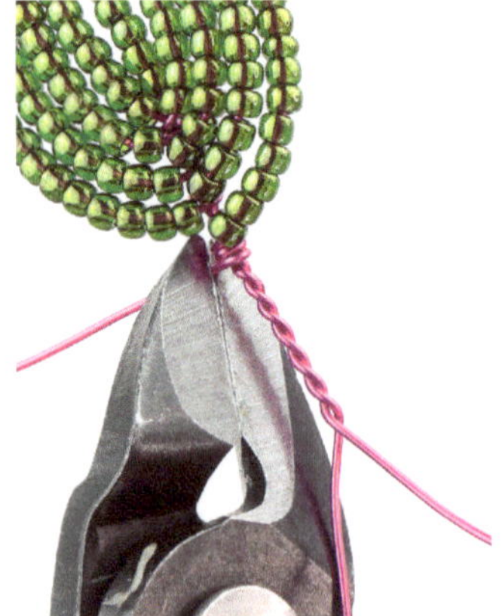

Reduce to two Bottom Wires: wrap off and remove working wire.

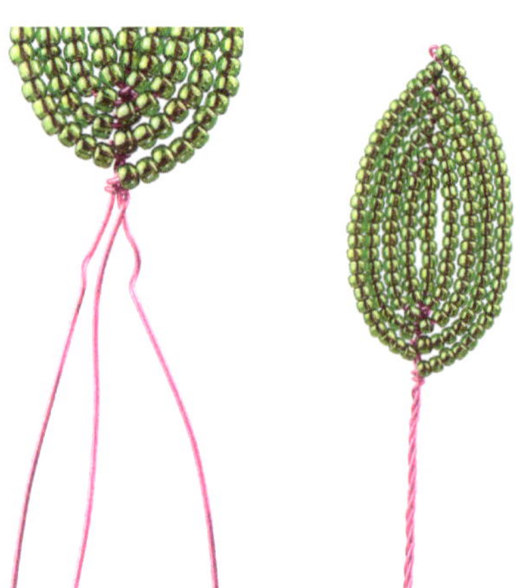

Three Bottom Wires: twist working wire into bottom wires.

BEEHIVE BASIC FRAME:

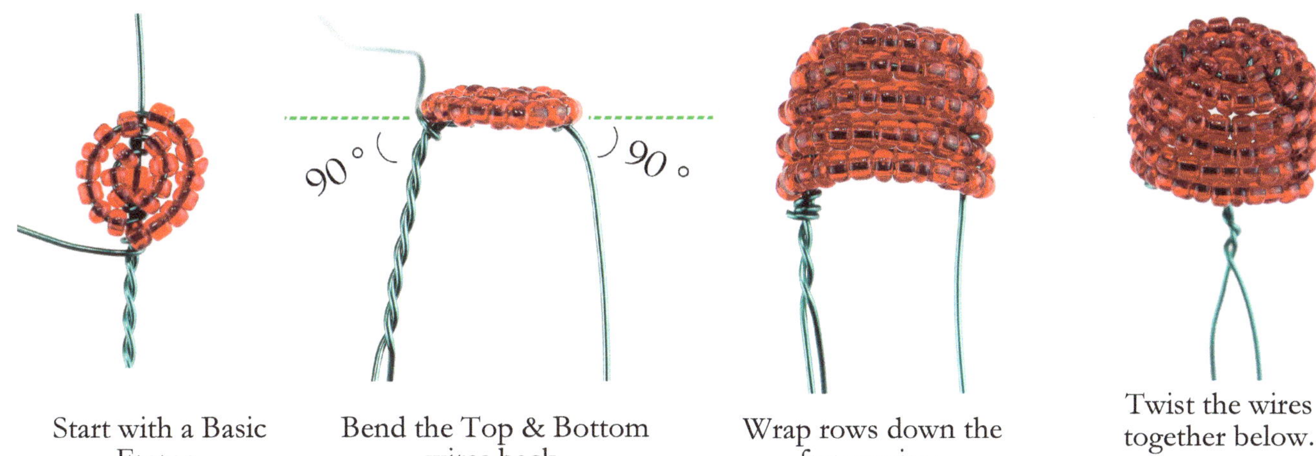

Start with a Basic Frame.

Bend the Top & Bottom wires back.

Wrap rows down the frame wires.

Twist the wires together below.

CONTINUOUS BASIC FRAME:

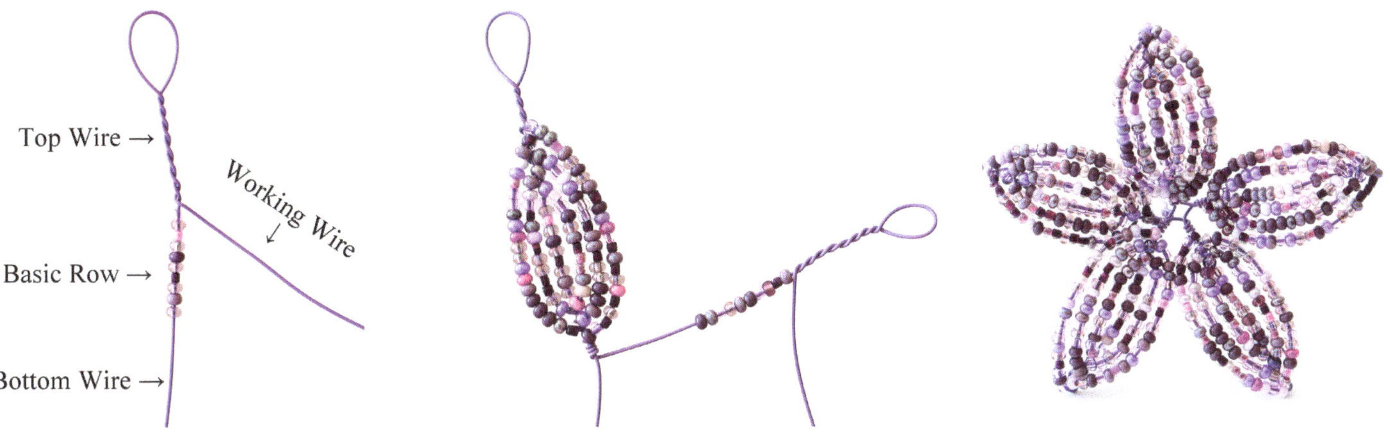

Flip the Basic Frame upside-down. Note the altered anatomy.

Wrap the rows. Leave a space below the second upside-down Basic Frame.

Repeat.
Cut and fold top wires back.

CONTINUOUS LOOPS:

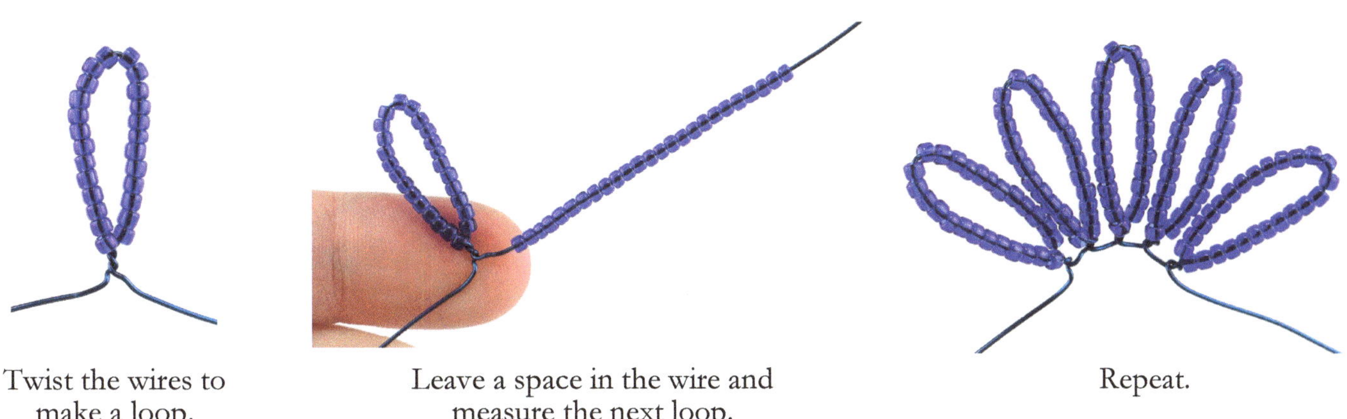

Twist the wires to make a loop.

Leave a space in the wire and measure the next loop.

Repeat.

Continuous Wraparound Loops:

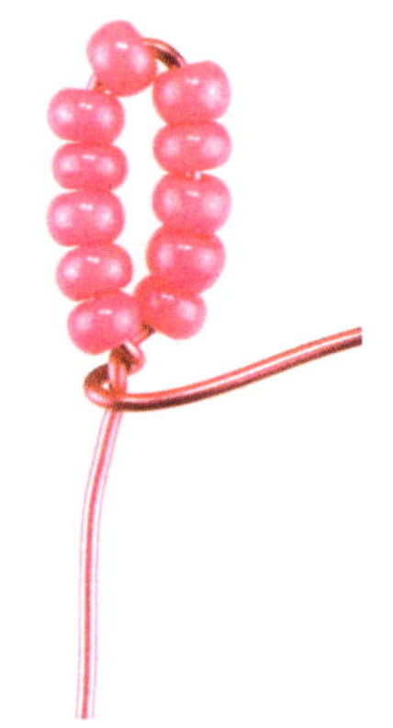

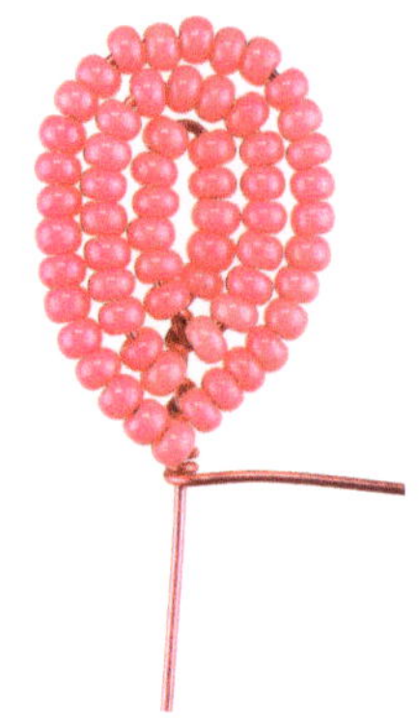

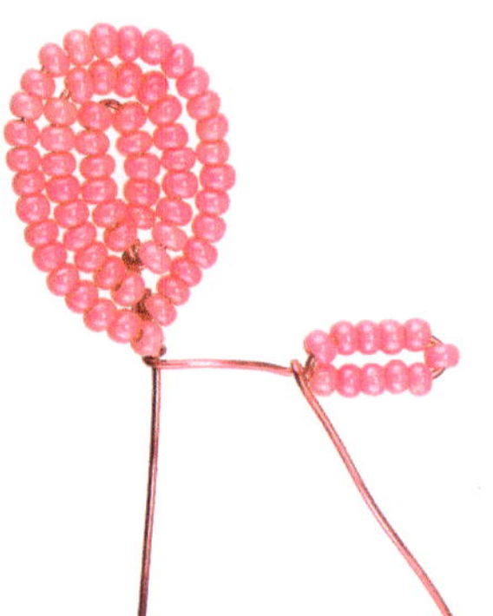

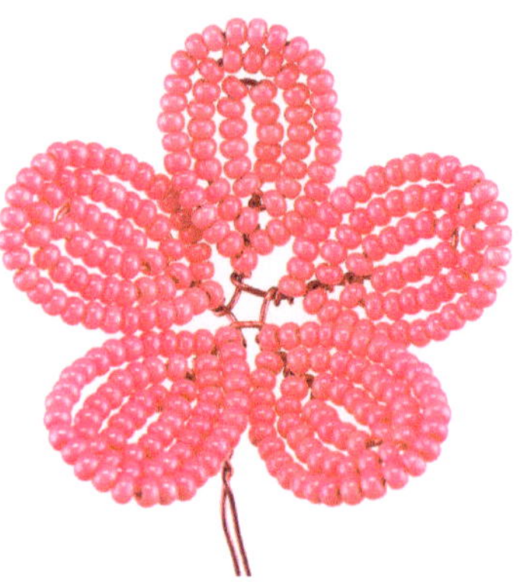

Make the Starting Loop.

Wrap rows around the starting loop.

Leave a space and make the next starting loop.

Repeat.

Extensions, Bottom Wire:

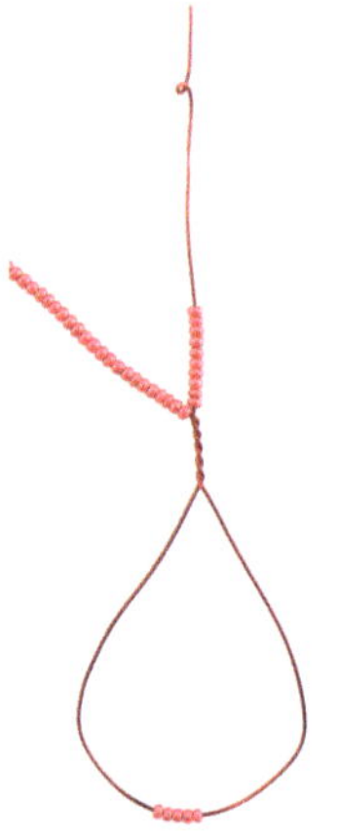

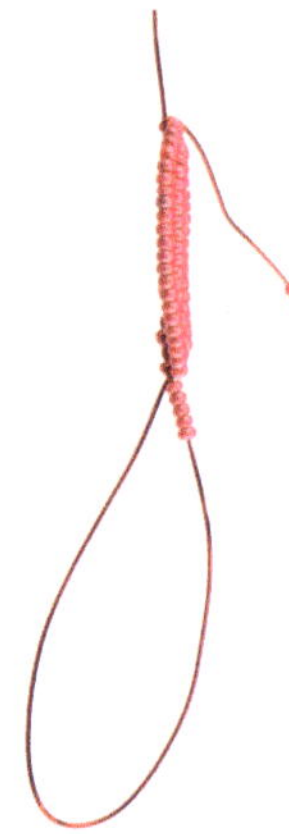

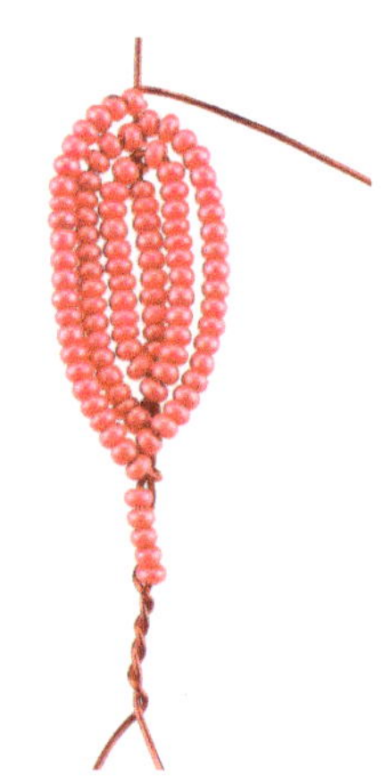

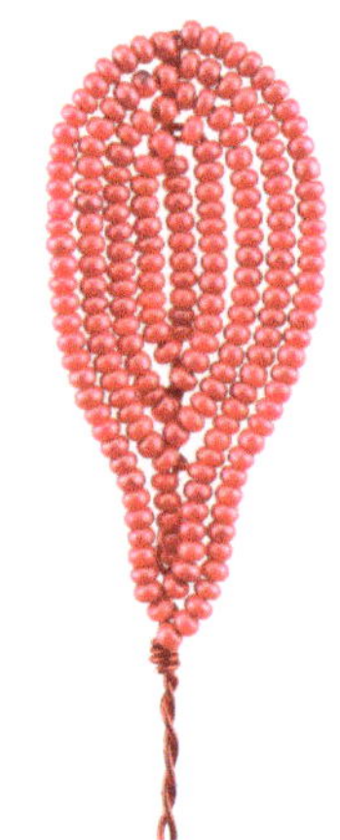

Add beads to bottom loop during frame construction.

Wrap Rows. Untwist bottom wires, slide beads up.

Twist bottom wires below extension with one wire behind the beads.

Wrap rows around extension.

Extensions, Top Wire:

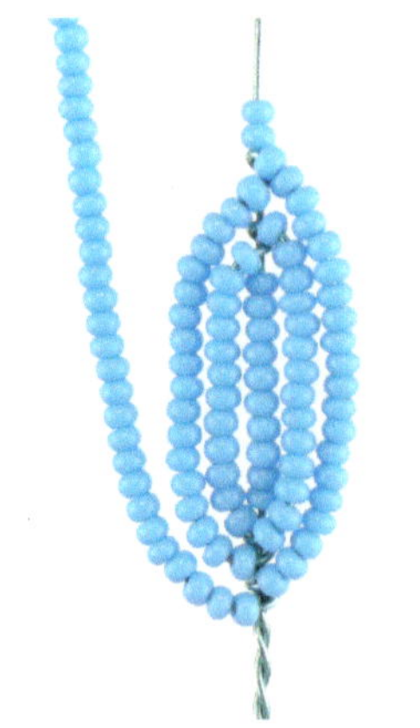

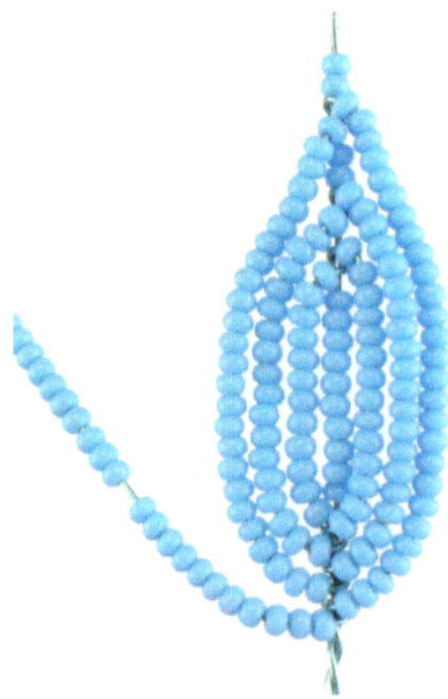

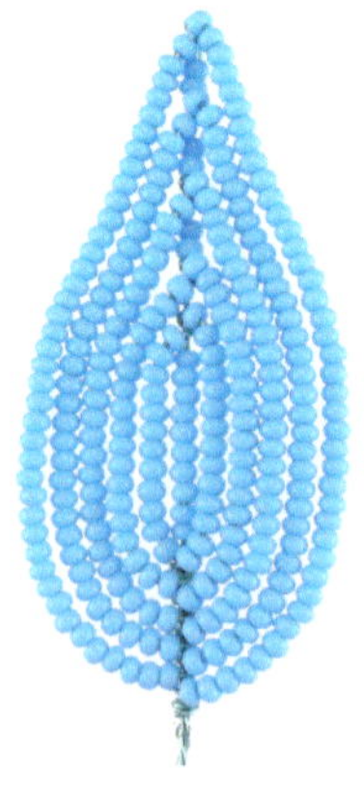

Add beads to the top wire.

Wrap rows around the extension beads.

Repeat as necessary.

FRINGE, TWISTED

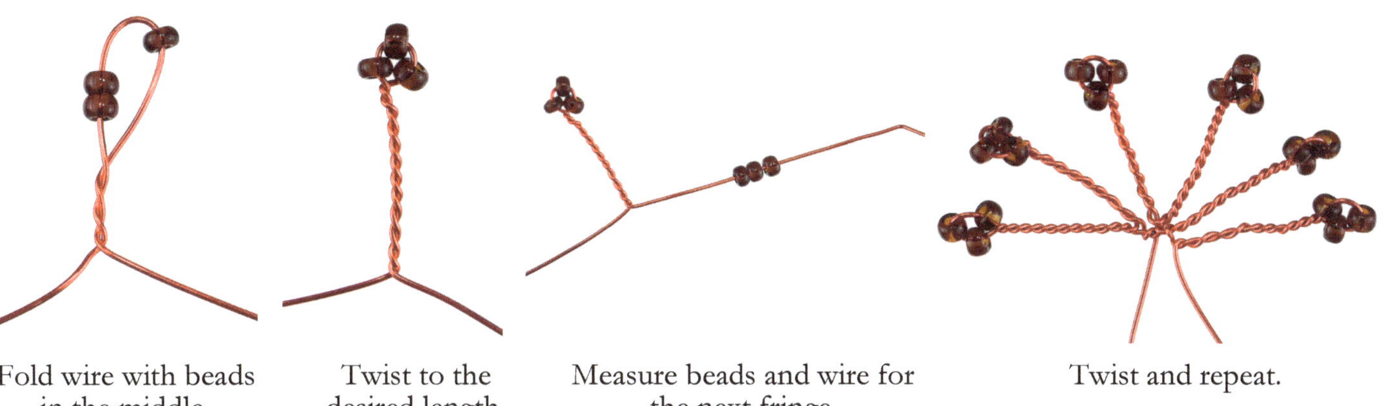

Fold wire with beads in the middle.

Twist to the desired length.

Measure beads and wire for the next fringe.

Twist and repeat.

FRINGE, WIRE-BACK

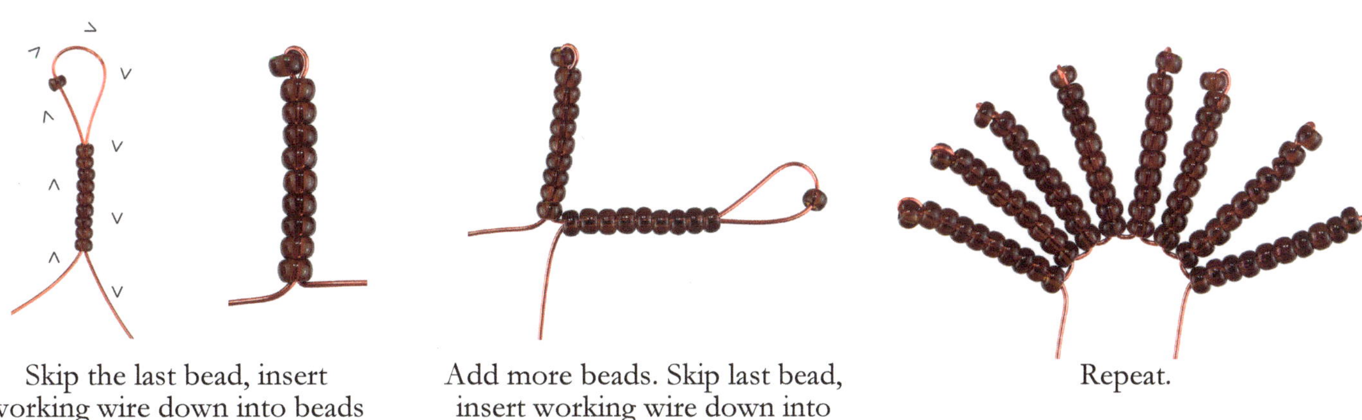

Skip the last bead, insert working wire down into beads below. Pull tight.

Add more beads. Skip last bead, insert working wire down into beads below.

Repeat.

LACING:

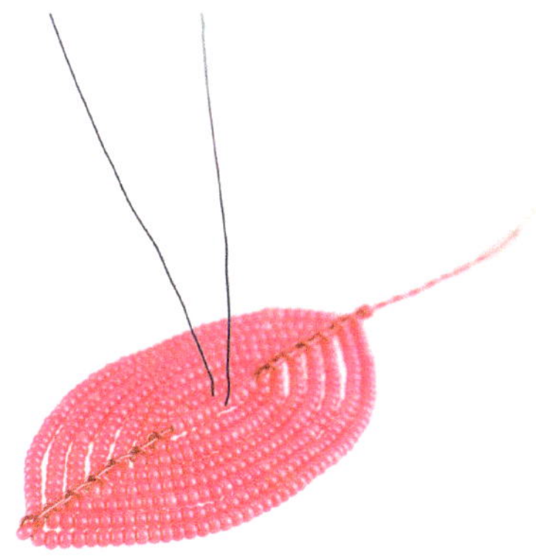

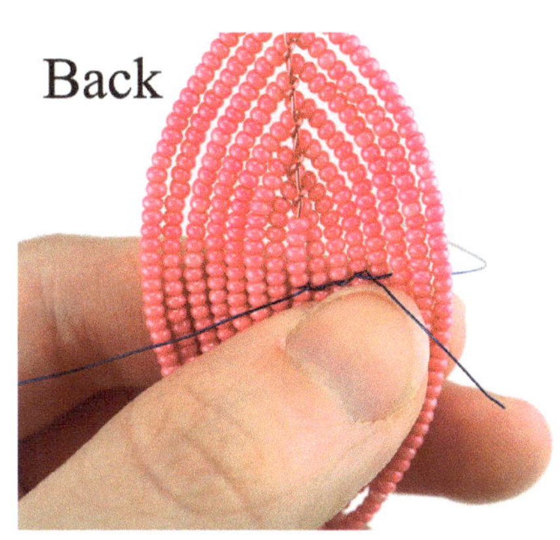

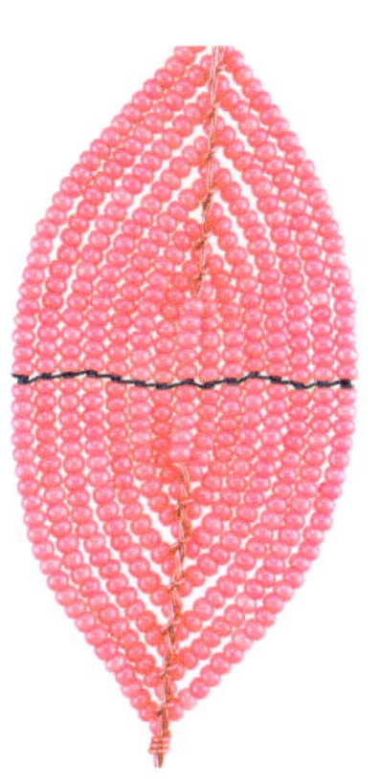

Fold lacing wire in half. Insert into front of Basic Row and pull to back. Cross the wires.

Start in the middle. Loop the wire around each row, crossing the wire over the back of the petal.

Weave both halves.

Lace-as-you-go:

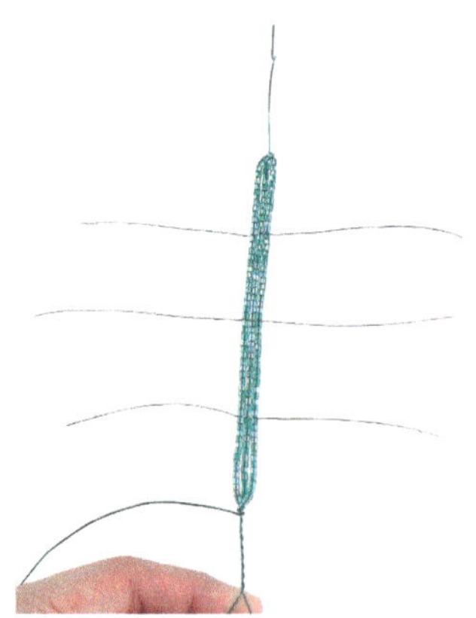

Add lacing wires after the first few rows.

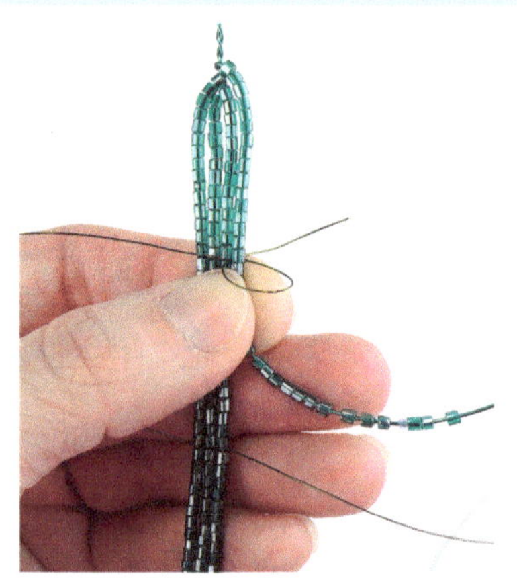

Wrap rows, looping each lacing wire around as you come to it.

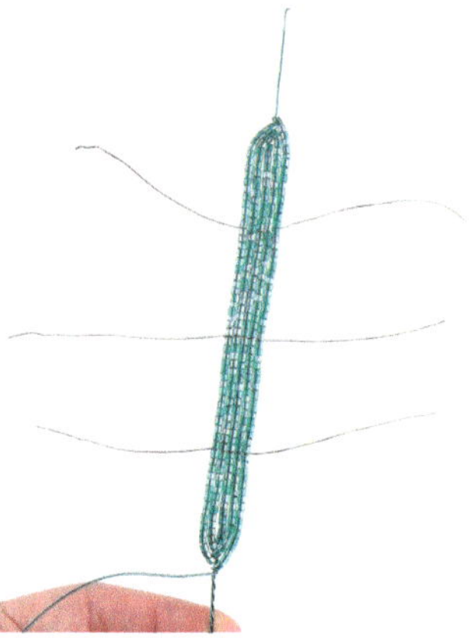

Repeat until the piece is finished.

Spokes:

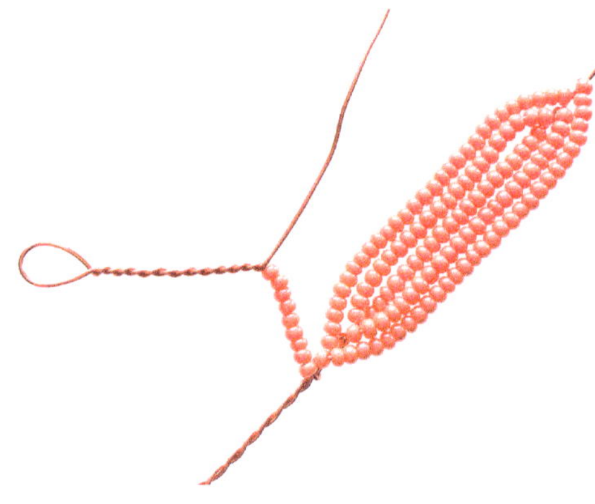

In a row, bend and fold bare wire in half and twist to form a new axis, called a spoke.

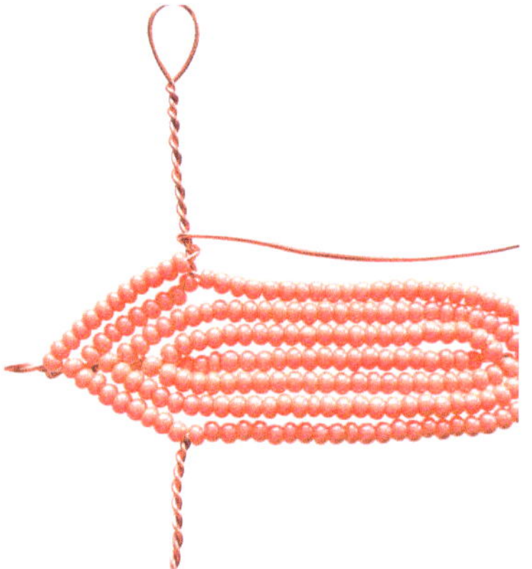

Wrap rows around each new spoke at a 45 degree angle to make a sharp point.

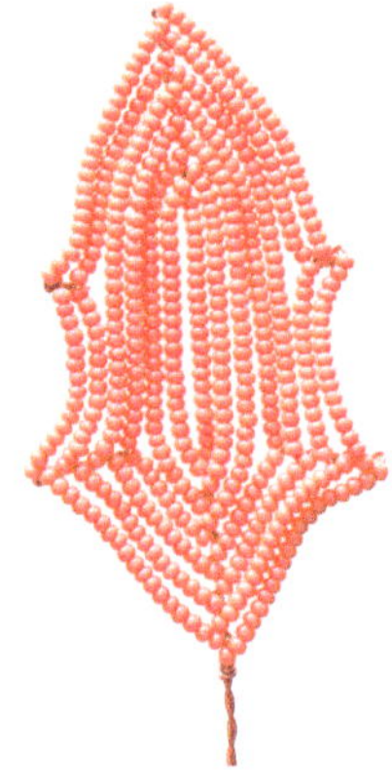

Clip spoke wires short and fold to the back.

Glossary

Assembly - The process of putting flower components together into a finished flower.

Assembly Wire - Wire used to attach flower components to the stem wire, or wire used to attach finished flowers to a frame.

Basic Frame (BF) - The most commonly used French Beading technique. It begins with a single row of beads in the center, with more rows of beads wrapped around it along two axis wires called the top and bottom wires.

Basic Row (BR) - The center, or starting row of a Basic Frame component.

Beehive Basic Frame (BBF) - An altered form of the Basic Frame which creates dome or cup-shaped components.

Bottom Loop - Part of the Basic Frame anatomy. The loop of wire below the bottom wire.

Bottom Wire - Part of the Basic Frame anatomy. The axis wire below the Basic row. Also, the wire below the Starting Loop in Continuous Wraparound Loops and Continuous Crossover Loops.

Bottom Wire Extension - Adding extra beads to the bottom wire after rows have already been wrapped in order to elongate the bottom and create a thinner point.

Continuous - Making multiple components on the same wire.

Continuous Basic Frame (CBF) - A technique that modifies the basic frame to make multiple basic frame type components on the same length of wire.

Continuous Loops (CL) - A French Beading technique that makes multiple simple loops on the same length of wire.

Continuous Wraparound Loops (CWL) - A modification of the Continuous Loop technique, in which additional loops are wrapped around a starting loop.

Copper Core Wire - The wire used for French Beading components. This wire is made from copper, with other metals and colored coatings applied to the outside.

Floral Tape - A specialized tape made from stretchy paper-like material that is used to assemble flowers.

Gauge - A term used to describe wire sizes in the United States (and a few other countries).

Lacing - Sewing across the back of a leaf or petal with a thin wire to hold rows together and provide extra support.

Lace-as-you-go - Lacing while you construct a petal or leaf, rather than after.

Pointed Bottom (PB) - Make the bottom of a component pointed by wrapping at a 45 degree angle at the bottom wire.

Pointed Top (PT) - Make the top of a component pointed by wrapping at a 45 degree angle at the top wire.

Round Bottom (RB) - Make the bottom of a component rounded by wrapping at a 90 degree angle at the bottom wire.

Round Top (RT) - Make the top of a component rounded by wrapping at a 90 degree angle at the top wire.

Starting Loop - The beginning, or center loop in the Continuous Wraparound Loop and Continuous Crossover Loop techniques.

Stem Wire - The wires exiting the bottom of a flower component, which are used to attach the flower to the flower stem. Also used to refer to the flower stem.

Support Wire - Extra wires added during or after construction to provide extra support for heavy components.

Tail Wire - A small section of wire left bare before and after a continuous component. These are generally twisted together to make the component's stem wire.

Top Wire - Part of the Basic Frame anatomy; the axis wire that extends above the Basic Row.

Top Wire Extension - Adding extra beads to the top wire after rows have already been wrapped in order to elongate the top of the petal and make it thinner.

Working Wire - The wire used to wrap rows. It is often strung with beads and feeds directly into the spool. Other times it is cut from the spool and beads are added to it to complete rows.

Resources

Below is a list of my favorite sources for beads and other supplies. This list was accurate at the time of publication in 2020, but because supply stores go in and out of business, they may not always be around. Because I am based in the USA, I am more knowledgeable about resources located there, but I've filled in as much as I can for other countries.

United States of America

Beads:

- ShipwreckBeads.com (Czech)
- FireMountainGems.com (Czech, Matsuno, Miyuki, Toho)
- AuraCrystals.com (Miyuki, Toho)
- EurekaCrystalBeads.com (Miyuki, Toho)
- PowwowSupply.com (Czech, Japanese)
- BeadedEdgeSupply.com (Czech, Japanese)
- BobbyBead.com (Toho)

Copper Core Wire:

- Parawire.com (Parawire brand)
- Beadalon.com (Artistic Wire brand)
- GreatCraftWorks.com (Artistic Wire)
- FireMountainGems.com (Zebra Wire)

Other Supplies:

- Papermart.com - floral tape, stem wires
- DMC.com - embroidery floss
- Local Craft Store - floral tape, stem wires, embroidery floss, wreath frames, felt
- Amazon.com - floral tape, stem wires, wreath frames

United Kingdom

Beads:

- GJbeads.co.uk
- Spellboundbead.co.uk
- SpoiltRottenbeads.co.uk
- londonbeadco.com
- BoundlessBeads.co.uk

Copper Core Wire:

- Wires.co.uk (Scientific Wire)

Other Supplies:

- Local Craft Store - floral tape, stem wires, embroidery floss, wreath frames, felt

Canada

Beads:

- beadfx.com
- beazu.com
- ibeadcanada.com
- thatbeadlady.com (Miyuki)
- thebeadstore.ca
- northernbeadcart.com
- Iguanabeads.com (Miyuki)

Copper Core Wire:

- Iguanabeads.com (Parawire)

Other Supplies:

- Local Craft Store - floral tape, stem wires, embroidery floss, wreath frames, felt

INDEX

About the Author

Lauren Harpster is a well-known and respected designer in the small, but growing world of French Beaded Flowers. Her passion shows not only in her detailed work, but also in her efforts to advance, promote, and preserve the art. This title is her third published book, with many more volumes to come. She lives in southern Utah with her husband and three children.

To learn more about the art of French Beaded Flowers, and to find more tutorials, videos, and designs by Lauren Harpster, visit BeadandBlossom.com.

"Learn How to Make French Beaded Flowers" is a new Facebook group run by Lauren Harpster and Fen Li, which focuses on teaching the art in a community setting.

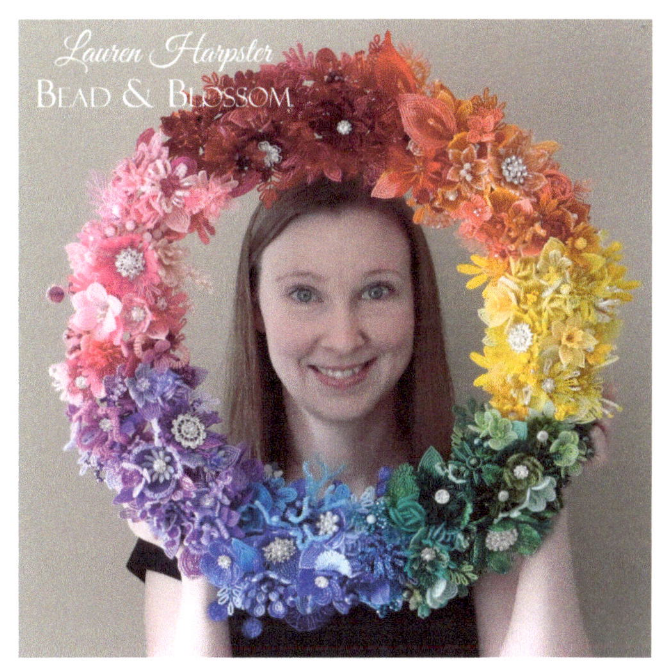

Other Publications:

"French Beading Patterns Volume One: Christmas Collection". Published Dec 2017.

"Learn French Beading: Beginner Course". Published Feb 2020.

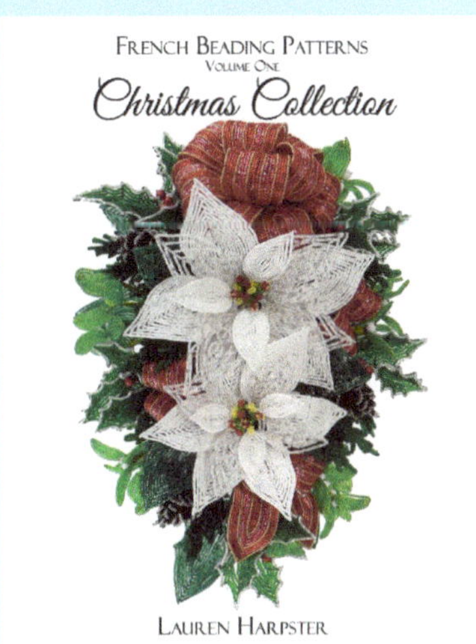

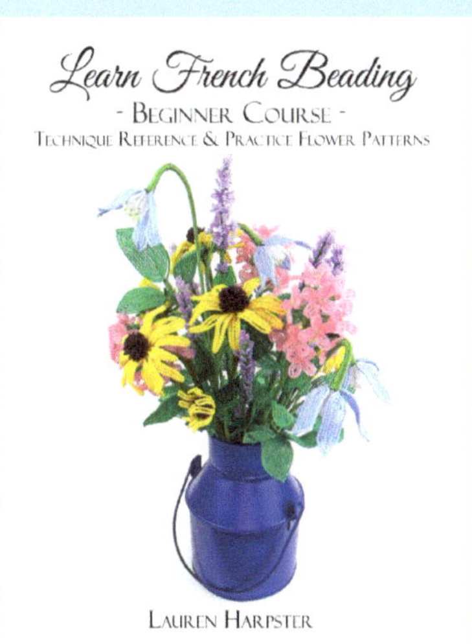

Bead & Blossom